Functional Analysis of Information Net
  Hal B. Becker

Functional Analysis of Information Pr
  Grayce M. Booth

Effective Use of ANS COBOL Compute.
  Laurence S. Cohn

The Database Administrator
  John K. Lyon

Software Reliability: Principles and Practices
  Glenford J. Myers

Software Reliability

Software Reliability

Principles and Practices

Glenford J. Myers

Staff Member,
IBM Systems Research Institute
Lecturer in Computer Science,
Polytechnic Institute of New York

A WILEY-INTERSCIENCE PUBLICATION

JOHN WILEY & SONS
New York • London • Sydney • Toronto

This publication is designed to provide accurate and
authoritative information in regard to the subject
matter covered. It is sold with the understanding that
the publisher is not engaged in rendering legal, accounting, or other professional service. If legal advice or
other expert assistance is required, the services of a
competent professional person should be sought.

*From a Declaration of Principles jointly adopted by a
Committee of the American Bar Association and a Committee
of Publishers.*

Library of Congress Cataloging in Publication Data:

Myers, Glenford J   1946–
  Software reliability.

  (Business data processing, a Wiley series)
  "A Wiley-Interscience publication."
  Bibliography: p.
  1. Computer programs—Reliability.   I. Title.

QA76.6.M93   001.6′425   76-22202
ISBN 0-471-62765-8

Printed in the United States of America

10 9 8 7 6 5

Jennifer
Andy
& Jeff

Preface

In the late 1960s, the fact that computer systems can make mistakes, and that these mistakes can have an effect on our lives, received a considerable amount of attention in the press. A typical "COMPUTER GOOFS!" news story might have described a department store customer who received a bill for $0.00, the customer's attempts to communicate this error to the store, and an endless stream of notices from the computer threatening to terminate the customer's account unless the bill was paid. Often, the easiest solution was actually to mail a check to the store for $0.00 or, as in one case, to have the incident publicized in the financial section of the *New York Times*.

Problems like this one are certainly undesirable, but their harm is usually limited to personal inconvenience. I would rather have an argument with a department store computer than be caught in a runaway computer-controlled train where a programming error is causing the train to attempt to accelerate to 1000 kilometers an hour instead of 100 kilometers an hour. In today's world errors such as this are now possible. Because data processing is touching our lives to an increasing extent, computer errors can now have such consequences as property damage, invasion of privacy, personal injury, and even loss of life.

This book was written to describe solutions to the problem of unreliable software. Every aspect of software production is examined, and solutions are expressed in two forms: *principles* and *practices*. Principles are major strategical approaches to the production of reliable software. Practices are smaller-scale tactical solutions to various aspects of the unreliability problem.

The book consists of four major parts. The first part defines software reliability, discusses the principal causes of software errors, and attempts to motivate the reader to read the remainder of the book. Part 2 contains a large set of principles and practices used in the design of reliable software. I use the word *design* in a broad sense, starting with the definition of requirements for a software system and ending with the coding of individual program statements.

Part 3 covers the broad area of software testing, a set of processes that consume vast percentages of data processing budgets and yet about which very little is known by most people. Although the key contributor to reliability is precise design, testing plays an important role in software reliability. A large set of proven principles and practices for testing is discussed.

Computer professionals will recognize that there are additional variables that affect reliability; many of these are discussed in Part 4. For instance, organizational structures, personalities, attitudes, management plans and motivation, programming tools, and the work environment all have a significant bearing on reliability. Part 4 also describes problems in current programming languages and computer architectures and suggests solutions to these problems. The subjects of mathematically proving program correctness and predictive techniques (reliability models) are also discussed.

This book only treats software reliability from the point of view of software errors. A large topic, the use of software to correct or circumvent hardware failures such as input/output device failures, is not covered in this book. Although this topic must obviously be considered in total system reliability, it is excluded because it is a separable topic that deserves the attention of another book and, in comparison to software reliability, it is fairly well understood.

This book should benefit anyone having an interest in the production of reliable software. People directly involved in software production, such as programmers, analysts, test personnel, programming managers, and data processing managers, should benefit the most. Programming language designers should find the material on programming languages, programming style, and computer architecture of interest. Software users, particularly those responsible for purchasing software or writing contracts for the development of new software, will gain insight into reliability and how it may affect their use of computer systems. Researchers should find all the material useful in obtaining an understanding of the reliability problem, examining the usefulness of past research, and understanding the promising areas for future research.

The book should be useful both as a reference book and as a text. The book will expose the university student to many of the real-world problems of software development. As a textbook, it can be used in senior or graduate-level computer science or software engineering courses on software development, providing that it is supplemented with actual experience such as a class project. I have used all of this material in graduate-level courses on software reliability at the IBM Systems Research Institute and the Polytechnic Institute of New York.

I thank many of my collegues at the IBM Systems Research Institute for valuable suggestions on the book. In particular, R. Goldberg and C. H. Haspel provided constructive criticism of most of the book, and B. G. Weitzenhoffer, C. J. Bontempo, and J. E. Flanagan provided valuable advice on material in Part IV. I must point out that certain material in the book can be considered as controversial; the opinions and views expressed are solely my own and do not necessarily represent the opinions and views of the people mentioned above nor the IBM Corporation.

GLENFORD J. MYERS

New York, New York
April 1976

Contents

PART 3

Software Testing

PART 4

Additional Topics in Software Reliability

Software Reliability

Concepts of
Software Reliability

CHAPTER **1**

Definition of
Software Reliability

The most significant problem facing the data
processing business today is the software problem that is manifested in two major complaints:
software is too expensive and software is unreliable. Most computer professionals recognize
the former problem as largely a symptom of the
latter. Because of the unreliable nature of
today's software, considerable expense is incurred in software testing and servicing. Although
this book focuses on the problem of unreliable
software, the problem of high cost is indirectly
confronted because of its relationship to unreliability.

It is interesting to note that the software
reliability problem as it exists today was
observed in the early days of computing:

> Those who regularly code for fast electronic com-
> puters will have learned from bitter experience
> that a large fraction of the time spent in preparing
> calculations for the machine is taken up in remov-
> ing the blunders that have been made in drawing
> up the programme. With the aid of common sense
> and checking subroutines the majority of mistakes
> are quickly found and rectified. Some errors,
> however, are sufficiently obscure to escape detec-
> tion for a surprisingly long time [1].

This observation was published by three
British mathematicians in 1952. Although

software errors were encountered before 1952, this seems to be the first recognition of the reliability problem, that is, that a considerable amount of time is required for testing and, even after this, some software errors still remain undetected.

IS THE MOON AN ENEMY ROCKET?

The immediate problem encountered in dealing with software reliability is one of definition: What is a software error and what is software reliability? Agreeing on standard definitions is important for avoiding such problems as a system user's stating that an error exists in his system and the system developer's replying, "No, it was designed that way."

The Ballistic Missile Early Warning System is supposed to monitor objects moving toward the United States and, if the object is unidentified, to initiate a sequence of defensive procedures starting with attempts to establish communications with the object and progressing potentially through physical interception and retaliation. An early version of this system mistook the rising moon for a missile heading over the northern hemisphere. Is this an error? From the user's (Defense Department's) point of view, it is. From the system developer's point of view, it may not be. The system developer may take the position that the requirements or specifications stated that action should be initiated for any moving object appearing over the horizon that is not a known friendly aircraft.

The point here is that different people have different views as to what constitutes a software error. Before we can begin discussing methods to eliminate software errors, we have to establish a definition of software errors. Rather than developing a definition from scratch, we can benefit by analyzing common definitions of software errors and determining their weaknesses.

WHAT IS AN ERROR?

One common definition is that a software error occurs when the software does not perform according to its specifications. This definition has one fundamental flaw: it tacitly assumes that the specifications are correct. This is rarely, if ever, a valid assumption; one of the major sources of errors is the writing of specifications. If the software product does not perform according to its specifications, an error is probably present. However, if the product does perform according to its specifications, we cannot say that the product has no errors.

A second common definition is that an error occurs when the software does not perform according to its specifications providing that it is used within its design limits. This definition is actually poorer than the first one. If a system is accidentally used beyond its design limits, the system must exhibit some reasonable behavior. If not, it has an error. Consider an air-traffic-control system that is tracking and coordinating aircraft over a particular geographic sector. Suppose that the original contract for the system specified that the system should be able to simultaneously handle up to 200 aircraft. However, on one particular day and for some conceivable reason, 201 aircraft appear in this sector. If the software system performs unexpectedly, say it forgets about one plane or aborts, then the software contains an error, even though it is not being used within its design limits.

A third possible definition is that an error occurs when the software does not behave according to the official documentation or publications supplied to the user. Unfortunately, this definition also has several flaws. There exists the possibility that the software *does* behave according to the official publications but errors are present because both the software and the publications are in error. A second problem occurs because of the tendency of user publications to describe only the expected and planned use of the software. Suppose that we have a user manual for a time-sharing system that states, "To enter a new command press the attention key once and type the command." Suppose that a user presses the attention key twice by accident and the software system fails because its designers did not plan for this condition. The system obviously contains an error, but we cannot really state that the system is not behaving according to its publications.

The last definition that is sometimes used defines an error as a failure of the software to perform according to the original contract or document of user requirements. Although this definition is an improvement over the previous three, it also has several flaws. If the user requirements state that the system should have a software error mean-time-to-failure of 100 hours and the actual operational system proves to have a mean-time-to-failure of 150 hours, the system still has errors (because its mean-time-to-failure is finite), even though it exceeds the user requirements. Also, written user requirements are rarely detailed enough to describe the desired behavior of the software under all possible circumstances.

There is, however, a reasonable definition of a software error that solves the aforementioned problems:

A software error is present when the software does not do what the user reasonably expects it to do. A software failure is an occurrence of a software error.

I expect two reactions to this definition. The software user's reaction will be, "Precisely!" The software developer may react with, "The definition is impractical, for how can I possibly know what the user reasonably expects?" The point is that the software developer, to design a successful system, must always understand what the system users "reasonably expect."

The word "reasonably" was placed in the definition to exclude such situations as a person's walking up to an information retrieval terminal in a public library and asking it to determine how much money he has in his checking account at the local bank. The word "user" describes any human being that is entering input into the system, examining output, or interacting with the system in any other way. A large software system (application programs, operating system, compilers, utility programs, and so on) will have a large number of different users, such as people communicating with the software through remote terminals or the mails (often people with no knowledge of computers or programming), application programmers, system programmers, and system operators.

The reader should now be able to grasp an elusive characteristic of software reliability: *software errors are not an inherent property of software.* That is, no matter how long we stare at (or test, or "prove") a program (or a program and its specifications), we can never find all of its errors. We may find a few errors, such as an endless loop, but, because of the basic nature of software errors, we can never expect to find them all. In short, the presence of an error is a function of both the software and the expectations of its users.

Although I will use this definition as the basic definition of a software error, it does have at least one flaw. Consider an airlines reservation terminal that instructs the clerk to "ENTER FLIGHT NUMBER AND DATE" to which he responds by entering "239,MAY10." The system responds with the message "INCORRECT DATE" because it expected the date in the form 10MAY. Is this a software error? According to our definition it may be, but I say it is not; it is probably a human factors problem. We could broaden the definition to cover situations such as this one by viewing them as human factors design errors in the software; however, we have to draw the line somewhere so I have chosen to exclude human factors problems from our definition of software error. Human factors is certainly an extremely important consideration in system design, but it is a separable area of study and is already dealt with elsewhere [2]. The subject of human factors arises again in Chapters 2 and 4.

WHAT IS RELIABILITY?

A second term that must be defined is *software reliability*. Again, we begin by examining the common definition of the term, which is the probability that the system will function for a particular period of time without encountering an error. The major problem with this definition is that it does not differentiate between types of errors. Consider an air-traffic-control system with two software errors, one which loses track of a plane and another which misspells a word in an operator message, for example, spelling TRANSAMERICAN as TRANSAMMERICAN. The severity of these errors differs considerably, which implies that reliability must be stated as a function of the *severity* of errors as well as their frequency. Accordingly, we define software reliability as follows:

Software reliability is the probability that the software will execute for a particular period of time without a failure, weighted by the cost to the user of each failure encountered.

Software reliability is thus a function of the impact that errors have on the system users; it is not necessarily a function of the actual magnitude of the error within the software system. For instance, a major design flaw could have only a negligible impact on the user. On the other hand, a seemingly trivial error could have a massive impact on the system user. For instance, the United States' first space mission to Venus failed because of a missing comma in a FORTRAN DO statement.

Reliability is not an inherent property of a program; it is largely related to the manner in which the program is used. The word *probability* in the definition actually represents the probability that a user will not enter a particular set of inputs that leads to a failure.

Within this book the term *reliability* is used rather loosely. At times it is simply used as a qualitative measure of the lack of errors in a program. The sense in which the word is used should always be obvious from the surrounding context.

ARE ENGINEERS SMARTER THAN PROGRAMMERS?

After the installation of a new computing system, a common remark for the data processing manager to make to the computer manufacturer is, "When we first installed our system the computer (the hardware device) worked fine but the operating system software was full of errors. Why are your engineers smarter than your programmers? Why don't you test your software to the same degree that you seem to test your hardware?"

The question is a perfectly reasonable one, but the answer is quite complicated. To begin with, the computer manufacturer probably spent considerably more money on software testing than on hardware testing, and it is obvious that software errors cannot be ascribed merely to lack of programmers' skill. The basic answer is that software is inherently much more complicated than hardware. The input domain of an operating system is magnitudes larger than the input domain of a central processing unit. For instance, the set of user manuals for IBM's OS/VS2 operating system and its related software is hundreds of times as voluminous as the manual describing the machine architecture of the IBM S/370 central processing units.

The basic input of a central processing unit (CPU) is a stream of machine instructions. To process a typical machine instruction, the CPU receives a fixed-size instruction (perhaps 16–36 bits in length) and several short bit strings (operands) in memory, implying that the input is in a rigid format. Furthermore, the execution of most instructions is not influenced to a great degree by the values of the operands and, in most CPUs, the execution of one instruction is independent of the execution of previous instructions. In comparison, the input domain of a software system is vastly larger; usually it is anything the human user decides to enter into the system. In most cases, the processing of an item of input is dependent on prior inputs.

A second area of difference is the relationship to the computing system's application. Hardware is largely application independent. One can use the same CPU to implement a hotel reservation system, a medical diagnostic system, or a simulation of the world's economic system. Most of the system's software, on the other hand, is highly sensitive to the particular application of the system.

A third area of difference concerns the nature of the elements (building blocks) of the products. Most hardware processors are collections of well-known building blocks such as memory arrays, registers, adders, busses, and gates. Any reasonable textbook on logic design describes optimal ways of building these devices. The engineer is primarily interested in the number, size, speed, and configuration of these devices to produce a processor meeting particular performance and cost goals. The building blocks available to the software designer are much more primitive in relation to the end result. His building blocks are the program statements available to him, collections of algorithms, and pieces of previous software systems.

The purpose of this discussion is not to compare the skills of the programmer and engineer but to point out that, in terms of achieving reliability, the software designer has a considerably more difficult job than the hardware designer. However, this must not be used as an excuse for unreliable software; in fact, the software designer has much to learn from the engineer. Many of the techniques used to produce reliable software relate to the moving of software development toward a disciplined field analogous to engineering.

HARDWARE RELIABILITY

To further understand software reliability, it is worthwhile to contrast it with hardware reliability. A hardware device can become inoperative because of three types of problems: design errors, manufacturing errors, and failures. A *design error* is an error that is initially present in every copy of a product. A design error might occur if parts of the memory of a CPU are unaddressable because of a logic design mistake in the memory addressing circuits. A *manufacturing error* is an error that is initially present in one or more copies of a product because of mistakes in the production of those particular copies. For instance, manufacturing errors occur because of such mistakes as poor soldering of connections or misrouting a wire. *Failures* are problems that are not initially present in a product but arise during its operation because of some physical phenomenon such as deterioration caused by molecular flaws, heat, humidity, friction, radiation, and so on. Examples of failures are the physical wear-out of a switch because of friction, loss of magnetism in a magnetic core from excessive heat, and failure of an integrated circuit because of slow deterioration of its insulation.

Figure 1.1 illustrates the change in the hardware instantaneous failure rate over time for a typical device. The curve can be analyzed by applying it to an automobile. The average automobile is initially unreliable because of design and manufacturing errors such as improper tuning, loose bolts, and missing parts. These problems are encountered and corrected early and the car reaches its reliability peak. After this initial period, there is a relatively constant failure rate during which the

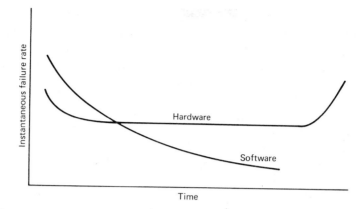

Figure 1.1   **The difference between hardware and software reliability.**

automobile's components fail randomly, usually following a Poisson distribution. As the automobile approaches the end of its useful life span, the failures are no longer random but appear at an increasing rate. The field of hardware reliability is primarily concerned with the middle period of random failure.

Software reliability is considerably different from hardware reliability. Software does not fail; it does not wear out. Furthermore, manufacturing errors (such as a mistake during the copying of a software system to a distribution tape) are not a consideration because they are relatively rare and easily detected. Software unreliability, then, is entirely attributable to design errors, that is, errors that are initially introduced during the production process. If we consider an environment where errors are corrected as they are detected (meaning they will never appear again), then software reliability usually changes according to the failure rate shown in Figure 1.1. Of course, this curve assumes that new errors are not introduced by the corrections for detected errors. This assumption is usually invalid.

Figure 1.1 shows that software and hardware reliability have inherently different behaviors. Hardware reliability is based largely on random failures; software reliability is based on predestined errors.

To emphasize this distinction between failure and error, consider the behavior of hardware failures and software errors in terms of dependence upon input data and time. Hardware failures are normally independent of the data being processed by the system. If a binary adder circuit is deteriorating and about to fail, the particular values of the data being processed have no effect on the failure. Software errors, on the other hand, are highly input dependent. The reason that a software error appears at a particular time is that some unique sequence of inputs is being processed at that time.

Hardware failures are highly time dependent. All physical devices have some useful life span, after which their failure rate increases rapidly. Software failures, although sometimes appearing to be a function of time, are actually a function of the current system input and the current system state. During the major portion of the life of a hardware device, failures are random and follow a Poisson distribution; a large field of study is based on this characteristic. Software failures are systematic, not random, events.

This matter of hardware and software reliability is discussed further in Chapter 18 in regard to attempts that have been made to apply hardware reliability mathematics to software.

THE HIGH COST OF SOFTWARE

As mentioned earlier, the two major problems in the software business are the excessive cost and unreliability of software. Proposed solutions to the cost problem often involve an attempt to raise "programmer productivity" by devising tools and techniques to allow programmers to work more quickly.

Figure 1.2 illustrates the relative costs of software over its lifetime

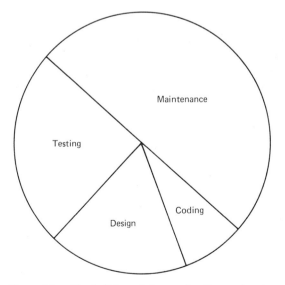

Figure 1.2   **Typical breakdown of software costs.**

for most typical large-scale efforts. The costs of maintenance (fixing errors and adding small changes after the system is initially installed) and testing account for approximately 75% of the cost of software. For instance, the SAGE system, a military defense system, had an average software maintenance cost of approximately 20 million dollars per year after 10 years of operation, compared to an initial development cost of 250 million dollars [3]. In typical releases of the IBM OS/360 operating system, approximately 60% (and as high as 76%) of the costs were incurred *after* the system was made available for use. In both cases the cost mentioned is for maintenance only. The maintenance *and* testing costs in these two cases probably exceeded 80% of the total costs. Although no one knows the annual world-wide costs for testing and maintenance, we do know that one organization, the U.S. Air Force, spent over 750 million dollars in 1972 on software testing [4].

It should be obvious that the high cost of software is largely due to reliability problems. Software costs are usually *not* significantly lowered by increasing programmer productivity if the latter is a measure of the speed of designing and coding the program. In fact, in some cases, attempts to increase programmer productivity can actually increase costs. The best way to dramatically reduce software costs is to reduce the maintenance and testing costs. This is achieved not by devising means to make programmers program faster, but by devising means to allow software to be designed with more precision and accuracy.

SOFTWARE EXPERIMENTATION

Throughout the book many conclusions are drawn about the "optimal" methodologies, tools, and techniques that should be used to achieve reliability. For most of these conclusions it is impossible to discuss firm experimental results that verify each conclusion, because of the extreme difficulty of performing experiments in software development. The reasons for this difficulty are listed below.

1. Software development is a labor-intensive (or more accurately "mind-intensive") industry. Thus experiments in software development are highly dependent on people. Most researchers agree that the most difficult subject for any experiment is the human being, because he (or she) is such a complicated and largely unknown system. For instance, in experiments designed to compare interactive versus batch computing, Sackman observed that there were differences of up to 28 to 1 in different programmers performing the

same task [5]. Often, these individual differences are more significant than the factors being studied in the experiment.

2. Software development experiments are prohibitively expensive. To study a single variable such as the effects of structured programming we might initiate two medium-sized projects, identical in all respects except that one uses structured programming and the other does not. Each project might last for a year and have a labor and computer-time cost of several million dollars. Next, to properly complete the experiment, we might repeat the same project a few times. We might also repeat it again in order to vary several other variables. The total duration of the complete experiment (studying only one factor of software development) may be several years at a cost of 10 to 20 million dollars. Even if the money for such an experiment were available, one would be faced with the problem of obtaining several hundred professional programmers for several years to devote to the experiment. Furthermore, someone may have invented something better than structured programming in the meantime.

3. There are hundreds of variables, many yet unidentified, that affect software development. Furthermore, these variables are not independent; many of them are related to one another. For instance, IBM's highly regarded New York Times project is often used as evidence of the value of structured programming and chief programmer teams [6]. However, the question of what percentage of the results is attributable to each technique and what percentage is due to other factors such as the high caliber of the programmers involved remains unanswered.

4. The few carefully planned experiments that have been performed have typically been single-individual projects involving student labor and small programs. One has to be extremely cautious in assuming that undergraduate students program like professional programmers and that results from small one-person projects can be extrapolated to large-scale many-person projects.

These difficulties are not intended as excuses or as discouragement to software experimenters. The intent is to indicate that, although the techniques described in this book have been observed to have a positive effect on reliability, there is little or no experimental evidence to serve as proof. Of course, it is possible to refuse to adopt any of the principles and practices discussed in this book until valid experimental proof is given, but this attitude entails the risk of not seeing any significant reliability improvements in software for a considerable time.

REFERENCES

1. R. A. Brooker, S. Gill, and D. J. Wheeler, "The Adventures of a Blunder," *Mathematical Tables and Other Aids to Computation,* **6** (38), 112–113 (1952).

2. J. Martin, *Design of Man-Computer Dialogues.* Englewood Cliffs, N.J.: Prentice-Hall, 1973.

3. R. H. Thayer, "Rome Air Development Center R & D Program in Computer Language Controls and Software Engineering Techniques," RADC-TR-74-80, Griffiss Air Force Base, Rome, N.Y., 1974.

4. M. Shelly, "Computer Software Reliability, Fact or Myth?," TR-MMER/RM-73-125, Hill Air Force Base, Utah, 1973.

5. H. Sackman, *Man-Computer Problem Solving: Experimental Evaluation of Time-Sharing and Batch Processing.* New York: Auerbach, 1970.

6. F. T. Baker, "Chief Programmer Team Management of Production Programming," *IBM Systems Journal,* **11** (1), 56–73 (1972).

CHAPTER 2

Errors—Their Causes and Consequences

In 1971 a large meteorological experiment was attempted by France. One hundred fifteen balloons containing measurement instruments were launched into the upper atmosphere and a satellite was launched to relay data between the balloons and ground stations. The balloons were designed to respond to two commands: a read command that directed the balloon to relay its data to the satellite and an abort command that detonated an explosive charge in the balloon in the event that the balloon went astray. Unfortunately, there was a software error in the system. Instead of reading data from the balloons, the software error caused the abort signal to be sent, destroying the 72 balloons in the line-of-sight path of the satellite.

To develop methods to achieve higher reliability in order to prevent errors such as this multimillion dollar mistake, one must first understand the underlying reasons for software errors. This understanding also aids in approaching such questions as: Is there something unique about the programming profession that attracts people who are mistake prone by nature? Are there inherent properties in software that makes it error-prone? Are these properties beyond our control or can we influence them?

One method often used to study the causes of errors is to collect error data and then group it into categories, for example, confirming that 17% of all errors are interface errors, 22% of all errors are attributable to incorrect sequencing of program statements, and so on. A second method is to group errors by the type of programming language statement containing the error, for instance, showing that 29% of all errors are found in IF statements, 13% of all errors are found in data declaration statements, and so forth.

Although these studies make interesting reading, they are not particularly useful in explaining how to eliminate errors. For instance, the first study implies that program statements should be sequenced correctly. Such a statement is of little use since no programmer knowingly attempts to sequence his statements incorrectly. The second study, implying that more errors occur in IF statements than in any other statement, might lead to the incorrect conclusion that IF statements should not be used in programs.

Studies like these are of limited benefit because they focus on the manifestations of errors rather than on the original causes of the errors. What is needed is an understanding of the underlying causes of software errors and some means of relating these causes to the software production process.

The single major cause of software errors is mistakes in translating information.

One can describe software production in simple terms as simply a set of processes that begins with a problem and ends with a large collection of detailed instructions that direct a computer in the solution of that problem. In other words, programming is problem-solving, and software is a collection of information (as opposed to physical objects) describing a solution of a problem. Software production, then, is simply a number of translation processes, translating the initial problem into various intermediate solutions until a detailed set of computer instructions is produced. Software errors are introduced whenever one fails to completely and accurately translate one representation of the problem or the solution to another more detailed representation.

Before a problem (such as unreliability) can be solved, the problem itself must first be understood. Realizing that translation errors are the reasons for software errors is extremely important, because that realization identifies our problem.

THE MACROSCOPIC TRANSLATION MODEL

The software error problem can be examined in greater detail by examining the different kinds of translation that occur in software production. A model of software production is illustrated in Figure 2.1. Before discussing the model, several considerations should be noted. The processes of software testing are excluded from this basic model.

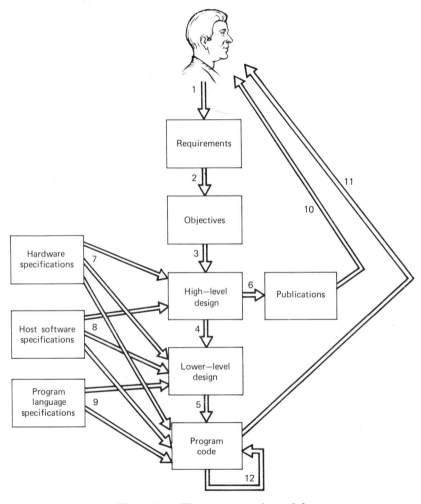

Figure 2.1   **The macroscopic model.**

The design processes are represented by only two steps, although in practice there usually are (and should be) more steps. The intent of the model is not to outline a recommended set of processes (this is done in Parts II and III), but to illustrate the basic kinds of translation that occur. Also, for now we disregard any overlap among processes and any feedback loops (for example, mistakes discovered during a particular process often require one to backtrack and correct work done in previous processes).

To get a better understanding of the translation problem, let us briefly examine each type of translation in Figure 2.1.

1. The process starts with the development of a description of the problem to be solved. This description becomes a statement of the requirements of the end-user. In some cases the user writes a requirements statement. In other cases the software producer writes the requirements statement, either by interviewing the user, researching the needs of the user, judging for himself the expected future needs of the user, or any combination of these.

   In each case there is ample opportunity for error; for example, the user may be unable to adequately express his needs, the user's needs may be misinterpreted, or there may be a failure to recognize *all* of the user's problem. Errors that occur at this level are obviously extremely costly.

2. The second process involves the translation of user requirements into objectives for the software product. Although this step does not entail a significant amount of translation, it does involve identifying and weighing a considerable number of tradeoffs (identified in Chapter 4). Software errors can be introduced during this step by misinterpreting the requirements, failing to identify the tradeoffs that must be considered, identifying the tradeoffs but making them incorrectly, and failing to establish necessary objectives that are not normally explicitly identified in user requirements.

3. The third step is concerned with transforming objectives into an external specification, a precise description of the entire system behavior from the user's point of view. In terms of the amount of translation that must occur, this step is the most significant step in software development. This makes step 3 the most error-prone step in software development in regard to the number and severity of errors.

4. Step 4 represents a number of translation processes that begin with an external description of the product and end by producing

a detailed design describing the large number of program statements that must be executed to implement a system having the specified external behavior. This step includes such processes as translating the external description into a structure of software components (e.g., modules) and translating each of these components into a description of procedural steps (e.g., flowcharts). Because we are dealing with larger and larger masses of information about the software product, the chances of introducing software errors during these processes are extremely high.

5. The last design process is the translation of the software logic specifications into programming language statements. Although a large number of errors are often made in this process, these errors tend to be relatively minor and easily detected and corrected. (This is not *always* the case, however, as you will see later on.)

A second type of translation occurs during this process: the translation of the source language representation of the program into object (machine-executable) code. This translation is normally done by a separate program, the compiler. Of course, the compiler itself occasionally contains errors that introduce errors into the program being compiled. However, we consider these errors as conditions outside of our control (unless the program we are producing is a compiler).

6. A software project has two outputs: the software itself and the publications describing the use of the software. The publications normally take the form of written manuals, although they could be stored within the computing system itself and retrieved, for instance, by the user at his terminal. Publications are usually written by translating the software external specifications into material that is oriented to particular kinds of users.

Publications have several influences on software reliability. For instance, if errors occur during the writing of the publications, the publications will not accurately describe the behavior of the software (unless identical errors are made in steps 4 and 6). The user will read the publications, use the software, and discover that the software does not behave as he expects—which is the condition that defines a software error. Of course, as mentioned in Chapter 1, even if the software and publications agree with one another, software errors may still be present (e.g., when translation errors are made in steps 1, 2, or 3 or when identical translation errors are made in steps 4 and 6).

7. During the development process, specifications for the system hardware serve as another form of input. For instance, the

designer of an operating system is dependent upon descriptions of the CPU hardware (e.g., the instruction set, interrupt mechanisms, and protection facilities) and all peripheral hardware attached to the system. The designer of an application system often depends on specifications of terminals and telecommunications lines. Any misunderstanding of these specifications may result in a software error.

8. Application software often interacts with the host software in the computing system for such services as input–output and dynamic allocation of resources. Misinterpreting the documentation of these host software services in another source of error.

9. The software product is ultimately expressed as source statements in at least one programming language. Misunderstanding the syntax or semantics of the programming language is yet another cause of software errors.

10. There are two forms of communication between the user and the software product: the publications describing the use of the product and the use of the software itself. Step 10 represents the user reading the publications and translating their content into an understanding of how he wishes to use the software.

To understand how reliability is affected by this process, assume we have a software product with a number of unknown errors. If the user is attempting to perform a function using the product and he cannot adequately determine how to do this by examining the publications (for example, because of poor organization or writing), he may attempt to experiment with the system. These attempts to use the system in unexpected ways often increase the probability of encountering the remaining software errors. Hence the quality of the user documentation, although it has no bearing on the number of software errors present, can affect the reliability of the product.

11. This step represents the user's direct interaction with the software, for example, entering input data from a terminal and examining the output produced. If the human factors are poor (the man–machine dialogue is poorly designed), the probability of the user's making a mistake is greater. Mistakes made by the user often lead to new and unanticipated conditions in the system, increasing the chances of encountering remaining errors.

12. As mentioned earlier, there are many feedback loops in this diagram that are ignored until later. However, one of these loops, step 12, is important enough to discuss at this point.

A considerable percentage of the world's software efforts

involve the alteration of existing software. Although the translation model in Figure 2.1 is a fairly good representation of this process as well, a major additional step that arises in the alteration process is the reading and understanding of the existing software code to understand how and where to add changes. This step occurs in maintenance activities (correcting software errors) and modification activities (adding new functions to existing products). Because of this, the software itself is usually not the end of the translation process; people have to translate the software to correct errors and add additional functions. Errors can obviously be introduced in this step, so attributes of the software, for example, features of the programming language used and programming style, require our attention.

This translation model describes how the vast majority of software errors originate. (Note also that many translation errors occur *within* each process.) This model is often viewed with surprise by the uninitiated, for their view is often that software errors are errors made by a programmer while writing his source code. Some software errors are due to causes not mentioned here, for example, dropping a card deck or transposing two characters while typing program statements on a terminal, but these errors represent only a small percentage of the errors and are usually easily detected.

This model is important because it describes the underlying causes of unreliability. We now have a set of known problems to solve. Many of the strategies in this book are based on this translation model. That is, techniques are discussed that minimize or detect the translation errors that occur in each of these steps.

THE MICROSCOPIC TRANSLATION MODEL

To obtain a better understanding of these translation problems consider the model represented by Figure 2.2. The person represents any person in the macroscopic translation model, for example, the user, analyst, designer, or programmer. This person is attempting to translate information about the product from form A to form B. To do this, he has to perform four basic steps.

1. He (or she) receives the information using his read mechanism R (the areas of the brain controlling his eyes and ears).
2. He stores this information in his memory M.

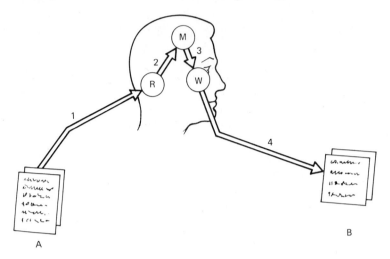

Figure 2.2   **The microscopic model.**

3. He retrieves this information from his memory, retrieves other information from his memory describing the translation process, performs the translation, and sends this to his writing mechanism *W* (the areas of his brain controlling his hands or mouth).
4. The information is physically dispersed by writing, typing on a terminal, or speaking.

Even though this is a simplistic model of this process, we can examine the errors generated in each step:

1. One of the greatest features of the human mind is its ability to comprehend input by matching it against a vast storehouse of past education and experiences. This is the principle behind the human's ability to "read between the lines," understand sentences that are grammatically incorrect, predict the ending of a movie, and so on. Unfortunately, these powerful abilities are sometimes the cause of software errors when they lead to imprecision in the translation process. Errors are introduced by misreading document *A*, seeing what is expected or wanted as opposed to what is actually there, making assumptions about missing facts, or simply overlooking information.

    These same abilities are often useful in the detection of errors. If errors are initially present in document *A*, we have the ability to detect them by recognizing conflicts with our previous experiences.

However, this is only useful if we go back to the producer of document *A* and question him about this conflict. Often, this is not done; we resolve the conflict ourselves, sometimes correctly, sometimes incorrectly, and proceed onward.

2. To remember most information accurately, we have to understand it. Software errors in this step result from misinterpreting or not understanding the input information. The information may be too complex, the person may not have the necessary educational background, or the information may be ambiguous.

3. The largest source of errors in this step is the phenomenon of forgetting: forgetting the input information *A* or forgetting how to perform the translation properly. Weaknesses in other mental abilities, such as clarity of thought and retrieval of related knowledge, also contribute errors.

4. The last step in which information can be altered or lost is step 4. Many people do not write or express themselves clearly, which obscures their output. If there is a large amount of output information, the person becomes impatient with the vast difference between his writing and thinking speeds. To overcome this he takes shortcuts or assumes that facts will be "intuitively obvious" to his audience. These faults increase the probability that the next person in the development process will make translation errors.

By now you probably have the impression that software errors are entirely caused by deficiencies in the human mind and that the only possible solution is the careful genetic breeding of today's best programmers. However, there are more realistic solutions to many of these translation flaws. The media that are used to express the different levels of a design (e.g., specifications, programming languages) influence the translation process. The design processes and attributes of the design itself, for example, its complexity, also significantly influence translation flaws. These solutions are discussed in Part II.

CONSEQUENCES OF ERRORS

When I was an undergraduate student I worked as a systems programmer in the college's computing center. One job I had after the installation of a new computing system was the development of an accounting system, that is, a program in the operating system to measure and record resource usage and an application program to maintain the accounting data and produce periodic reports. Because

disk storage space was at a premium, I had to optimally pack department, project, and user records on the disk tracks within the accounting
data set.

A few years later at a computer conference I ran into the computing
center director. He shattered my pride in this system by telling me of
an error that had just been discovered. An attempt to add a new project
in a particular department caused an overflow to a second disk track
for that department. I had planned for this condition but unfortunately
made an "off-by-one" error; an IF-GREATER-THAN-OR-EQUAL
statement should have been an IF-GREATER-THAN statement.

I am sure many readers have had this experience. A system may
operate successfully for several years with its users becoming confident
in its operation until it unexpectedly fails when hidden errors suddenly
surface because of new conditions.

In preparing the manuscript for this book I used a text editing and
processing program. The program functioned fairly well, but it
consistently failed at one particular place in the book. When processing
Chapter 1 it printed the definition of software reliability as:

> Software reliability is the probability tha
> software will execute for a particular peri
>
> o
>
> time without a failure, weighted by the cost t
>
> o
>
> the user of each failure encountered.

It almost seemed that I had struck a sensitive nerve in the software:
the program did not like my definition of reliability! Actually, all that
happened was that I formatted my lines in a way that the designer of
the text processing program did not anticipate.

Data processing trade magazines often publicize humorous stories
about classic software errors (humorous to all except those involved)
such as the insurance system that canceled a policy for no apparent
reason and prevented its being reinstated, a magazine subscription
program that suddenly sent every copy of the magazine to one address,
a loan system that sent a monthly bill for $212,958.72 when the balance
of the loan was only $2342.55, and a railroad system that lost freight
cars. Errors in voting systems have given votes to the wrong candidates,
lost votes entirely, and even in one case given all the votes to a single
candidate (only the last error was easily recognized). An error in a large
warehouse data base system caused records of the contents of the
warehouse to be destroyed, causing, among other things, the firm to lose
track of 15 tons of frozen liver that had been placed in an unre-
frigerated compartment. A school system grading program recognized

only two-digit test scores, resulting in students with scores of 100 receiving failing grades. A programmer who just completed converting his company's payroll program from an IBM 1401 system to an IBM 360 system opened his pay envelope and discovered that his salary had been reduced to $0.00.

Fortunately, most of these errors had no severe consequences. However, there is another set of classic errors that have resulted in disasters or near-disasters. A software error in the onboard computer of the Apollo 8 spacecraft erased part of the computer's memory. Eighteen errors were detected during the 10-day flight of Apollo 14. The concern over software errors in the Apollo program was expressed by the following statement [1]:

> The world's most carefully planned and generously funded software program was that developed for the Apollo series of lunar flights. The effort attracted some of the nation's best computer programmers and involved two competing teams. Checking the software was as thorough as the experts knew how to make it. In the aggregate, about $660 million was spent on software for the Apollo program. Yet, almost every major fault of the Apollo program, from false alarms to actual mishaps, was the direct result of errors in computer software.

Critical software errors have not been limited to just the Apollo program. A 1963 NORAD exercise was incapacitated because a software error caused the incorrect routing of radar information. The U.S. Strategic Air Command's 465L Command System, even after being operational for 12 years, still averaged one software failure per day [2]. An error in a single FORTRAN statement resulted in the loss of the first American probe to Venus. Worst of all, errors in medical software have caused deaths [3] and an error in an aircraft design program contributed to several serious air crashes [4], although information on these errors is, as one might expect, sketchy.

These first two chapters should have given you an appreciation of the software reliability problem. As our society becomes increasingly computerized, the consequences of unreliability become increasingly severe. Fortunately, there *are* solutions for many aspects of the reliability problem; the remainder of this book discusses these solutions.

REFERENCES

1. E. Ulsamer, "Computers—Key to Tomorrow's Air Force," *AIR FORCE Magazine,* **56** (7), 46–52 (1973).
2. R. H. Thayer, "Rome Air Development Center R & D Program in Computer Lan-

guage Controls and Software Engineering Techniques," RADC-TR-74-80, Griffiss Air Force Base, Rome, N.Y., 1974.

3. B. W. Boehm, "Software and its Impact: A Quantitative Assessment," *Datamation*, **19** (5), 48–59 (1973).

4. P. Naur and B. Randell, Eds., *Software Engineering: Report on a Conference Sponsored by the NATO Science Committee.* Brussels, Belgium: NATO Scientific Affairs Division, 1968, p. 121.

Designing Reliable Software

CHAPTER 3

Basic Design
Principles

Software development encompasses two categories of tasks: design and testing. Part 2 is
concerned with the design tasks and the types
of testing that can occur in the design processes.
Part 3 discusses the types of software testing
that should occur after the design is finished.

The word *design* has an ambiguous meaning
in the software business today. Many organizations arbitrarily restrict "design" to a description of the early project activities and use words
such as implementation, development, and
programming to describe later activities.
Unfortunately, there are no industry-wide
conventions for these terms; different organizations group different processes under these
headings, which leads to confusion when trying
to compare two projects. Furthermore, these
arbitrary distinctions tend to create "caste"
systems because programmers often consider
the job of a "designer" to be more prestigious
than the job of an "implementer."

To overcome these problems, I use the word
design as it is defined in the dictionary: "to
fashion according to a plan." This covers
software activities beginning with the establish-
ment of requirements and objectives and ending with the writing of program statements, providing that we recognize that there are distinct

stages of design. The phrases *software development, software engineer-ing,* and *software production* are used to describe the total software cycle. This chapter discusses a number of principles that are common to all of the design stages.

FOUR APPROACHES TO RELIABILITY

All design principles and practices for reliability can be grouped in four categories: *fault avoidance, fault detection, fault correction,* and *fault tolerance.* Fault avoidance describes the principles and practices that minimize or eliminate the existence of errors. Fault detection is concerned with functions within the software that detect the presence of errors. Fault correction describes software functions that correct errors or their resulting damage. Fault tolerance is a measure of the software system's ability to continue to operate in the presence of errors.

Fault Avoidance

Fault-avoidance techniques are those design principles and practices whose objectives are to prevent errors from ever existing in the software product. Most of the techniques focus on the individual translation processes and are concerned with the prevention of errors during the processes. These techniques fall into the following categories:

1. Methods of managing and minimizing complexity, since complexity is a major cause of translation mistakes.
2. Methods of achieving greater precision during translation.
3. Methods of improving the communication of information.
4. Methods of immediately detecting and removing translation errors. These methods are concerned with the detection of errors at each translation step rather than deferring the discovery of errors until the program instructions are produced and tested.

It should be obvious that fault avoidance is the optimal strategy for software reliability. The best way to achieve reliability is to avoid creat-ing errors in the first place. However, it is always impossible to guarantee the absence of errors. The remaining three categories are geared to the assumption that errors will be present.

Fault Detection

Assuming the software will contain some number of errors, the next best strategy is to provide the software with the means to detect its own errors. Although we are concerned with the detection of software errors, the concept is illustrated for the detection of hardware failures in the dialogue in the movie "2001: A Space Odyssey":

COMPUTER: I AM HAVING DIFFICULTY MAINTAINING CONTACT WITH EARTH. THE TROUBLE IS IN THE AE-35 UNIT. MY FAULT PREDICTION CENTER REPORTS THAT IT MAY FAIL WITHIN 72 HOURS.

Most fault-detection techniques involve detecting failures as soon as possible after they arise. Immediate detection has two benefits: the effects of the error can be minimized and the later difficulty a human will have in taking information about the error and locating and correcting it will also be minimized.

Fault Correction

Fault-correction techniques go one step farther; after an error is detected, either the error itself or the effects of the error are corrected by the software. Fault correction is a viable technique in designing reliable hardware systems. Some hardware processors have the ability to detect faulty components and begin using identical spare components. Similar techniques for software are nonexistent because of the inherent difference between hardware failures and software errors. If a particular software module contains an error, identical "spare" modules will also have the same error.

The remaining ideas of correction are attempts to repair any damage caused by the error such as damaged data base records or system control tables. Damage-correction techniques are of limited benefit because they require one to predict in advance a few possible types of damage and to design software functions to undo the damage when it occurs. This appears to be a paradox because if one knew in advance what errors would occur, one could take additional steps to avoid these specific errors. Unless fault-correction functions can be generalized to correct many types of damage, fault avoidance is a better investment. Rather than design an operating system function that detects and corrects a damaged chain of tables or control blocks, one would be better off designing the system so that only one module has access to the chain, and then intensively attempting to verify the correctness of this module.

Fault Tolerance

Fault-tolerant strategies are concerned with keeping the software system functioning in the presence of errors. Strategies fall into three groups: dynamic redundancy, fallback methods, and error isolation.

1. The concept of *dynamic redundancy* originated in hardware design. One approach to dynamic redundancy is a processing technique known as *voting*. Data is processed in parallel by multiple identical devices and the output of these devices is compared. If a majority of the devices produce the same result, that result is assumed to be the correct one. Again, because of the nature of software errors, if an error is present in one copy of a software module, the same error will exist in every copy of the module, so the voting concept appears to be of no use. An approach sometimes suggested to circumvent this problem is to produce several copies of a module, where those copies are *not* identical. That is, all the copies perform the same function but either different algorithms are used or different programmers design the different versions of the module. This approach fails for the following reasons. It is often difficult to produce dissimilar versions of a module that perform the identical function. Also, additional software has to be produced either to execute these versions of the function in parallel or execute them sequentially and then compare the results. This additional software adds a new layer of complexity to the system, which, of course, is counter to the basic idea of fault avoidance, that is, to attempt to minimize complexity in the first place.

    A second approach to dynamic redundancy is to execute these spare copies of the function only when the results from the primary copy are detected as incorrect. If the results of a function are incorrect, the system automatically invokes a spare function. If the results from this spare are incorrect, another spare is invoked and so on. Although Randell [1] outlines a nice method for this, this approach has most of the weaknesses listed above. Also, it seems likely that on a project with a fixed amount of resources, each "spare" implementation of a function will receive less design and testing attention than the single copy would have received if dynamic redundancy had not been used.

2. A second set of fault-tolerant techniques is called *fallback* or degraded-service methods. These methods are normally only appropriate when it is essential for the software system to shut-down

gracefully. For instance, in a process-control system, if a software error is detected that is causing the system to fail, a separate back up piece of software may be loaded and executed to guarantee the safe shutdown of all processes being controlled by the system. Similar functions are often necessary in operating systems. If an operating system detects that it is about to fail, the system may load a separate kernel of functions that have the responsibility of notifying all terminal users of the pending failure and saving any critical data in the system.

3. The last set of fault-tolerant techniques fall into the category of *error isolation*. The basic premise here is to attempt to isolate errors to a minimal part of the software system so that if an error is encountered, the total system does not become inoperable; either isolated functions within the system become inoperable or particular users can no longer continue to function. For instance, many operating systems adopt a strategy of isolating errors to particular users so that after an error occurs only a subset of the users of the system is affected and the system as a whole remains operable. Telephone switching systems try to recover from errors by terminating phone connections rather than risking a total system failure. Other error-isolation techniques are concerned with protecting each program in the system from errors in other programs. An error in an application program running under an operating system should affect only that program. It should not affect the operating system or other application programs in the system.

Of the three groups of fault-tolerant techniques, only the third group, error isolation, is feasible for most software systems.

An important point to consider with these four approaches is that fault-detection, fault-correction, and fault-tolerant techniques are somewhat counter to fault-avoidance techniques. In particular, detection, correction, and tolerance involve the addition of functions to the software itself. These additional functions not only increase the complexity of the software product, but they themselves can contain software errors. As a basic guideline, *all* the fault-avoidance techniques that are discussed and many of the fault-detection techniques are applicable to any software project. Fault-correction and -tolerant techniques are not widely applicable to software today. However, this is an application-dependent consideration. If a particular application, say, a real-time application, must remain operable in the presence of errors, then correction and tolerant techniques may be desirable. Applications

	Fault Avoidance	Fault Detection	Fault Correction	Fault Tolerance
Principles	Chaps. 5, 6, 8	None	None	None
Practices	Chaps. 4, 5, 6, 8, 9	Chaps. 7, 8	Chap. 7	Chap. 7

Figure 3.1   **Relationships between chapters and reliability methods.**

in this category include telephone-switching systems, process control systems, aerospace systems, air-traffic-control systems, and general operating systems.

Figure 3.1 maps these techniques to their appropriate chapters in the book. *Principles* are application-independent strategies for software reliability. System design, program design, and module design principles are discussed for fault avoidance. There are no known principles for the remaining three categories. *Practices* are smaller-scale, generally application-dependent, tactics for software reliability. Practices in these four categories are discussed in the chapters shown in Figure 3.1.

THE DESIGN PROCESSES

The design of any software product always involves several distinct forms of design. In well-managed projects these processes are explicitly identified so that checkpoints can be established, methodologies can be chosen, and the "goodness" of the design can be measured after the completion of each process. In poorly managed projects some or all of these processes are not explicitly identified; each process still occurs in some fashion but some of them occur implicitly, implying that checkpoints, methodologies, and measurements are never established.

Figure 3.2 is a model of the design processes for the typical large-scale software project. Note that the model is methodology independent. All these activities must occur in some form in any development effort, independent of the programming language used, whether the end-user wrote the initial requirements, whether "structured programming" is used, and so on.

The first step produces a set of requirements, that is, a statement of what the user expects of the product. The following step is concerned

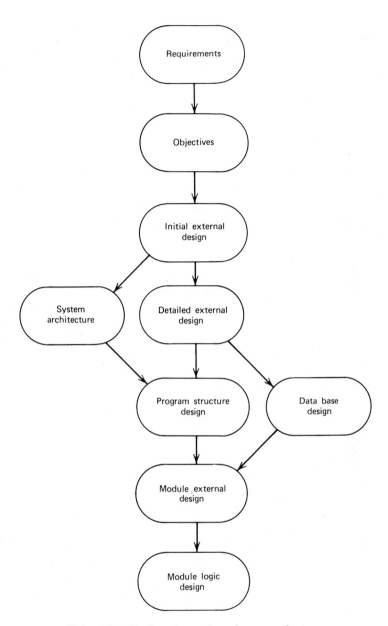

Figure 3.2   **Design stages for a large project.**

with setting objectives, which are the goals of both the product and project. Next, a high-level external design is performed. This step is defines the user interface but excludes much of the detail, such as exact input and output formats.

The initial external design leads to two parallel processes. The detailed external design process completes the user interface, describing it in utmost detail. The system architecture process decomposes the system into a set of programs, subsystems, or components and defines the interfaces among them. These two steps lead to the process of designing the program structure, which involves taking each program, component, or subsystem and designing their modules, module interfaces, and module interconnections. The next process, module external design, is the precise definition of all module interfaces. The last step, module logic design, is the design of the internal logic or procedure of each module in the system, including the expression of this logic as program statements.

The remaining design process shown in Figure 3.2 is data base design. This is the process of defining any data structures external to the software, for example, the design of file records or data base records.

Figure 3.2 illustrates the basic dependencies among the design processes, but it is not intended as a description of a sequential work plan for any particular project. In particular, overlap between these steps is often possible and usually desirable. Figure 3.2 shows what design processes have to be completely finished before another design process can be completed. For instance, it is necessary to complete the module external design for all modules in a system before the module logic design can be completed. However, the module logic design for some modules can certainly be completed before the module external design for all modules is finished. This form of overlap between adjoining steps is often desirable. Note, however, that there should be *no* overlap between two steps that are not adjoining one another. For instance, the module logic design process should not begin before the program structure design is finished. As a second example, the system architecture should not be started before the system objectives have been fully defined.

Also remember that in any real design effort, the picture of the flow of design processes is not quite this simple. There is a considerable amount of feedback between processes. For instance, flaws may be discovered in the objectives during one of the external design steps, requiring one to back up momentarily to correct the flaw in the objectives. During the program structure design it may suddenly be discovered that a function described in the external specifications is infeasible or extremely costly, possibly requiring a tradeoff and alteration of the external specifications.

Figure 3.2 can, with modifications, also serve as a model for small projects. The system architecture and data base design processes are often not present in single-program projects, and the initial and detailed external design processes are often merged into one step.

COMPLEXITY

Complexity, being a principal underlying cause of translation errors, is one of the major causes of unreliable software. Complexity is both difficult to define precisely and to quantify. However, we can say that the complexity of an object is some measure of the mental effort required to understand that object.

In general, the complexity of an object is a function of the relationships among the components of the object. For instance, to some extent the complexity of an external design of a software product is a function of the relationships among all of the external interfaces of the product, for example, relationships among user commands and the relationships established between outputs of the system and inputs to the system. The complexity of a system architecture is a function of the relationships among subsystems. The complexity of a program design is a function of the relationships among the modules. The complexity of a single module is a function of the connections among the program instructions within the module.

Two concepts can be adapted from general systems theory to combat complexity in software [2]. The first concept is *independence*. This concept simply says that, to minimize complexity, we must maximize the independence of each component of a system. Basically, this involves partitioning the system so that the high-frequency dynamics of the system fall within single components and the intercomponent interactions represent only the lower-frequency dynamics of the system.

The second concept is *hierarchical structure*. Hierarchies allow the stratification of a system into levels of understanding. Each level represents a set of aggregate relationships among the parts in the lower levels. The concept of levels allows one to understand the system by hiding unnecessary levels of detail. For instance, the system we call "man" appears to be hierarchy. The social scientist can study interactions among people without worrying about their internal construction. The psychologist works at a lower level in the hierarchy. He may be concerned with various logical and physical processes within the brain, but he is not concerned with the internal construction of the regions of the brain. Farther down the hierarchy, the neural scientist deals with the structure of the basic components of the brain. However, he can study the brain at this level without having to worry about the molecular structure of a particular protein in a neuron. The organic chemist is interested in the composition of complex amino acids from such components as carbon, hydrogen, oxygen, and chlorine atoms. On the lowest levels, the nuclear physicist studies the system from the point of view of the elementary particles within an atom and the relationships among the particles.

The point is that hierarchies enable one to design, describe, and understand complex systems. If one could not take such a view of man, the social scientist would have to deal with man as an immense and complex set of subatomic particles. Obviously, this detail would overwhelm him and make infeasible even the meager understanding that we have of man today.

To these two complexity-reducing concepts (independence and hierarchical structure), I would add a third: *making connections apparent* when they do occur. A basic problem in many large software systems is the immense number of unknown side-effects among the system's components. These side-effects make systems impossible to understand. We can safely say that a system that cannot be understood is a system that was originally difficult to design with any assurance of reliability.

A software design solution at any level always has some underlying form or organization. To minimize complexity we need techniques for discovering this inherent form so that the design can be partitioned along it. For instance, in external design, partitioning the system according to its inherent form is called *conceptual integrity* [3]. The chapters dealing with system architecture and program structure design discuss techniques to discover this inherent form in order to decompose the system into a set of components with a high degree of independence. In program logic design, a discipline called *structured programming* attempts, among other things, to fit all program logic into a few basic standard forms.

THE USER RELATIONSHIP

Chapter 1 stated that a software failure occurs when the system fails to do what the user reasonably expects it to do. At that time, a common question from the software developer was presented, namely, "How can one possibly know what the eventual user will reasonably expect of the system?" In any proper system development effort, this question should never arise. If the system developer has little or no knowledge of what the user will reasonably expect the software system to do, then the software project will never be successful.

Two common mistakes in software projects are failure to involve the end-user of the product in the decision-making processes and failure to understand the user's culture or environment. There is a tendency in many projects purposely to exclude the user from the decision-making process. The usual reason is that the software developer feels that if the user does become involved, he will never make up his mind; his requirements will be constantly changing. There is a small degree of validity in this concern, but in practice the advantages of user involvement far outweigh this potential disadvantage. The second fault in software projects is that the software designer often has little or no understanding of the user's environment, that is, what the user's problems are and how the user will use the software system. There are, for example, people involved with the design of operating systems who have never themselves used an operating system. There are programming language designers who have never attempted to implement an application system in a high-level programming language. There are data base management system designers who have never attempted to implement a data base application. These problems cannot help but lead to significant software errors.

The only obvious way to overcome these problems is to maintain a significant degree of contact with the user throughout the development cycle. Relationships must be established with the end-user community so that the end-user is heavily involved in the decision-making process in the requirements, objectives, and external design phases. User involvement in later processes is also desirable, particularly in the testing process where the user can give the system developer a great deal of insight as to how the system should be tested. Be cautious, however, in involving the user in detail on which he is not competent to pass judgment. For instance, it is reasonable to involve the user in the design of the external characteristics of the system but unreasonable to involve him in such activities as reviewing the logic design of a particular module in the system.

The disadvantage mentioned earlier is that the user may potentially alter his requirements on the system. Note, however, that this has nothing to do with the user's direct involvement in the project. If the requirements on the system are going to change, they will change regardless of whether the user is directly involved in the project. In fact, if the user is not directly involved, the designer will probably not learn of the changing requirements until it is too late. If the user is directly involved, he may have a greater appreciation of the costs of any change. If this condition of changing requirements is planned for correctly, user involvement can be turned into an advantage.

User involvement in the development of new proprietary unannounced products is *not* infeasible. Although the product is not being developed for any particular user, the software developer probably has a good idea of his prospective customers. Legal nondisclosure agreements can be signed to allow one or more prospective customers to participate in the design of the product before it is publicly announced.

Overcoming the second problem of understanding the user's culture requires that the designers of the software have a thorough understanding of the user's business. A common ineffective practice is to send the key designers of the system off to the sites of existing systems. The designers are given cursory presentations about the existing systems but no in-depth knowledge of how these systems are used or what their real problems are. If I were designing an airlines reservation system, one of my first steps would be getting a temporary job as an airlines reservation agent. After a few weeks I would have a real appreciation of the user's environment and perhaps a number of ideas for improving and increasing the productivity of this environment.

PROBLEM SOLVING

Most software development activities are problem-solving activities. External design is the solution of the problem, "Translate a set of product objectives into an external specification," where the objectives are the given and the external specification is the unknown. In the module logic design problem, the given is the module external specification and the unknown is the program code for the module. Debugging is the construction of a correction for a software error (the unknown) from a description of symptoms of the error (the given).

It is surprising that software developers receive no formal education or training in general problem-solving techniques. In teaching courses on software design I have observed that the successful solutions to complex design problems come from the students who either consciously or subconsciously apply general problem-solving rules.

One of the best discussions of problem-solving is Polya's *How To Solve It* [4]. Although it is slanted toward geometry problems and mathematical puzzles, most of the techniques are applicable to software design. Since software problems, unlike most mathematical problems, have no single "right" solution, I have slightly altered and rearranged Polya's technique. This is outlined in Figure 3.3 and discussed as follows.

Understand the Problem

The worst mistake that can be made in problem solving is the failure to thoroughly understand the problem. Understanding a problem involves understanding its two components: the data and the unknown. The data are all the given primitive facts for the problem and the relationships among the facts and the unknown. Digesting the data for a complex problem is a large but absolutely necessary task. What is needed is a thorough grasp of the "big picture" of the data, suppressing most of the detail but also storing it away for easy recall later on. There are many ways to achieve this. For example, some people physically cut

---

Problem Solving

1. Understand the problem
   Study the data.
   Study the unknown.
   Are the data sufficient for a solution? Contradictory?
2. Devise a plan
   What must you achieve?
   What design methods will be used?
   Have you seen the same problem before?
   Do you know a related problem? Can you use its result?
   Can you solve a more specialized or analogous problem?
   Can you solve part of the problem?
3. Carry out the plan
   Follow the plan to solve the problem.
   Check the correctness of each step.
4. Review the solution
   Did you use all of the data?
   Check the correctness of the solution.
   Can you use the result or the method for other problems?

Figure 3.3   **Steps for solving design problems.**

a specification into pieces and paste all of these pieces in a planned order on an office wall. This allows them to see the "big picture" while also enabling them to locate the detail.

The second part of the problem is the unknown. The designer must understand the form that the solution must take. If the problem is the detailed external design of a program, for instance, the designer must understand the purpose of an external specification, its audience, its format, and so on.

In examining the problem, the designer must also examine the data to ensure that it is sufficient to solve the problem and to ensure that parts of the data do not contradict each other.

Devise A Plan

Before starting the solution, a plan must be developed to direct the solution. Failure to do this is another common mistake. For example, software designers who take the time to understand a problem, but then immediately start the solution without taking time to plan their design effort, might end up with a good solution but not before making many unnecessary false starts.

The first part of the plan is to consider what the solution is intended to achieve. Ten people may have ten different opinions as to the "right" answer to a design problem; the designer must consider those particular aspects of the solution that require the most emphasis. Unfortunately, in most projects designers are given too much leeway in this area; each designer on the project makes tradeoffs based solely on his own opinions, leading to a system with many inconsistent decisions. The idea of *project objectives,* discussed in Chapter 4, is a solution to this problem. Project objectives establish project-wide goals for each design solution.

A key ingredient of successful design is methodology. As part of his plan, the designer must select an appropriate methodology for the particular design process.

A second set of ingredients includes experience, education, and the solutions of previous problems. The software business has evolved to the point where it is extremely rare that a designer will be faced with a problem that has not already been solved in part or in whole. For instance, the designer of a new operating system should realize that hundreds of operating systems have already been designed and many textbooks exist on the design of operating systems. The designer faced with a sorting problem should realize that many sorting algorithms have already been invented and evaluated. The intelligent problem solver will search his own experience and the experience of others to see if the problem has already been solved.

Even if an existing solution cannot be found, a related problem has probably been solved. The designer of an airlines reservation system might realize that it has many similarities with other reservation systems such as hotel reservation systems. He may then be able to locate and use elements of the solution of a hotel reservation problem.

If all else fails, an effective method is to solve a more specialized problem or only part of the problem. If the problem contains an overwhelming amount of detail or complexity, the designer should consider attempting to simplify the problem by discarding most of the detail. One of two positive results will occur: either he will later see how to alter his simplified solution to add in the discarded detail, or he will have greater insight into the eventual solution, allowing him to discard his simplified solution and begin again.

Carry Out The Plan

The next step is actually to solve the problem according to the planned approach. Since most solutions involve a large set of progressive steps, the designer should attempt to verify the correctness of each step during the solution process.

Review The Solution

After a solution has been completed, the last step involves testing the solution. The designer should review the data to ensure that he made use of all relevant data in his solution. An effective technique is to review the problem statement word by word, crossing out each fact used in the solution and then checking the relevance of each uncrossed word. The designer must also verify the correctness of the problem solution.

DESIGN CORRECTNESS

An explicit part of each design process must be the verification of the output, that is, attempting to find translation errors that arose during the process. The reasons for this are shown in Figure 3.4. Not only is the cost of correcting an error much smaller the earlier in the project it is discovered, but the probability of fixing the error correctly is much greater in an early phase than it is if the error is encountered during a later phase such as during system testing.

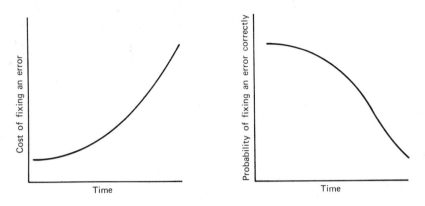

Figure 3.4   **Motivation for early detection of design errors.**

Although the verification of each particular design process is discussed in succeeding chapters, a general philosophy for verification is the *n-plus-and-minus-one rule.* A vital consideration in design verification is getting the proper individuals involved. The "proper" individuals are people with a vested interest in locating any flaws. The *n*-plus-and-minus-one rule is:

Given that the design for phase n must be verified, the verification should be done by the designer(s) of phases n − 1 and n+1.

As an example, suppose we have completed the system architecture phase. Looking back at Figure 3.2, we see that the *n* − 1 designers are the authors of the initial external specifications and the *n*+1 designers are the designers of the program structure. These are the appropriate people to "test" the system architecture.

The premise behind this is that any verification or testing process must be a destructive, even sadistic, effort. The attitude must be to find every conceivable fault or weakness in the system design, not to look at the system design to show that it is correct. The *n* − 1 designer, the external designer, is motivated to find flaws because his attitude is usually "Let me see how the system architects took my perfect external design and introduced errors." The *n*+1 designer is equally motivated to find flaws, but for a different reason. His feelings are "My input is the system architecture, so I should uncover any flaws in it and ensure that I can understand it before I start my work."

This philosophy is another one that is almost intuitively obvious, yet rarely practiced. If need be, formal procedures should be established to ensure that it occurs. It works for every design process shown in Figure 3.2. Naturally it has to be altered slightly for the first and last processes and for any two sequential processes performed by the same people.

REFERENCES

1. B. Randell, "System Structuring for Software Fault Tolerance," *IEEE Transactions on Software Engineering,* **SE-1** (2), 220–232 (1975).
2. H. A. Simon, *The Sciences of the Artificial.* Cambridge, Mass.: MIT Press, 1969.
3. F. P. Brooks, *The Mythical Man-Month: Essays on Software Engineering.* Reading, Mass.: Addison-Wesley, 1975.
4. G. Polya, *How To Solve It.* Princeton, N.J.: Princeton University Press, 1971.

CHAPTER 4

Requirements, Objectives, and Specifications

Software errors first creep into a product when requirements and objectives are established. The cause of most of these errors is a misunderstanding of the needs of the user. More errors originate when the requirements or objectives are translated into external specifications. Unfortunately, too few people place sufficient emphasis on these processes. The need for this emphasis is nicely summarized by Williams [1]:

> There is nothing, absolutely nothing, that can cause a more devastating outcome of a development activity than an incomplete and/or incorrect knowledge and corresponding specification of system and software requirements.

ESTABLISHING REQUIREMENTS

Software projects can be divided into three categories: user-driven, user-reviewed, and user-independent projects. In a *user-driven* project the software requirements are developed directly by the user organization. The software developer is a subcontractor to the user organization and the requirements represent all or part of the contract. As an example, many software projects for the United States government fall into this category. The government agency develops a rather lengthy set of requirements that are bid upon by software vendors.

In a *user-reviewed* project the software requirements are either developed by the software developer, or are developed in a joint effort between the software developer and the user organization. In this type of project the user organization has approval rights on the requirements and usually on later types of specifications, particularly the external specification.

In a *user-independent* project the responsibility for establishing requirements falls on the software developer. Most projects involved with the development of generalized marketable products fall into this category. However, as mentioned in the previous chapter, it is still vital to obtain some sort of user involvement in this type of project.

The purpose of software requirements is to establish the needs of the user for a particular software product. In doing this the user-reviewed category of projects is the most desirable. It is desirable, of course, to deeply involve the potential user of a product in the requirements process. It is also desirable to involve the software development organization in the process. A problem in the user-driven project is that the software developer is *not* involved, increasing the chances of misinterpreting or misunderstanding the requirements. User-driven and user-independent projects must be planned to achieve this dual involvement.

The requirements for a medium- or large-size system should be developed by a small team of individuals. One member of the team must be a key representative of the user organization, a representative with sufficient authority to make decisions. Note, however, that this person is typically not an actual end-user of the system. Because of this, a second representative on the team must be an individual who will actually use the system. For instance, in developing the requirements for an airlines reservation system, this representative should be an experienced reservation clerk. The development organization must also be represented on the team. One representative should be a person who will eventually have a key role in the external design process. Another team member might be a person who will have a key role in one of the internal design processes. The goal here in terms of reliability is to ensure that the user requirements are specified as accurately and precisely as possible and to ensure that the software development organization can translate these requirements into a system design with a minimum number of errors.

It is not my intention to describe the actual process of establishing requirements. The process involves the analysis of existing systems, interviewing users, performing feasibility studies, and estimating benefits. Techniques for these activities are described elsewhere in texts on systems analysis [2].

Automated systems for describing and manipulating requirements have been developed but are of limited use [3, 4]. These systems, such as Information Algebra, ADS, and TAG, are oriented toward small, specialized, and extremely well-defined problems.

One manual and semiformal method for describing requirements is the HIPO (Hierarchy plus Input-Process-Output) technique [5]. A HIPO diagram is drawn for each major required function; the diagram highlights the input and output data for the function and the basic processing steps. A *visual table of contents* is prepared showing the hierarchical organization of these functions.

Figures 4.1 and 4.2 are diagrams from a proposal for an on-line program-library system [6]. Each block in Figure 4.1 represents a major user function. Figure 4.2 is the HIPO diagram for one of these blocks.

When this technique is used, the diagrams are normally drafted by the software organization and presented to the user for his inspection. The diagrams do not imply anything about the final structure of the program, nor should they be written in programming jargon. Their objective is to provide the end-user with a graphical overview of the product, hopefully to allow him to say, "Yes, that is what I want this program to do."

In using this technique it is important to realize that HIPO diagrams only express functional requirements. Other types of requirements (e.g., reliability, performance, or cost) must be separately described.

Little can be said about the methods for verifying the correctness of requirements other than that the user is responsible for checking the requirements for completeness and accuracy and the developer is responsible for checking feasibility and understandability. In reviewing requirements it is desirable to set priorities for each requirement to give the software developer guidance in making tradeoffs in later design processes.

SOFTWARE OBJECTIVES

The second process in software development is the development of objectives. Objectives are specific goals for the software product.

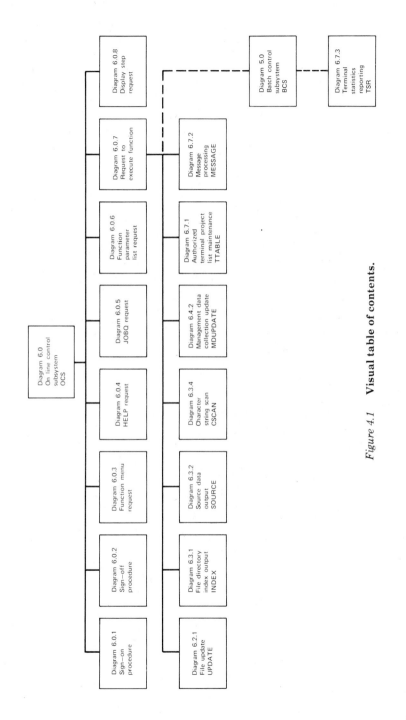

Figure 4.1 **Visual table of contents.**

49

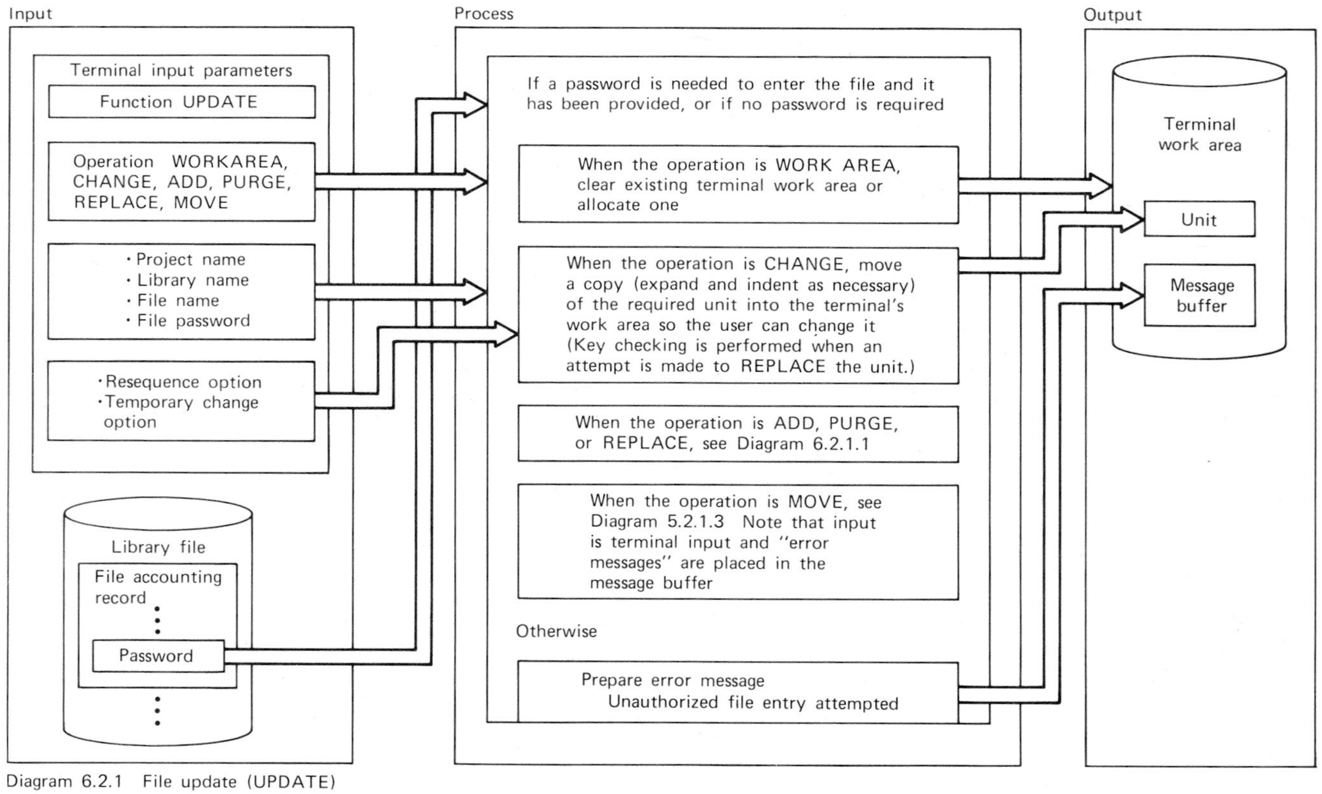
Input
Process
Output
Terminal input parameters
Function UPDATE
Operation WORKAREA, CHANGE, ADD, PURGE, REPLACE, MOVE
· Project name
· Library name
· File name
· File password
· Resequence option
· Temporary change option
Library file
File accounting record
Password
If a password is needed to enter the file and it has been provided, or if no password is required
When the operation is WORK AREA, clear existing terminal work area or allocate one
When the operation is CHANGE, move a copy (expand and indent as necessary) of the required unit into the terminal's work area so the user can change it (Key checking is performed when an attempt is made to REPLACE the unit.)
When the operation is ADD, PURGE, or REPLACE, see Diagram 6.2.1.1
When the operation is MOVE, see Diagram 5.2.1.3 Note that input is terminal input and "error messages" are placed in the message buffer
Otherwise
Prepare error message
Unauthorized file entry attempted
Terminal work area
Unit
Message buffer
Diagram 6.2.1 File update (UPDATE)

Figure 4.2 **HIPO diagram.**

Establishing software objectives is primarily a process of establishing tradeoffs. For instance, it is not inconceivable to have a requirements document with the following statement:

Maximize the reliability, efficiency, adaptability, generality, and security of the system, while minimizing its cost, schedule, storage usage, and terminal response time.

A statement like this is useless because many of the factors in the statement directly conflict with one another. The purpose of objectives, then, is to establish goals for the product and tradeoffs among those goals where necessary.

Common mistakes made in the objectives process are:

1. Failing to have written objectives.
2. Having a cursory set of written objectives where vital specific objectives are left unstated.
3. Stating objectives for the product, but stating them in such a way that they conflict with one another. The result is that the individual programmers on the project will resolve the conflicts for themselves, each person resolving them in a different way. A 100-person project will then end up with tradeoffs being made at least 100 different ways, resulting in an unpredictable outcome.
4. Recognizing the need for specific objectives but defining objectives for only the product, failing to define objectives for the project. A software development effort needs two distinct sets of objectives: *product objectives,* which define the goals of the product from the user's viewpoint, and *project objectives,* which are goals within the project such as schedules, cost, degree of testing, and so forth.

UNDERSTANDING THE TRADEOFFS

As mentioned earlier, the objectives process requires considering tradeoffs between conflicting requirements. Mistake 3, failing to define the necessary tradeoffs on a system-wide basis, is a common and serious mistake.

Software objectives can be grouped into ten major categories, reliability being one of the categories. To make meaningful tradeoffs it is necessary to understand the relationships among these categories. Since this book is primarily concerned with the reliability category, we discuss the relationships between reliability and the nine other categories.

Generality

Generality is a measure of the number, power, and scope of user functions. A requirements or objectives document would (hopefully) never say, "Maximize generality"; it would list the specific user functions needed.

Reliability and generality conflict because "generalized" products are normally larger and more complex. The resolution of this conflict should not imply that software products must be extremely specialized, however. This conflict can be lessened by avoiding any generalizations of the product that are of little or no benefit to the user. For instance, some compilers have so many options that it takes several pages simply to list them. It is likely, also, that some of these options have never been used. These unnecessary options complicate the compiler, undoubtedly leading to errors.

The generality-versus-reliability conflict is the most difficult tradeoff to make and the one that requires the most thought. One must remember that each element of the user interface, however small, has some negative effect on reliability. Each software function must be weighed in terms of its real benefit to the user versus its effect on reliability.

Human Factors

A product's human factors are a measure of the product's ease of understanding, ease of use, difficulty of misuse, and the resulting frequency of user errors. Although "humanizing" the user interface can increase system complexity and thus have a negative effect on reliability, human factors and reliability objectives are generally not in conflict. Many of the lingering errors in operational systems arise when new conditions suddenly occur. These new conditions are often the result of an unexpected action by a user. Good human factors minimize the chances of unexpected user actions, decreasing the chances of encountering any lingering errors.

Adaptability

Adaptability is a measure of the ease of extending the product, such as adding new user functions to the product. Adaptability and reliability are, surprisingly, compatible. A distinct advantage of many of the design techniques for reliability discussed in later chapters is their positive effect on extensibility or adaptability. That is, not only do these design techniques lead to more reliable software, but they also lead to products that are easier to extend.

Maintainability

Maintainability is a measure of the cost and time required to fix software errors in an operational system. Maintainability and reliability are compatible because maintainability is closely related to adaptability. Also, reliability techniques such as fault detection and error isolation have a positive effect on maintainability.

Security

Security is a measure of the probability that one system user can accidentally or intentionally reference or destroy data that is the property of another user or interfere with the operation of the system. Security measures involve the careful isolation of user data, the isolation of user programs from one another, and the isolation of user programs from the operating system. Security measures, being similar to error isolation measures, are usually compatible with reliability goals.

Documentation

Documentation objectives are concerned with the quality and quantity of user publications. Documentation objectives and human factors objectives are similar in that they are concerned with the ease of understanding and use of a product. Because of this, documentation objectives are not in conflict with reliability objectives.

Product Cost

The cost of a software product includes the cost of the original development of the product plus the cost of maintaining the product. In Chapter 1 the relationships between reliability and the current excessive cost of software were discussed; it was shown that the excessive cost of software is largely due to excessive numbers of errors. Thus it is thought that the objectives of high reliability and minimal development and maintenance costs are not in conflict.

Schedule

Another key objective in any project is to produce the product by a certain date. The benefits of a product are usually closely related to its availability date. Many of the relationships between reliability and the cost of software also apply between reliability and schedules. One major cause of schedule slippages is reliability problems. For instance, people have a tendency to grossly underestimate the time needed for testing. The actual time needed for testing is closely related to the number of software errors remaining in the product after its design is completed, and this time can be reduced by minimizing the number of errors generated during the design processes. Objectives to maximize reliability and minimize elapsed development time are compatible, providing, of course, that the elapsed time objectives are not so extreme as to allow an insufficient amount of time for adequate design.

Efficiency

The relationships between efficiency or performance and reliability are extremely complex. For instance, reliability measures can add additional instructions that must be executed (e.g., for fault detection and recording), add additional overhead because of a hierarchical structuring of the system, and discourage obscure and tricky coding, thus increasing the program's execution time and storage requirements. On the other hand, an unreliable system cannot be said to be "efficient" no matter how fast it executes. In short, all blanket statements about reliability and efficiency (except this one) are wrong.

Execution speed can be categorized into two measures: instantaneous speed (such as terminal response time or the processing time for a transaction) and throughput (the total work performed over a large time period). Reliability and instantaneous speed are somewhat incompatible, while reliability and throughput are usually not in conflict (throughput is a function of a large number of factors including the percentage of time that the system is operable). An analogy can be found in automobile racing. A dragster is a system where instantaneous speed is the objective. Since a drag race lasts for only a few seconds, the designer is not interested in reliability. He attempts to minimize the car's weight and does not really care if the car falls apart after each race. On the other hand, a race such as the Indianapolis 500 is more concerned with throughput objectives. In designing a car for an endurance race the durability of the car is often more important than its top speed. The designer is concerned with minimizing pit-stops for repairs, optimizing engine lubrication and cooling, protecting the driver in crashes, and so on.

The computing industry has undergone several phases of efficiency and reliability tradeoffs. In its early years, when computer hardware was unreliable and the applications were lengthy batch-processing scientific programs, efficiency reigned. The programmer was concerned with squeezing every possible second out of his program so that it had a chance of running to completion before the hardware failed. Because of the batch-processing environment, if the programmer encountered an error he simply corrected it and reran his program.

In the 1960s the industry entered a second phase, which has continued until the present and in which it will remain for some time. The reliability and speed of computer hardware increased by orders of magnitude. Applications went on-line, controlling critical processes and becoming an integral part of the day-to-day operation of many corporations. Inefficiencies are tolerable in most of these applications, but errors are not. To quote an acquaintance of mine in data processing at State Farm Automobile Insurance [7]:

> State Farm's software systems service some 15,000,000 policyholders and process some 2.3 billion dollars in premiums every year. With that many dollars and people dependent upon the accuracy of the system, reliability must take precedence over efficiency. Then, too, State Farm is an auto insurance company, and as such is subject to the whims of some 50 state insurance commissioners and state legislatures. In other words, program modification is a way of life. Therefore, maintainability is also more important than efficiency.

While the industry is in this second phase, any software developer who sacrifices reliability in favor of efficiency could be considered as acting irresponsibly. (As with everything else, there are exceptions, but they should represent only a small percentage of today's software projects.) Computer hardware is steadily becoming cheaper and faster. Software inefficiencies can be tuned later if necessary; unreliability is much more difficult to rectify. The results of inefficiencies are usually predictable (longer waits); the results of unreliability are unpredictable and often disastrous.

It is conceivable that the industry will enter a third phase, possibly toward the end of the century. Although perfect reliability will remain an unreachable goal, the industry may evolve to a point where software development becomes such a precise discipline that achieving high reliability becomes the normal case. At this point designers can turn their attention back to efficiency, solving, for example, the artificial intelligence problems that are infeasible today because of their computational complexity. Until that time, however, the focus must be on software reliability, sacrificing efficiency where necessary.

WRITING SOFTWARE OBJECTIVES

A good set of software objectives defines the goals of a software product without implying any particular implementation and specifies how tradeoffs are to be made in later design processes. As mentioned earlier, two types of objectives must be established: product and project objectives.

Product Objectives

Product objectives define the software goals from the users' point of view. Product objectives must contain the following categories of information:

1. *Summary.* The objectives should start with a brief statement of the overall purpose of the product.
2. *User Definition.* If the product is a large system with a variety of users, these different user roles should be defined.
3. *Detailed Functional Objectives.* This category outlines the functions that must be provided from the users' points of view.
4. *Publications.* Objectives must be established for the documentation to be supplied to the user, including the types of documentation and the audience for each type.
5. *Efficiency.* This category includes all efficiency or performance goals such as response time, throughput rates, and resource usage, as well as required performance measurement and tuning aids.
6. *Compatibility.* If the particular product must be compatible with other products or previous products, these objectives are listed under this category. Pertinent international, national, and corporate standards should also be identified.
7. *Configurability.* This group of objectives specifies the various hardware and software configurations supported by the product, any other software products upon which this product is dependent, and optional ways of selecting parts of the product, if applicable.
8. *Security.* This category describes the security objectives of the product. If the product is involved in financial matters (e.g., an

off-track betting system or inventory-control system), auditing facilities must be identified.

9. *Serviceability.* Goals for the cost and time to repair errors are listed in this category, along with any software functions needed to achieve these goals, such as diagnostic programs.

10. *Installation.* Objectives here include methods and aids for placing the product in operation.

11. *Reliability.* Reliability objectives, like all of the other categories, are highly dependent on the particular type of product. However the following topics should be considered:

    a. Mean time to failure should be defined for each type of failure (system, user, and specific function) and also by the severity of the failure.
    b. Mean time to restart the system after a failure.
    c. Goals for the number of software errors, categorized by severity and time of discovery.
    d. The consequences of system failure or the loss of any critical functions.
    e. The tolerable amount of data loss in the event of a failure.
    f. Vital information that must be protected from failures.
    g. Necessary fault-detection functions.
    h. Necessary fault-correction functions.
    i. Necessary fault-tolerant functions.
    j. Detection and recovery from user errors and hardware failures.

Project Objectives

Project objectives are goals to be met *during* the development processes, goals that are not directly manifest in the final product. Project objectives must be formally established, for, as Weinburg and Schulman [8] have shown, diverse and unexpected results occur when programmers do not work under a common set of project objectives. Project objectives should contain the following information:

1. Cost goals for each process.
2. Project schedules.
3. Objectives for each testing process.
4. Adaptability goals outlining the degree of adaptability or extensibility that must be achieved.
5. Maintainability goals outlining considerations for maintaining the product.

6. Reliability levels that must be achieved after each development process to achieve the product reliability objectives.
7. Objectives for the internal documentation during the project.
8. Criteria for measuring the product to determine its readiness for use.

More detail on most of these points can be found in later chapters, particularly in Part 3.

Guidelines for Objectives

It is vital that objectives be *clear, visible, reasonable,* and *measurable.* Any objective that cannot be understood is useless. Objectives should never be hidden from the software developers; they must be made visible to *everyone* on the project. Objectives should be achievable, since case studies of classic projects have shown that beginning the project with infeasible goals is often the major reason for failure. All objectives must be stated in sufficient quantitative terms to allow measuring the final product to the objectives. One of the testing processes described in Part 3 involves testing the product to the product objectives.

Each objective must be detailed enough to permit the design processes to proceed, but must not imply a particular design solution. Dependencies among objectives must be identified so that, if a particular objective is altered or cannot be achieved, the designer can easily determine which other objectives will be affected. Priorities should be established for all objectives (e.g., on a scale from "absolutely necessary" to "nice, but not vital") to define the way tradeoffs should be made.

An effective documentation technique is to list specific "nonobjectives" as well as objectives. This eliminates many "assumption" or "reading between the lines" errors by clearly illustrating what this product is *not* intended to do. Obviously, the nonobjectives of any product are almost infinite. However, by predicting any misunderstanding that might arise, one can develop a small list of nonobjectives to minimize misunderstanding.

Evaluating the Objectives

To evaluate the objectives, the *n*-plus-and-minus-one rule suggests involving the author of the requirements and the designer of the initial external specification. However, because the objectives pervade every aspect of the project, additional involvement in the evaluation is necessary. Key representatives from the user community and the design, test, maintenance, and publications activities should be involved in the evaluation process.

The first step is to match the objectives with the requirements to ensure that each requirement has been correctly translated. Each objective should be evaluated in light of the guidelines in the preceding section. Because of their importance, objectives should be personally evaluated by several levels of management in both the user and programming organizations.

EXTERNAL DESIGN

External design is the process of describing the intended behavior of a product as it would be perceived by a human observer external to the product. The purpose of external design is the "engineering" of the external (usually human) interfaces of the product without regard to its internal construction. The external design is expressed in an external specification, which has a wide audience that includes the user (for review and approval), the writers of the user documentation, all programmers involved with the project, and all personnel involved with the testing of the product.

Producing a complete and correct external specification is the most challenging problem in software development today. As we saw in Figures 2.1 and 3.2, the external specification is involved in more translation steps than any other design document.

Although no methodology exists for external design, a valuable principle to follow is the idea of *conceptual integrity* [9]. Conceptual integrity is the harmony (or lack of harmony) among the external interfaces of the system; the concept implies that is is better to have one set of coherent harmonious functions than a possibly larger set of independent and uncoordinated functions. Seemingly good features that do not integrate with the other features should probably be discarded rather than have them complicate the user interface.

Conceptual integrity is a measure of the uniformity of the user interface. A system without conceptual integrity is a system with no underlying uniformity; such a system results in an overly complicated user interface and additional complexity in the software structure. Since conceptual integrity is only a concept, it is difficult to describe in detail because it varies from application to application. As an example, a time-sharing system with conceptual integrity would have at least the following characteristics. All features available to a foreground (terminal) user are available to a background (batch) user and vice versa. The foreground interface and the background interface are identical. That is, instead of entering commands from a terminal, a user can enter the same commands as a background job. All commands have an inherent symmetry with respect to syntax, names, operands, conventions, and defaults. The semantics of all commands is similar. For instance, if the operand "FILE" on a particular command tells the system to send the output to a file instead of the terminal, then all commands having a similar option should use the word "FILE." Terminal characteristics, prompting, and error messages are common for all commands.

The easiest way *not* to achieve conceptual integrity is to attempt to produce an external design with too many people. The magic number seems to be about two. Depending on the size of the project, one or two people should have the responsibility for the external design.

The previous statement will perhaps have shocked the reader who is currently designing a new operating system, a programming language, or a hospital information system and with thirty other people is writing the external specification. Experience has shown, however, that the probability of success drops drastically as the number of designers exceeds two, even for a large product. That is not to say that only two people should participate in this design process; what it does imply is that only a few people should have the responsibility for the process, including the making of all decisions and the writing of the specification. In a large project these few people require supporting researchers, assistants, draftsmen, secretaries, and so forth. This supporting cast has the roles of information gathering and processing, but not design, decision making, or the actual writing of specifications.

Who, then, should these select responsible people be? To start with, they definitely should not be programmers or college graduates with computer science degrees. This process of external design has little or nothing to do with programming; it is more directly concerned with understanding the users' environment, problems, and needs and the psychology of man–machine communications. Furthermore, this trend of external design increases as new computing applications touch more end-users who have no knowledge of computing. Programmers and computer science graduates generally have no education or training in this type of design. They may be experts in programming languages, algorithms, programming techniques, compiler theory, testing, and debugging, but they have little or no experience in the end-uses of computers, human-factors engineering, and man-machine psychology. It would be reasonable to use programmers as external designers on products intended for use by programmers, such as a programming language or a debugging tool, but it would be unwise to expect a programmer to perform the external design of an operating system or a truck-dispatching system.

Because of its difficulties and its increasing importance in software development, external design requires some type of specialist. The specialist must understand the fields mentioned above and should also have a familiarity with all phases of software design and testing to understand the effects of external design on these phases. Candidates that come to mind are systems analysts, behavioral psychologists, operations-research specialists, industrial engineers, and possibly computer scientists (providing their education includes these areas, which is rarely the case). Several organizations have tried giving the job of the actual writing of the specification to professional writers (their user-manual writers). This is not recommended because it adds another translation step (designer to writer to specification). However, it is often desirable to involve these writers in the design process because of their valuable user-oriented perspective.

DESIGNING THE USER INTERFACE

In designing the external interfaces of the product the designer is concerned with three areas that have relationships with software reliability: minimizing user errors, detecting user errors when they do occur, and minimizing complexity. Martin's *Design of Man-Computer Dialogues* [10] is an excellent introduction to this subject. For additional case studies of the external design of interactive systems, see Orr's *Conversational Computers* [11].

As mentioned earlier, this book is concerned with software errors, not user errors. However, there is a relationship between the two. User errors increase the probability of arriving at unanticipated states in the system. Minimizing user errors does not decrease the number of software errors, but it does increase software reliability by decreasing the probability of encountering any remaining errors. Guidelines for minimizing user errors in interactive systems are listed below. Analogies for most of these guidelines can be made for batch-processing programs.

1. Tailor the interface to the training and intelligence of the user and the pressure under which the user is working. For instance, one should expect that the user interface of a banking system would be

considerably different depending on whether the user is a bank customer or a trained teller. I am reminded of a farfetched example of what not to do: a hospital information system displayed dates on terminals in the following form:

$$2.5 \times 10^1 \text{ OCT } 1.969 \times 10^3$$

2. Design the information entered by the user to be as brief as possible, but not so brief that it loses its meaning. In doing this consider the frequency with which the average user will use the system (e.g., frequent or occasional use) and whether the user is under stress during his or her use of the system.

3. Have conceptual integrity among the types of inputs entered and also among the outputs. For example, all reports, graphical displays, and messages should have the same formats, style, and abbreviations.

4. Provide a "help" facility, a separate set of functions that provide the user with information if he becomes confused or forgets particular interfaces to the system. One example of a sophisticated help facility is in the Berkeley Time-Sharing System [12]. For instance, the user could enter the message "?HELP! HOW CAN I TERMINATE AN EDIT?" and receive a 50-word explanation of how to return from edit mode to command mode.

5. Avoid making the user angry at the system, which may lead to some unexpected input conditions. Avoid abusive or sarcastic output and communicate in his language, not computer gibberish.

6. Always give some sort of immediate acknowledgement to any input entered. Without this, the user may have some doubt over whether the input was received correctly, leading him to reenter the input, which may result in an error situation.

In addition to minimizing user errors, the system must also properly deal with user errors when they do occur—and they will occur no matter how well the interfaces are designed. For instance, terminal operators on the New York SPRINT system, a police car dispatching system, entertained themselves during slack periods by trying to fail the system by keying in invalid messages [10]. Guidelines for detecting user errors are listed as follows:

1. Design the system so that it recognizes *any* input data. If the information entered is not what the system defines as valid, inform the user.

2. If the user is entering a complex transaction through many

messages or prompting sequences, give him a chance to verify it before it is acted upon, as shown below.

USER: 222,AA,23MAY,2F
COMPUTER: YOU NEED 2 FIRST-CLASS SEATS ON AMERICAN AIRLINES FLIGHT 222 FROM ORD (CHICAGO) TO JFK (NEW YORK) ON 23MAY, LEAVE 8:00 PM, ARRIVE 10:30 PM. CORRECT?

3. Design the system so that user errors are detected immediately. If a user enters the message "SEND FREIGHT CARS F23 AND F42 FROM CHICAGO TO DES PLAINES ON TRAIN 883," the system should immediately verify that these two cars are already in Chicago and that there is a train 883 going from Chicago to Des Plaines. There are two reasons for this immediate verification. First, the user may be dispatching a series of freight cars, his plan of action being dependent on having dispatched F23 and F42 to Des Plaines. If he discovers later on that F23 is in Pittsburgh instead of Chicago, his entire plan may be invalid, requiring him to have a way to "back out" all of his dispatching messages. Also, if the error is undetected, the software system may get confused and end up with records showing F23 in Pittsburgh and Des Plaines simultaneously.

4. Where accuracy is vital, design redundancy into the input data. In a banking system one might require the customer's name to be keyed in with the account number in order to detect errors in entering the account number. A second possibility is to make the account number self-checking by making the last digit some arithmetic combination of the previous digits [13].

The remaining area of reliability is minimizing the complexity of the external design in order to minimize the internal complexity of the system, as well as minimize user errors. A common belief is that a "humanized" external design has to be complicated, containing fancy prompting techniques, many options, and automatic error correction such as spelling correction. This belief is incorrect.

A design issue that always arises in the external design of an interactive system is whether or not to prompt the user to reenter parts of the input data that are incorrect. Assume a user enters the command

EDIT   GJMPROGSET.1   TYPE(TEXT)   DISP(80)

and the system discovers an error: TEXT is not a valid operand of keyword TYPE. Should the system prompt the user for a correction such as issuing a message "INVALID TYPE. ENTER TYPE FIELD"? First of all, the user is now confused. Does he enter the keyword and the operand or just the operand? Rather than be faced with this dilemma, it would be easier for him simply to reenter the command. Also, prompting for corrections requires the system to make assumptions about what is correct and what is not. What if TEXT was not really the error? Suppose the input would have been correct if he said FILE instead of EDIT? What does the user do now?

This type of prompting should be avoided because it confuses the user and tremendously complicates the software. If you argue that this type of prompting is necessary in your system because your input commands are so lengthy that reentering the command takes too much time, one can counter by saying that your input commands are poorly designed.

A second complexity problem is offering the user too many options. IBM's OS/360 operating system has an installation process called a SYSGEN (system generation) that allows the system to be tailored when it is installed. This resulted in almost every OS/360 installation having a unique version of the operating system, complicating IBM's maintenance job. This, in turn, led to the speculation that it would have been cheaper for IBM to totally omit this SYSGEN process and to provide each installation with enough "free" storage to hold the parts of the system that it did not require.

Whenever there is indecision over whether to provide the user with an option, the answer today is too often to provide the option. In a system I recently used it took two pages in the user manual to simply list (without describing) all of the options on a command to invoke a PL/I compiler. Not only did this confuse me for a while in trying to figure out how to compile my PL/I program, but it complicated the compiler, undoubtedly leading to errors. Generally, a large set of options is no favor to the user. The designer must consider every option carefully in terms of its utility versus the confusion and the added complexity. When in doubt it is safer to omit the option. The number of minor options available in a product is not going to influence its salability. Also, options may have a negative effect on the potential customer in that they indicate that the designer has an imprecise understanding of exactly how the system is to be used.

The last area of complexity is systems that make assumptions about the input data such as the assumptions involved in attempting to correct spelling mistakes. Such schemes are not only complex but they are often dangerous. Consider a hospital system to which the user requests four cc of ethyl alcohol, and suppose the user hits an extra key resulting in the input message "RETHYL ALCOHOL." The system does not recognize the first word so it sends it through an algorithm that decides the user really meant to enter "METHYL ALCOHOL." Anyone that has ever taken a freshman chemistry course should recognize the huge difference between the two: ethyl alcohol intoxicates; methyl alcohol kills.

The message then, in designing a user interface for a reliable product, is to provide a uniform and simple interface, to expect anything as input, and to immediately detect as many errors as soon as possible.

WRITING THE EXTERNAL SPECIFICATION

A well-done external specification is a large document. An effective way to manage such a large document is to adopt a hierarchical organization. A technique I recently used was to subdivide the specification into *major facilities*, then *facilities,* and then *functions.* One of the major facilities was the library manager. A facility under this major facility was the security administrator facility. A function in this facility was the REPORT-SECURITY-INCIDENTS command.

Chapter 2 showed external design as consisting of two processes: initial and detailed external design. Assuming the specification is hierarchically organized, these two processes simply represent checkpoints in the top–down design of the system according to the hierarchy. The first step is to outline the major facilities (or whatever the first-level breakdown is), then the facilities, then the user functions, and last the detail for each user function. Initial external design represents the first three steps. The system is designed to the level where each user function is identified but its precise syntax, semantics, and output are left undefined. This has two purposes: it places a management checkpoint in the middle of the lengthy external design process and it allows verification of an intermediate level of the design with the user and to the objectives.

The detailed external design for each user function should specify the following types of information:

1. *Input description.* This is a precise description of the syntax (e.g., format and valid values and ranges) and semantics of each user input to the function. An "input" might be a command, control card, input form, response to prompting, or an analog signal.
2. *Output description.* This is a precise description of all outputs from the function (e.g., terminal responses, error messages, reports, analog control signals). The outputs should be related to the inputs

in a cause-and-effect manner; that is, the reader should be able to discern the output generated for any particular input. The output of the function must also be specified for any invalid input.

3. *System transformations.* Many external functions, in addition to generating external outputs, also alter the state of the system. Any such system transformations should be described here, but remember that this is an external specification, implying that transformations must be described from the user's point of view. For example, a warehouse system might have an "order" command that is used by a salesman to initiate an order. This function has two outputs: an invoice that is transmitted to the shipping department and a confirmation message to the salesman's terminal. It also has two system transformations: updates to the inventory file and a record of the order on the audit file.

4. *Reliability characteristics.* This is a description of the effects of any possible failure of the function on the system, files, and user. I have found that including this section has a small, but positive, psychological effect on reliability. In a project developing an interactive system, I requested that the statement "any error in this command must not cause a system failure" be placed in this section for each command. Although the people designing the internal structure of the system would never knowingly allow an error in a user command to cause an overall system failure, this statement served as a constant reminder of that fact.

5. *Efficiency.* This is a description of any efficiency constraints deemed necessary for the function, such as elapsed time and storage usage. Efficiency can rarely be specified as an absolute because it is influenced by the hardware configuration, telecommunication line speeds, the efficiency of all other concurrently executing programs, the number of terminal users active, and so on. To circumvent this problem, one or more standard hardware configurations and work-loads can be specified elsewhere in the specification and then the efficiency of individual functions can be specified in relation to these.

6. *Programming notes.* The external specification must describe the product from the user's point of view and avoid constraining the internal design. However, it is occasionally necessary to convey ideas or· hints about the internal design of the function. This practice should be minimized but, where necessary, this section is used to convey the information.

For any complex user function the task of relating outputs and system transformations in a cause-and-effect manner to inputs is not a trivial job. The *decision table* is an excellent answer to this problem.

Figure 4.3 is a decision table for a SHIP-PART command in a warehouse system. The command has three operands: a customer number, part number, and quantity. This decision table, supplemented by a small amount of descriptive material, makes an excellent external specification of the command. Decision tables provide a graphical and rigorous way of showing the relationships between the inputs and outputs. To appreciate the utility of decision tables, try expressing the relationships in Figure 4.3 in an alternative form: an English narrative description.

The decision table is a useful technique for software reliability. Decision tables are unique in their characteristic of being a communication vehicle between the external designer, the user, and the programmer. Decision tables in external specifications can easily be comprehended by a user reviewing the specification. Furthermore, decision tables in external specifications are an ideal input to programmers designing the internal logic of the product. This dual use of decision tables reduces translation errors. Mechanical techniques are also available to review decision tables for incompleteness, redundancies, and ambiguities [14]. For instance, these techniques could be used on Figure 4.3 to ensure that it covers all input conditions. Because many software errors are due to unexpected conditions, these mechanical techniques are quite valuable.

For some inexplicable reason, decision tables are not widely used. Decision table techniques are rarely included in programmer education, either in industry or universities. Because of their contributions to reliability, decision tables should be an important part of the repertoire of the software developer.

After discussing the detail required in a quality external specification, one sometimes hears the reaction, "Yes, this may be the ideal but I cannot possibly provide this level of information without first constructing the system." The people with this opinion are sometimes right and sometimes wrong. When they are right, what they are saying is that they are working on a research project. A *development project* produces a product that can be designed in a phased top-down and outside-in manner. A *research project* is a project where the goals and outcome are not (or cannot be) determined in advance. I am not trying to downgrade research; it is certainly valuable. However, the designer should know what type of project he is faced with because research projects, because of their very nature, cannot have fixed schedules or cost estimates. Most current software projects are development

Ship-part command

	1	2	3	4	5	6	7	8	9	10	11	12
Command syntax valid?	Y	Y	Y	Y	Y	Y	Y	Y	Y	Y	Y	N
Customer number valid?	Y	Y	Y	Y	Y	Y	Y	N	N	N	N	
Part number valid?	Y	Y	Y	Y	Y	N	N	Y	Y	N	N	
Quantity > 0 and integer?	Y	Y	Y	Y	N	Y	N	Y	N	Y	N	
Customer credit OK?	Y	Y	Y	N								
Enough parts in stock?	Y	Y	N									
Will stock be under order limit?	Y	N										
Send notice to shipping dept.	X	X										
Send Message 1 to terminal	X	X										
Send Message 2 to terminal			X									
Send Message 3 to terminal				X								
Send Message 4 to terminal					X		X		X		X	
Send Message 5 to terminal						X	X			X	X	
Send Message 6 to terminal								X	X	X	X	
Send Message 7 to terminal												X
Send Notice 1 to purchasing dept.	X											
Send Notice 2 to purchasing dept.			X									
Decrement quantity in inventory file	X	X										
Record transaction in audit file	X	X										

Figure 4.3   **Decision table.**

projects; few projects involve inventing anything for the first time. The focus of this book is on development projects, although the reader should recognize that some development projects may need to be preceded by research projects.

In summary, the external specification describes every possible input to the system (both valid and invalid) and the system's reaction to each input. The external specification must precisely and completely describe the external interfaces while implying little or nothing about the internal construction of the product.

VERIFYING THE EXTERNAL SPECIFICATION

Completion of the external design represents a crucial turning point in the project. The external design process and the previous processes focused on the user–product interfaces; the remaining design processes focus on the internal software structure. For this reason, and because of the difficulties previously discussed in producing a quality external specification, verifying the correctness of the external specification is of utmost importance.

In this verification step, a positive attitude must be taken toward errors. The goal of any verification or testing process is to find as many faults as possible; the aim is not to show that the specification has no errors. Understanding this subtle distinction is quite important. It is also important to verify the specification while it is still in its rough form since there is often a psychological barrier to making improvements once a document is in its "final" printed form.

There are six verification techniques that can be used on the external specification. These techniques are not mutually exclusive alternatives; I recommend using all of them.

n-Plus-and-Minus-One Review

Again, the n-plus-and-minus-rule can be applied, with the n-minus-one people looking for translation errors and the n-plus-one people looking for problems that will lead to errors in the subsequent processes.

The initial external specification is evaluated by the people responsible for the objectives, system architecture, and detailed external design. The specification should be matched against the objectives by reviewing each objective and then determining whether it is adequately reflected by the specification.

The detailed external specification should be evaluated by the people responsible for the initial external design, program structure design, and data base design and the people responsible for writing the user documentation.

User Review

It is vital to obtain review and approval of the initial and detailed external specifications from the user organization. If for some reason this cannot be done (e.g., a user-independent project), then a separate "devil's advocate" team should be formed within the software development organization with the task of evaluating the specifications from the user's point of view.

Decision Tables

If decision tables are used in the specifications (and they should be), then mechanical techniques can be used to check for completeness (finding any omitted circumstances) and ambiguities (identical conditions leading to different outputs or transformations).

Manual Simulation

An effective technique for evaluating the detailed external specification is generating test cases and then using the detailed external specification to simulate the behavior of the system. This process of evaluating a design document by "executing" it with test cases is often called a *walk-through.*

To test a single external function the following actions would occur. One person (*not* the author of the specification) would first develop a set of "paper test cases" for the function: a list of particular inputs (valid and invalid) for the function. This person and the author of the specification then simulate each of these inputs entering the system, using the specification as a description of the behavior of the system. Whenever the specification does not correctly and completely describe the outputs and transformations for a particular input, an error has been discovered. Before the walk-through process begins, it is usually necessary to establish an initial state of the system (such as describing a simple initial content for any files) and then update this state description as transformations occur.

This process can also be used to test combinations of functions by generating test cases that describe complex scenarios of inputs.

It is important to note that the goal of any of these evaluation sessions is to find errors but not to create on-the-fly corrections. The correcting of errors should be deferred until all possible errors have been discovered. It is also important to have someone other than the author of the specification create the test cases and interpret the specification, since the author would tend to "read between the lines."

Terminal Simulation

A more sophisticated walk-through technique is to play a "man hidden in the empty computer" game. Rather than simply reading a list of test cases as in a manual simulation, the tester sits at a terminal and enters test cases and examines output just as if the terminal were connected to the actual software product. To simulate the system, another person sits at another terminal, armed with the specification. A small program in the computing system connects these terminals together by displaying any input entered from the tester's terminal on the human simulator's terminal, and giving the human simulator commands to direct output to the tester's terminal. The human simulator performs the same activities as in the manual simulation, that is, examining the input received from the other terminal, examining the specification to find the correct output, keeping track of system transformations, and sending output back to the other terminal.

The connecting program is quite simple. If the terminals are typical typewriter-like terminals, the human simulator needs commands to read from and write to the test terminal and to recognize any actions taken at the test terminal, such as the use of an attention key. If the terminal is a CRT-display terminal, the human simulator must have functions to format the screen of the test terminal and to recognize any special-purpose keys such as function keys.

This technique is valuable because it aids in finding any human factors flaws in the design, as well as problems in the specification. The technique is useful during the external design process to study human factors alternatives.

Cause–Effect Graphs

Cause–effect graphing is a technique adopted from engineering circuit design that allows the designer to represent a specification as a boolean logic diagram. Its primary purpose is to serve as a rigorous way of generating optimal test cases for software testing. However, because it involves a detailed analysis of the specification, it has a secondary benefit of finding errors in the specification. Cause–effect graphing is discussed in Chapter 12.

PLANNING FOR CHANGE

Changing requirements is a fact of life in software development. These changes come from technological advances, social changes (e.g., new legislation), changes in people, suggested improvements, and the discovery of errors. The experienced software developer is aware of this fact of life; he has planned for change, has oriented his design so that changes are not traumatic events, and knows how to manage change so that it does not upset the reliability of his product.

The first rule in managing change is to keep all documentation up-to-date throughout the entire project cycle. A common mistake is to produce a quality set of objectives and external specifications and then fail to update them when changes occur. This is a poor practice because the objectives and specifications now no longer accurately reflect the product, leading to communication problems and to problems in using the objectives and specifications in the testing processes discussed in Part 3.

The second rule is to "freeze" the output of each design process at particular points in time. "Freezing" does not imply that changes can no longer be made; it simply implies that changes must pass through a formal approval process. Requirements and objectives should be frozen after their approval. External specifications should be frozen after they have successfully passed the verification step.

The approval process for changes to a frozen document is usually called a *design change process*. Design change requests are initiated by the user or the software developers. Each design change request is evaluated for its benefits and effects on the product such as schedule, cost, reliability, security, and efficiency. A small committee usually has the responsibility of approving or disapproving each change (or deferring it for future implementation). Each approved change must be immediately reflected in the appropriate design documents. In evaluating a proposed change to a prior decision, remember that other decisions may have subsequently been based on this decision. Failing to consider all ramifications of a design change is a common mistake.

The third rule in managing change is to verify each change to the same degree that each initial function was verified. Another common mistake is to spend a sufficient amount of time carefully verifying an external specification but then failing to perform the same verification on changes. Because design changes are made under heavier pressure, they are highly susceptible to error and must be carefully verified.

The last rule is to ensure that all changes are made at the proper level. A programmer designing the internal logic of a module may make a change but fail to recognize that the change alters the external characteristics of the product. The software and the specifications are now out of step, resulting in a software error. There is no easy solution to this problem other than making everyone aware of the problem.

REFERENCES

1. R. D. Williams, "Managing the Development of Reliable Software," *Proceedings of the 1975 International Conference on Reliable Software.* New York: IEEE, 1975, pp. 3–8.
2. J. E. Bingham and G. W. P. Davies, *A Handbook of Systems Analysis.* New York: Halsted, 1972.
3. D. Teichroew, "A Survey of Languages for Stating Requirements for Computer-Based Information Systems," *Proceedings of the 1972 Fall Joint Computer Conference.* Montvale, N.J.: AFIPS Press, 1972, pp. 1203–1224.
4. J. D. Cougar and R. W. Knapp, *System Analysis Techniques.* New York: Wiley, 1974.
5. *HIPO—A Design Aid and Documentation Technique.* GC20-1851, IBM Corp., White Plains, N.Y., 1974.
6. N. Tinanoff and F. M. Luppino, "Structured Programming Series, Volume VI, Programming Support Library (PSL) Specifications," RADC-TR-74-300, Volume VI, IBM Federal Systems Div., Gaithersburg, Md., 1974.
7. P. Fandel and L. Milligan, "PL/I Structured Programming Case Study," *Proceedings of the 39th Meeting of GUIDE International.* New York: GUIDE International Corp., 1974, pp. 585–605.
8. G. M. Weinburg and E. L. Schulman, "Goals and Performance in Computer Programming," *Human Factors,* **16** (1), 70–77 (1974).
9. F. P. Brooks, *The Mythical Man-Month: Essays on Software Engineering.* Reading, Mass.: Addison-Wesley, 1975.
10. J. Martin, *Design of Man-Computer Dialogues.* Englewood Cliffs, N.J.: Prentice-Hall, 1973.
11. W. D. Orr, Ed., *Conversational Computers.* New York: Wiley, 1968.
12. M. W. Pirtle, "HELP," in W. D. Orr, Ed., *Conversational Computers.* New York: Wiley, 1968, pp. 96–101.
13. T. Gilb, *Reliable EDP Application Design.* New York: Petrocelli/Charter, 1974.
14. M. L. Hughes, R. M. Shank, and E. S. Stein, *Decision Tables.* New York: McGraw-Hill, 1968.

CHAPTER 5

System Architecture

System architecture is the process of partitioning a large software system into smaller pieces. These pieces have a variety of labels such as programs, components, subsystems, and levels of abstraction.

The system architecture process is a necessary step in the design of systems but not in the design of programs. If the external specification describes a software *system*, the next design step is system architecture, followed by the program structure design process. If the external specification describes a *program*, the system architecture step is unnecessary. The immediate problem, then, is to distinguish between systems and programs. Unfortunately, these words have no precise definition. The dictionary is of no help in this regard because objects ranging from operating systems to subroutines to DO loops all fit the definition of system.

We can say that a software system represents a set of solutions to a set of distinct but related problems, and then rely on intuition to distinguish systems from programs. For instance, an operating system, an airlines reservation system, and a data base manager are examples of systems and therefore must pass through the system architecture process. A text formatting command in a time-sharing system, a compiler, and an inventory-control program are examples of single programs and do not require the system architecture process.

Every software design methodology has two parts: a set of desired characteristics of the solution and guidelines for the solution process itself. In developing a design methodology, one normally starts by defining the desired characteristics of the solution and then later develops the thought process required to arrive at the desired solution. Because of this one can expect more to be known about the desired properties of the solution than the thought process. We have already encountered this in external design; certain desirable attributes were listed in Chapter 4, but the actual process of external design is still largely ad hoc. In module logic design, ending up with a structured program is the desired solution and one particular thought process is called *step-wise refinement.*

In terms of these two parts of a design methodology, system architecture is the least understood design process. Not only is the thought process undefined, but the desired characteristics of the system structure are only beginning to be understood. The following sections outline several currently ill-defined approaches to system design.

LEVELS OF ABSTRACTION

The idea of levels of abstraction was originated by Dijkstra [1, 2]. A system is partitioned into distinct hierarchical pieces, called levels, that meet certain design criteria. Each level is a group of closely related modules. The purpose of the levels is to minimize the complexity of the system by defining the levels to be highly independent from one another. This is accomplished by hiding properties of certain objects of the system such as resources and data representations within each level, thus allowing each level to represent an "abstraction" of these objects.

There are two general structures of these levels, shown in Figures 5.1 and 5.2. In Figure 5.1 the problem is viewed as developing a "user machine" starting with a low-level hardware machine or operating system. A progression of levels called *abstract machines* is defined so that each higher machine is built upon the lower machines, extending their capabilities. Each level can only reference (call) one other level: the level immediately subordinate to it.

In the structure of Figure 5.2 the levels are not complete abstractions of the lower levels, allowing any level to reference any or all of the lower levels.

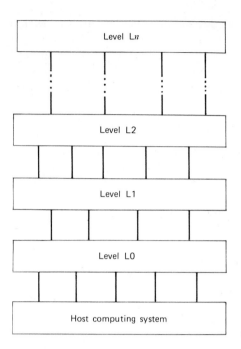

Figure 5.1 **Levels of abstraction.**

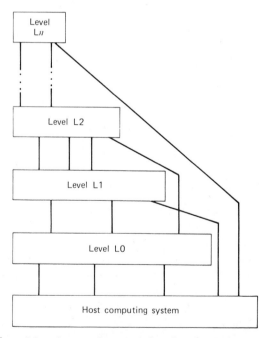

Figure 5.2 **A second approach to levels of abstraction.**

Although the current definition of the levels of abstraction method is itself quite abstract, certain properties of the levels are beginning to be recognized:

1. Each level knows absolutely nothing about the properties, or even existence, of higher levels [3]. This is the fundamental property of levels of abstraction that significantly decreases the connections and assumptions among parts of the software system, thus decreasing complexity.
2. Each level knows nothing about the insides of any other level. All communication among levels is done through rigid, predefined interfaces.
3. Each level is a group of modules (separately compiled subroutines). Some of these modules are internal to the level, that is, they cannot be referenced from other levels. The names of the remainder of the modules are potentially known by a higher level. These names represent the interfaces to the level.
4. Each level contains certain resources and either hides these resources from the other levels or provides some abstraction of the resources to other levels. For instance, in a file management system, one level might contain the physical files, hiding their organization from the remainder of the system. Other levels might own resources such as catalogs, data dictionaries, and protection mechanisms.
5. Each level can also support an abstraction of the data within the system. In a data management system, one level might represent any file as a tree structure, thus isolating the actual physical structure of the file from all other levels.
6. The assumptions that each level makes about the other levels must be minimized [4]. Assumptions can take the form of relationships that must hold prior to execution of a function, data representations, and environmental factors. In an automobile insurance system this might imply that all knowledge of the state-dependent insurance laws is hidden in one level and all knowledge of the characteristics of the input mechanisms (e.g., display terminal, typewriter terminal, optical character reader, telecommunications message) is hidden in another level.
7. Connection between levels is limited to explicit arguments passed from one level to another. Levels cannot share global data [5]. Furthermore, it is desirable to totally eliminate all global data (even within levels) in a system [6].
8. Each level should have high strength and loose coupling as defined in Chapter 6. This means that each function performed by a level of

abstraction should be represented by a unique entry point. Arguments passed between levels should be single data elements rather than complex data structures.

The levels-of-abstraction approach to system design has not been widely used to date. The two most well-known uses were in the design of small-scale operating systems, the THE system [1, 2] and the Venus system [7]. The THE system is a small operating system that was developed by six people at the Technological University in Eindhoven, The Netherlands. The system is a batch-processing system with multiprogramming and virtual storage (via paging). The system consists of five levels of abstraction, presumably in the structure of Figure 5.2.

Level 0 contains the functions of CPU dispatching and process (task) synchronization. This level is the only level aware of the multiprogramming aspects of the system, including the number of processors (CPUs).

Level 1 is responsible for memory management, including management of the paging drum. No other level is aware of the paging mechanism. In fact, no other level knows that this is a virtual storage system.

Level 2 handles all communications between higher levels and the operator's console. No other level knows the characteristics of the operator's console or the number of consoles.

Level 3 is responsible for the buffering of the input and output streams. The other levels are unaware of this process, including the characteristics of the input/output devices and which particular devices are being used.

The user (application) programs sit at level 4.

The system was designed and tested in a bottom-up manner starting with level 0. The levels of abstraction minimized the number of internal states in the system, allowing the correctness of each level to be informally verified after it was designed and permitting "exhaustive testing" of the final product. This led the principal designer (E. Dijkstra) to make the rare statement that "the resulting system is guaranteed to be flawless" [1].

To anyone who has experienced the trauma of making significant changes to an operating system (such as converting an operating system into a multiprocessing and/or virtual memory system), this organization appears to have many benefits. Not only are modifications limited to isolated parts of the system, but the levels of abstraction show precisely what parts have to be altered.

Although the reliability results were outstanding, the THE system is, in fact, a primitive operating system in many respects. For instance, it contains no secondary storage other than the paging drum, so there is no file management problem.

A second project using levels of abstraction was the Venus system [7]. This was a broader project than the THE system in that it included the hardware design as well. In fact, the lower levels of abstraction (CPU dispatching and virtual memory management) were actually implemented as microprograms.

A remaining benefit of levels of abstraction is *portability*: the ease of modifying an application to operate on a different computing system. Since all of the interfaces to the host operating system are in level 0 and all interfaces to any data management facility would be isolated in another level, the application can be modified to execute under a different operating system or a different data management system by replacing only a single level.

Although the levels-of-abstraction approach is currently quite vague, the ideas appear to be of value for the initial structuring of large systems (both operating systems and application systems). Although current uses of the approach have been in a bottom-up manner (lower levels are designed before higher levels), the concept can be used in a top-down manner. For the few designers who have the job of designing a total computing system (hardware and software), there are significant advantages in using it in a top-down manner; it allows the designer to postpone decisions as to whether any given function will be implemented in hardware or software until late in the design cycle when cost–performance studies can be made.

PORT-DRIVEN SUBSYSTEMS

A second system design technique is called *port-driven* or *queue-driven* subsystems [8–10]. This method is primarily concerned with the communication techniques among subsystems, components, or programs, contrasted to the levels of abstraction concept, which is primarily concerned with the proper distribution of function among hierarchical levels of the system.

Mechanisms to interconnect pieces of a system can be grouped into three categories. Mechanisms in the first category, such as the GO TO statement, interrupts, and the "supervisor call," pass control (execution flow) from one piece to another without explicitly passing data. Mechanisms such as the procedure or subroutine call fall into the second category; they transfer both control and data to another part of the system. The third category, port-driven mechanisms, includes methods of transferring data without transferring control.

With the port-driven mechanism, the system is divided into a set of subsystems, each having one or more input ports or queues. A port is simply a list of the current input messages (parameter lists) to a subsystem. Each subsystem is viewed as an asynchronous process; that is, all subsystems are executing in parallel. If a subsystem wants to transfer some data to another subsystem, it places the data on an input port of the other subsystem. If a subsystem is ready to process some data, it reads it from one of its input ports. These two communication mechanisms are called SEND and RECEIVE.

The port mechanism tends to increase the independence of subsystems by freeing them of most timing dependencies on one another. Furthermore, the subsystems do not have to be aware of the *location* of each other. Only the send/receive mechanism need know the location of each subsystem (e.g., in the same virtual memory or machine as another subsystem, in a different virtual memory, or in a different computing system). The port mechanism also has several test-ing, debugging, and auditing advantages that will be discussed later.

Figure 5.3 is an illustration of a subsystem (called a *process* to dist-inguish it from non-port-driven subsystems). The process has one or more *primary input ports,* one for each function of the process. The process can execute a statement or command such as:

RECEIVE PORT1(A,B,C)

which takes the next message from input port PORT1 and assigns the arguments in the message to parameters A, B, and C. The process can send data to other processes by executing a statement such as:

SEND DATAMGR(X,A)

which forms a message from arguments X and A and places the message on some port called DATAMGR.

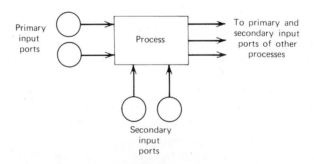

Figure 5.3   **Direct port configuration.**

The process may have a second set of input ports called *secondary input ports.* These ports are used to communicate with subordinate processes. If a process needs to perform a read from a data base in order to perform its function, it might send a message to the data base manager and then expect to receive the result on a secondary port. The input message to the data base manager would typically contain an argument telling the data base manager the name of the secondary port.

The process in Figure 5.3 is part of a *direct configuration.* That is, processes communicate directly by sending a message to an input port of another process. The process in Figure 5.4 is part of an *indirect configuration.* Processes of this type have output ports. Rather than sending a message to an input port of another process, they send messages to their output ports. Output ports are connected to input ports of other processes through a separate specification such as job control language statements. A typical statement might be:

CONNECT OUTPORT2 OF PROCESS ABC TO INPORT1 OF PROCESS XYZ.

Whenever process ABC sends a message to its output port OUTPORT2, the send/receive mechanism will route the message to INPORT1 of process XYZ. Therefore, output ports do not physically exist; they are aliases for input ports of other processes.

Figure 5.5 is a diagram of an information-retrieval system using a direct configuration. The terminal manager is a continually executing process (as are the four other processes). It polls the terminal devices on the system and, whenever a command is received from a terminal, it sends a message to the interpret-command subsystem consisting of two arguments: the terminal command and a terminal identifier. The terminal manager also performs a second function: writing output lines on terminals, for which it has an input port.

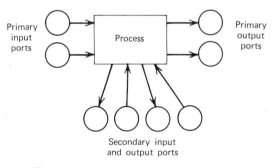

Figure 5.4   **Indirect port configuration.**

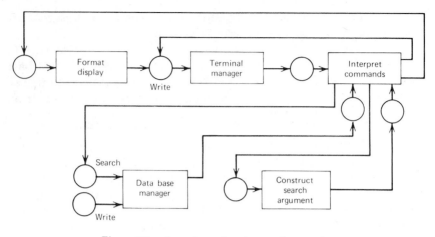

Figure 5.5   **A system structure using ports.**

The interpret-command subsystem continually reads from its single primary input port. When it receives a terminal command it uses two subordinate subsystems to construct a search argument and search the data base. When it has completed a search it sends the result of the search, along with the terminal identifier, to the format-display subsystem. If the interpret-command subsystem detects an error, such as an invalid command, it sends an error message (and terminal identifier) to the input port of the terminal manager and then receives another message from its input port. The operation of the remaining processes is straightforward. Note that the data base manager has a second primary input port for writing information into the data base, which is not used in this system.

The Send/Receive Mechanism

The send/receive mechanism is a separate subsystem that is invoked whenever a subsystem executes a SEND or RECEIVE statement. The following functions should be considered in developing the send/receive mechanism:

1. A SEND function as described above.
2. A RECEIVE function that suspends the process issuing the RECEIVE if no message is available. The suspended process resumes execution when a message is placed on one of its input ports.

3. A CONDITIONAL-RECEIVE function that allows the process to continue execution if no message is available.
4. CREATE-PORT and DESTROY-PORT functions to allow subsystems to dynamically create and destroy ports.
5. CONNECT and DISCONNECT functions, if the send/receive mechanism has to know which subsystems are in communication with each other.
6. "Hiding" the location of a subsystem from all other subsystems by providing intermemory and interCPU communication mechanisms (e.g., shared files, channel-to-channel adapters, telecommunications lines).
7. Representing ports as queues (first-in, first-out), stacks (last-in, first-out), or some other data structure such as a list ordered on a priority basis.
8. Interface checking (checking correspondence between arguments and parameters) or data conversion between arguments in "sent" messages and parameters in "received" messages.
9. Disk back-up of the current contents of all ports to provide a checkpoint/restart function in the event of an error.
10. Journaling of all messages (useful in diagnosing errors).
11. Optional monitoring of all messages for specific values (useful in diagnosing errors).

Each subsystem should be a separate task, allowing them to execute in parallel on a multiprogramming or multiprocessing system, although this characteristic is not a vital part of the concept.

The easiest way to develop a send/receive mechanism is to use the mechanism, if available, in the host computing system. If it is necessary to develop your own mechanism, see Knott [11] for an example of the interfaces and Knuth [12] for the algorithms.

Other Considerations

The send/receive mechanism itself meets the definition of a level of abstraction in that it provides an abstraction (the port concept), owns resources (the physical ports), and hides information from the remainder of the system (the physical characteristics of the ports and the physical location of each subsystem). In fact, the two concepts can be used together by defining each port-driven subsystem as having the characteristics of a level of abstraction. The structure of a real-time system employing both concepts is outlined in Figure 5.6 [13].

The port concept can also be used as a memory device for

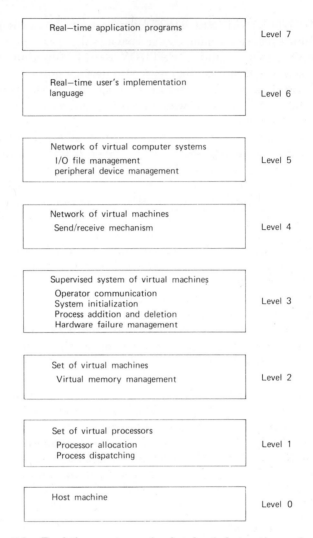

Figure 5.6   **Real-time system using levels of abstraction and ports.**

subsystems. Each subsystem can have one or more "private ports," that is, ports to which it sends and from which it later receives messages.

The port concept has many testing and debugging advantages because it places a central mechanism in the middle of all intersubsystem communications. In addition to the monitoring and tracing functions mentioned above, the send/receive mechanism could send a copy of all messages to a terminal to allow a human debugger to "watch" the operation of the system. By allowing ports to be connected to input/output devices such as terminals, subsystems can be simulated. Assume one has implemented the system in Figure 5.5 except for the data base manager. The system can be tested without the data base manager by typing a RECEIVE command at a terminal to obtain each message placed on the data base manager's input port. The data base manager is simulated by making up a suitable result for each search request and using a SEND command to transmit the result to the proper secondary input port for the interpret-command subsystem.

Unfortunately, the current state of both the port approach and levels-of-abstraction approach is that they both describe the desirable attributes of the system design solution without describing the design process itself. Undoubtedly, this will be rectified in the future. However, both approaches are useful today in giving the designer a number of guidelines for software system design.

SEQUENTIAL PROGRAMS

A significant percentage of the systems being designed today are still the traditional batch-processing systems, where the system is divided into a set of sequential programs that communicate from one to another through secondary storage files. For instance, a system to process property insurance premiums might consist of a program that edits and consolidates the weekly input, followed by a sorting program, then a master-file update program, and then a report-generation program.

Although this type of design has been performed for at least the last 25 years, no methodology has been developed other than the not-too-helpful suggestion to "draw a flowchart of the system and then divide it up into programs." However, several ideas from levels of abstraction and composite design [6] can be adapted. Each program should know nothing of the programs running at an earlier time in the sequence. Assumptions among programs should be minimized. Each program should hide certain system resources from the other programs. Each program should have functional strength and a minimal degree of coupling with the other programs (see Chapter 6).

DOCUMENTATION

The output of the system architecture process is design documentation describing the decomposition of the software system into its major parts (components, subsystems, programs, processes, or levels of abstraction). The documentation should describe the function or functions of each component, the precise interfaces among the components, and the system structure. The system structure should be expressed in all of the following forms:

1. The control-flow hierarchy of the system (i.e., the "calling structure" of the components).
2. The data-flow structure of the system.
3. The task (parallel process) hierarchy (i.e., the "mother/daughter/ sister" relationships among tasks).
4. The memory structure of the system. This only applies if the components do not all reside in a single addressable memory (e.g., one virtual memory or one storage region).
5. A mapping of the software structure to the hardware configuration (e.g., which components own or communicate with which input/ output devices).

Ideas for the actual description of function, interfaces, and structure can be found in Chapters 6 and 8.

VERIFICATION

Because the system architecture process is only vaguely understood today, its verification is also largely undefined. Two verification steps should be taken using the n-plus-and-minus-one method and the walkthrough method.

The objective of the n-plus-and-minus-one review is to uncover any translation errors made during the system architecture process and to minimize any future translation errors when using the system architecture as input to later design processes. Figure 3.2 implies that this review is performed by the designer of the initial external specification and by the about-to-be designers of the program structure of each component. The $n - 1$ designer looks for incomplete and inaccurate translations from the external design. The $n + 1$ designers check the system architecture for feasibility and understandability. Because the system architecture process is often performed in parallel with the detailed external design process, it is also important to match the outputs of the two processes to uncover errors.

A walk-through process similar to the one described in Chapter 4 for external design can also be used effectively. Test cases are developed and then manually "walked-through" the component structure, looking for incomplete or mismatching interfaces and missing or incomplete function. It is important to include at least one test case for system start-up, another for system termination, several for representative types of transactions entering the system, and a few test cases describing invalid inputs and unusual system states.

REFERENCES

1. E. W. Dijkstra, "The Structure of the THE-Multiprogramming System, *Communications of the ACM*, **11** (5), 341–346 (1968).

2. E. W. Dijkstra, "Complexity Controlled by Hierarchical Ordering of Function and Variability," in P. Naur and B. Randell, Eds., *Software Engineering: Report on a Conference Sponsored by the NATO Science Committee*. Brussels, Belgium: NATO Scientific Affairs Division, 1968, pp. 181–185.

3. G. Goos, "Hierarchies," in M. Beckman et al., Eds., *Advanced Course in Software Engineering*. Berlin: Springer-Verlag, 1970, pp. 29–46.

4. D. L. Parnas, "Information Distribution Aspects of Design Methodology," *Proceedings of the 1971 IFIP Congress*, Booklet TA-3. Amsterdam: North-Holland, 1971, pp. 26–30.

5. B. H. Liskov, "A Design Methodology for Reliable Software Systems," *Proceedings of the 1972 Fall Joint Computer Conference*. Montvale, N.J.: AFIPS Press, 1972, pp. 191–199.

6. G. J. Myers, *Reliable Software Through Composite Design*. New York: Petrocelli/Charter, 1975.

7. B. H. Liskov, "The Design of the Venus Operating System," *Communications of the ACM*, **15** (3), 144–149 (1972).

8. E. Morenoff and J. B. McLean, "Inter-Program Communications, Program String Structures and Buffer Files," *Proceedings of the 1967 Spring Joint Computer Conference*. Montvale, N.J.: AFIPS Press, 1967, pp. 175–183.

9. R. M. Balzer, "Ports—A Method for Dynamic Interprogram Communication and Job Control," R-605-ARPA, Rand Corp., Santa Monica, Ca., 1971.

10. R. M. Balzer, "An Overview of the ISPL Computer System Design," *Communications of the ACM*, **16** (2), 117–122 (1973).

11. G. D. Knott, "A Proposal for Certain Process Management and Intercommunication Primitives, Part I," *Operating Systems Review*, **8** (4), 7–44 (1974).

12. D. E. Knuth, *The Art of Computer Programming, Volume 1, Fundamental Algorithms*. Reading, Mass.: Addison-Wesley, 1968.

13. P. G. Sorenson and V. C. Hamacher, "A Real-Time System Design Methodology," *INFOR*, **13** (1), 1–18 (1975).

CHAPTER 6

Program Structure Design

The next software design process is the design of the program structure, which includes the definition of all modules in the program, the hierarchical structure of the modules, and the interfaces among the modules. If the product being designed is a single program, the input to this process is the detailed external specification. If the product is a system, the input is the detailed external specification and the system architecture, and this process is the structural design of all components or subsystems in the system.

The traditional method of managing complexity is the idea of "divide and rule," often called "modularization." However, in practice this idea has often been ineffective in reducing complexity. Liskov [1] has pointed out three reasons for this failure:

1. Modules are made to do too many related but different functions, obscuring their logic.
2. Common functions are not identified in the design, resulting in their distribution (and varied implementation) among many different modules.
3. Modules interact on shared or common data in unexpected ways.

A design methodology called *composite design* [2] is the design principle discussed here for program structure design. Composite design actually consists of two sets of principles: a set of explicit design measures that solve the three problems listed above plus many additional problems, and a set of thought processes for decomposing a program into a set of modules, module interfaces, and module relationships. Composite design leads to a program structure of minimal complexity, which has proven to increase reliability, maintainability, and adaptability.

MODULE INDEPENDENCE

The primary way to make a program less complex is to decompose it into a large set of small, highly independent modules. A module is a closed subroutine that can be called from any other module in the program and can be separately compiled (note that this excludes the PL/I internal procedure and the COBOL "performed" paragraph). High independence can be achieved by two optimization methods: maximizing the relationships within each module and minimizing the relationships among modules. Given that a program will eventually consist of a set of program statements where the statements will have some relationships among themselves (both in terms of function performed and data manipulated), what is needed is the foresight to organize these statements into separate boxes (modules) such that the statements within any module are closely related and any pair of statements in two different modules are minimally related. The goals are to isolate a single function to each module (high module strength) and to minimize the data relationships among modules by using formal parameter-passing methods (loose module coupling).

MODULE STRENGTH

Module strength is a measure of the relationships within a module. Determining the strength of a module involves analyzing the function or functions performed by the module and then fitting the module into one of seven categories. The categories were established partially to quantify the "goodness" of particular types of modules.

Before proceeding it is necessary to define what is meant by the *function* of a module. A module has three basic attributes: it performs one or more *functions*, it contains some *logic*, and it is used in one or more *contexts*. Function is an external description of the module; it describes what the module does when it is called, but not *how* it does it. Logic describes the internal algorithm of the module, in other words, how it performs its function. Context describes a particular usage of a module. For instance, a module with the function "squeeze the blanks from a character string" might be used in the context "compress teleprocessing message." To see the difference between function and logic, consider a module with the function: compile a PL/I program. This module may be the top module in an 83-module compiler or it may be the only module in the compiler. In either case its function remains the same but its logic is much different. Therefore, the function of a module can be viewed as the summation of the module's logic plus the functions of all subordinate (called) modules. This definition is recursive and applies to any module in a hierarchy.

The design goal is to define modules such that each module performs one function (such modules are said to have *functional strength*). To understand the need for this goal, the scale for the seven categories of module strength is explored as follows, starting with the weakest type of strength.

A *coincidental-strength* module is a module in which there are no meaningful relationships among its elements. It is difficult to give an example of such a module since it performs no meaningful function. The only way to describe the module is by describing its logic. One way a module of this type might occur is in an after-the-fact "modularization" of a program, where we discover identical sequences of code in several modules and decide to group these together into a single module. If these code sequences (although appearing to be identical) have different meanings in the modules in which they originally appeared, this new module has coincidental strength. A module of this sort is closely related to its calling modules, implying that almost any modification of the module on behalf of one of its callers will cause it to operate incorrectly for its other callers.

A *logical-strength* module is a module that, during each invocation, performs one selected function from a class of related functions. The selected function is explicitly requested by the calling module, for instance by the use of a function code. An example is a module whose function is to read or write a record to/from a file. The main problem with this type of module is the use of a single interface to reflect multiple functions. This leads to complex interfaces and unexpected errors in instances where the interface is modified to reflect a change in one of the functions.

A *classical-strength* module is a module that sequentially performs a class of related functions. The most common examples are "initialization" and "termination" modules. The major problem with modules of this type is that they usually have implicit relationships with other modules in the program, making the program difficult to understand and leading to errors when the program must be modified.

A *procedural-strength* module is a module that sequentially performs a class of related functions, where the functions are related in terms of the procedure of the problem. The "problem" is the reason for writing the program. An example of a problem is: write a program to regulate the temperature of the primary boiler. Problems to a certain extent dictate the procedure of the program. For instance, the problem might state that upon receiving signal x, valve y should be turned off and the temperature should be read and logged. A module whose function is "turn off valve y, read boiler temperature and record it on journal" has procedural strength. The only reliability problem is that the code for the set of functions may be intertwined. Note that this type of module, in common with most other types, has other non-reliability-related problems, as shown by Myers [2].

A *communicational-strength* module is a module with procedural strength but with one additional relationship: *all* of its functions are related in terms of data usage. For instance, the module "read next transaction and update master file" has communicational strength since both functions are related by their use of the transaction. Again, the functions may tend to be intertwined, but the risk of making a mistake while performing a modification is somewhat less since the functions are more closely related.

Informational strength is next on the scale. However, I defer discussion of it for a moment.

A *functional-strength* module is a module that performs a single specific function such as "turn off valve y," "execute EDIT command," or "summarize the week's transactions." Functional strength is the highest (best) form of module strength.

Note that a functional-strength module could also be described as a set of more-detailed functions. For instance, a "summarize transaction tape" module could have been described as "initialize summary table, open transaction file, read records, and update summary table." The reader may look at this and have the feeling that by just rewording the module's description its strength has been lowered. The resolution is that if these "lower functions" can rationally be described as a single "higher" well-defined function, the module has functional strength.

The remaining type of strength is *informational strength.* An informational-strength module is a module that performs several functions, where the functions operate on the same data structure and each function is represented by a unique entry point. A module with two entry points, one having the function "insert entry into symbol table" and the other having the function "search symbol table," has informational strength. This type of module can be viewed as the physical grouping of certain functional-strength modules to achieve "information hiding" [3], such as hiding all knowledge of a particular data structure, resource, or device to within a single module. In the example mentioned, all knowledge of the symbol table structure and location are hidden within one module. The advantage in this is that whenever some aspect of the program can be hidden within a single module, the independence among the program's modules increases. The design goal mentioned earlier is now modified to include informational-strength modules, as well as functional-strength modules, as the goal.

Although the preceding discussion focused only on the relationship between module strength and susceptibility to errors, module strength also affects the adaptability of the program, the difficulty of testing individual modules, and the degree to which a module is usable in other contexts and other programs [2]. The strength scale was ordered by weighing all of these attributes.

Note that a module may fit the descriptions of several types of strength. For instance, a communicational-strength module also fits the definition of procedural and classical strength. A module is always classified as having the highest strength whose definition it meets.

MODULE COUPLING

The second primary way to maximize module independence is by minimizing the connections among modules. Module coupling, a measure of the data relationships among modules, is concerned with both the mechanism used to pass data and the attributes of the data itself. Every pair of modules in a program can be analyzed and fit into either one of six categories of coupling or else be categorized as having no direct coupling.

The design goal is to define module interfaces so that all data passed between modules is in the form of explicit simple parameters. Again, to understand the importance of this goal, the six categories of coupling are explored below, starting with the tightest form of coupling (the worst case).

Two modules are *content coupled* if one *directly* references the contents of the other. For instance, if module A somehow references data in module B by using an absolute displacement, the modules are content coupled. Almost any change to B, or maybe just recompiling B with a different version of the compiler, will introduce an error into the program. Fortunately, most high-level languages make content coupling difficult to achieve.

A group of modules are *common coupled* if they reference the same global data structure. A set of PL/I modules that reference a data structure declared as EXTERNAL are common coupled to one another. FORTRAN modules referencing data in a COMMON area and groups of modules referencing a data structure in an absolute storage location (including registers) are also examples of common coupling.

There are a large number of problems associated with common coupling. All of the modules are dependent on the physical ordering of the items within the structure, implying that a change to the size of one data item affects all of the modules. Use of global data defeats attempts to control the access that each module has to data. For example, IBM's OS/360 has a large global data structure called the communications vector table. The inability to control access to this table (and other global tables) has led to a number of reliability and adaptability problems. Global variable names bind modules together when they are originally coded. This means that the reuse of common-coupled modules in future programs is difficult if not impossible.

The use of global data also reduces a program's readability. Consider the following piece of a program:

```
DO  WHILE  (A);
    CALL  L  (X,Y,Z);
    CALL  M  (X,Y);
    CALL  N  (W,Z);
    CALL  P  (Z,X,Y);
END;
```

If A is not a global variable and if other bad coding practices are avoided (such as overlaying A and W, X, Y, or Z), we can state that the loop cannot terminate. If A is a global variable, we cannot immediately determine if the loop can terminate. We have to explore the insides of modules L, M, N, and P, and also the insides of all modules called by these four modules, to understand the DO loop!

The case against global data is becoming as important as the case against the GO TO statement and is beginning to receive attention in the professional literature [4, 5, 6].

A group of modules are *external coupled* if they reference the same global data item (single-field variable). For instance, a set of PL/I modules referencing a variable (not a structure) declared as EXTERNAL are external coupled with one another. External coupling has many of the problems associated with common coupling. However, the problem of dependence on the physical ordering of items within a structure is not present in external coupling.

Two modules are *control coupled* if one explicitly controls the functions of the other, for instance by the use of a function code. Control coupling and logical strength usually occur together; thus the major problem here is the same one as associated with logical strength: the use of a single complex interface to reflect one of many functions. Control coupling also often implies that the calling module has some knowledge of the logic of the called module, thus lessening their independence.

A group of modules are *stamp coupled* if they reference the same nonglobal data structure. If module A calls module B passing B an employee personnel record and both A and B are sensitive to the structure or format of the record, then A and B are stamp coupled.

Stamp coupling should be avoided where possible because it creates unnecessary connections between modules. Suppose module B only needs a few fields in the personnel record. By passing it the entire record, B is forced to be aware of the entire structure of the record and the chances of module B's inadvertently modifying the record are increased. (It seems fair to say that the more extraneous data to which a module is exposed, the greater the opportunity for error.)

Stamp coupling can often be eliminated by isolating all functions performed on a particular data structure to an informational-strength module. Other modules may need to name the structure, but they know only its name (address), not its format. This technique is illustrated later in this chapter.

Two modules are *data coupled* if one calls the other and all inputs to, and outputs from, the called module are data item parameters (not structures). Suppose in the example above that module B's function is to print an envelope for an employee. Rather than giving B the personnel record, we could pass it the employee's name, street, apartment, city, state, and zip code as arguments. Module B is now not dependent on the personnel record. A and B are more independent and the probability of an error in B is lower since the programmer of B has less data to deal with.

As was the case for module strength, module coupling affects other attributes that have not been discussed, such as adaptability, the difficulty of testing modules, the reusability of modules, and the ease or difficulty of multiprogramming [2].

A pair of modules can fit the definition of several types of coupling. For instance, two modules could be both stamp coupled and external coupled. When this occurs the modules are defined to have the tightest (worst) type of coupling that they exhibit (in this case external coupling).

The measures of strength and coupling can be used to evaluate an existing design or as guidelines in producing a design for a new program. They should not imply, however, that a design with instances of strengths and couplings below the ideal is necessarily a poor design. The strength and coupling measures are guidelines. A designer may decide, based on some tradeoff, to define a logical-strength module. However, when he does this, he should be able objectively to explain his reasons and also to realize the implications of his tradeoff. This is certainly better than going about the business of design in an intuitive and haphazard manner.

High module strength and low coupling contribute to module independence by minimizing the interactions and assumptions among modules. The following three design criteria defined by Holt [7] present a good summary of these effects:

1. The complexity of a module's interactions with other modules should be less than the complexity of the module's internal structure.
2. A good module is simpler on the outside than on the inside.
3. A good module is easier to use than to build.

FURTHER GUIDELINES

In addition to strength and coupling, there are other guidelines that have an effect on module independence. These guidelines are summarized as follows.

Module Size.   Module size has a bearing on a program's independence, readability, and difficulty of testing (e.g., number of paths). One could satisfy the criteria of high strength and minimal module coupling by designing a program as one huge module, but it is unlikely that high independence would be achieved by doing so. The use of a large number of modules is desirable, for modules represent explicit barriers within the program, thus reducing the potential number of interconnections among program statements and data. As a general rule, modules should contain between 10 and 100 executable high-level language statements.

Predictable Modules.   A predictable module is a module whose function is independent of its past history of use. A module that internally keeps track of its own state across invocations (e.g., setting a "first-time switch") is unpredictable. All modules should be predictable, that is, they should have no "memory" from one invocation (call) to another. Interesting elusive time-dependent errors occur in programs that attempt to call an unpredictable module from several places in the program.

Decision Structure.   Whenever possible it is desirable to arrange modules and decisions in those modules so that modules that are directly affected by a decision are subordinate to (called by) the module containing the decision. This tends to eliminate the passing of special parameters representing decisions to be made and also keeps decisions affecting program control at a high level in the program hierarchy.

Minimized Data Access.   The amount of data that each module can reference should be minimized. Avoiding common, external, and stamp coupling is a big step in this direction. The designer should try to isolate knowledge of any particular data structure or data base record to a single module (or a small subset of modules), possibly by using informational-strength modules. The global data problem should not be solved by passing a single huge parameter list to all modules. Following these rules will minimize the scope of data access that each module has, reducing the consequences of errors and making errors easier to isolate.

Internal Procedures.   An internal procedure or subroutine is a closed subroutine that physically resides in its calling module. Internal procedures should be avoided for several reasons. Internal procedures are difficult to isolate for testing (unit testing), and they cannot be called from modules other than the modules physically containing the procedures. This violates the objective of "reusability." Of course, an alternative is to insert copies of an internal procedure into all modules needing it. However, this often leads to errors (copies of the same procedure often become "nonexact copies") and complicates program maintenance (when the procedure is changed all modules using it must be recompiled). Lastly, unless a great deal of discipline is used during the coding process, internal procedures will have poor degrees of coupling with their calling modules. If a need for an internal procedure arises, the designer should consider making it a module.

COMPOSITE ANALYSIS

Module strength, coupling, and the other guidelines discussed are valuable in evaluating alternatives in a design but they do not explicitly identify the design thought process. Within composite design is a process called *composite analysis,* a top-down design reasoning process. Composite analysis involves an analysis of the problem structure and how data is transformed as it flows through the problem structure. This information is used to decompose the problem into a "layer" of modules. Each module is then viewed as a subproblem, the analysis is repeated for this subproblem, and so on.

In using composite analysis there are three basic decomposition strategies. In decomposing any subproblem, one of the following strategies is used. *STS (source/transform/sink) decomposition* involves breaking the problem into functions that acquire data, alter its form, and then deliver the data to some point outside of the problem. *Transaction decomposition* involves breaking the problem into "sister" functions that process unique types of transactions. *Functional decomposition* involves breaking the problem into functions that perform data transformations. STS decomposition is normally used to decompose the problem initially into the first layer of modules, and then either STS, transaction, or functional decomposition is used on each subproblem, the one used being dependent on characteristics of the subproblem.

Transaction and functional decomposition are basically intuitive processes and little more can be said about them. STS decomposition, however, is a more sophisticated process and can be summarized in these five steps:

1. Outline the structure of the problem, picturing it as three to ten processes based on data flow through the problem.
2. Identify the major input stream of data entering the problem and the major output data stream leaving the problem.
3. Trace the major input data stream through the problem structure. As you do this you will notice two effects: the input data stream will change form, becoming more abstract as you follow it into the problem structure, and you will eventually hit a point where the input stream seems to disappear. The point at which the input stream last appears is called the *point of highest abstraction* of the input stream.

    Perform a similar analysis of the output data stream, starting at the "end" of the problem structure and working backward. Identify the point at which the output stream first appears in its most abstract form.

These points are of interest because they divide the problem into its most independent pieces.

4. The two points identified break the problem structure into pieces (normally three). Describe these pieces of the problem structure as functions and define modules (again, normally three) that perform each of these functions. These modules become subordinate modules to the module being decomposed.

5. Define the interfaces to these modules. At this time you should be interested only in identifying the kind of data in each interface. That is, identify descriptive input and output arguments without being concerned about their precise nature (order, attributes, and representation). A subsequent design process (module external design, described in Chapter 8) will define the detail of each interface.

The decomposition process is continued down the module hierarchy until a stopping point is reached. The general guideline telling when to stop is whenever a module is reached whose logic seems "intuitively obvious" (meaning it probably will contain 50 statements or less).

The output of the analysis process is a hierarchical block diagram showing the structural relationships of all modules (who calls whom), the functions of each module, and the interfaces among the modules. Notation for this diagram is described in Myers [2].

COMPOSITE ANALYSIS EXAMPLE

The easiest way to understand composite analysis is to see its application on an example. This same example is used in later chapters to illustrate other design and testing processes.

In deciding on an appropriate example I immediately ran into several problems. The example cannot be a large program; it must be textbook size, yet it also must not be trivial. An application program (e.g., a payroll program) might not hold the interest of system programmers and even many application programmers; a component of an operating system would have an equally limited appeal. To compromise I chose a *loader,* a program that is midway between an application program and an operating system. A second reason for selecting a loader as an example is my feeling that most readers will be at least vaguely familiar with the function of a loader.

As mentioned at the beginning of the chapter, a detailed external specification is the input to the program structure design process. Rather than supply such a specification for the loader, I simply describe the functions of the loader and its inputs and outputs in sufficient detail to allow us to design its structure.

The function of the loader is to load a program into main storage, ready for execution (some loaders also initiate the execution of the program, but this detail is disregarded here). The input to the loader is a file (referred to as INFILE) containing one or more object modules produced by a compiler. The loader can have a second input: a program library file (referred to as PROGLIB) containing a large library of object modules that may be needed in the loaded program. The loader has two outputs: the loaded program in main storage and an output file (referred to as OUTFILE) containing a memory map showing the main storage locations of the modules in the loaded program, and a list of error messages, if any.

INFILE is a sequential file containing one or more object modules. PROGLIB is some type of indexed or partitioned file where object modules are stored as separate entities. All object modules have the same format: one or more ESD (external symbol dictionary) records describing external symbols and external references in the module, two or more TXT (text) records containing the object (machine) code for the module, followed by zero or more RLD (relocation dictionary) records describing any address constants in the module, and an END record. Each ESD record contains a symbol name, the type of symbol (module name, entry-point name, or reference to an external name), and the relative offset of the symbol within the module. The first TXT record contains the size of the object code for the module. Each following TXT record contains a section of the object code along with a length field describing the amount of object code on this record. The RLD records describe any address constants within the module, addresses that must be relocated when the module is assigned a particular main storage address. An RLD record contains the offset of an address constant in the object code and the number of the corresponding ESD record (each address in an object module is relative to an external symbol). For address constants that will point to areas within the module, the corresponding ESD record is the ESD for the module name (primary entry point). For address constants that will point to other modules, the corresponding ESD record is the ESD for the external reference to the other module.

To load a program, the loader has to perform the following functions:

1. Move the object code for each module in INFILE into assigned main storage locations.
2. Ensure that all external references are matched. For example, if module A is being loaded and it contains a CALL statement to module B, the loader must ensure that module B is also loaded. If module B is not in INFILE, it is loaded from PROGLIB if it is found there. Note that module B may then contain external references to other modules that must subsequently be matched.
3. Relocate all address constants. An address constant is a data area in a program that contains the address of another data area. We will assume that all address constants have a single fixed length. The compiler has no knowledge of what main storage locations the program will be loaded into, so the compiler puts *relative* addresses in the address constant fields. For an address constant pointing to a location within the same module, the compiler assigns it the offset of the location relative to the beginning of the module. Address constants pointing to external references are initialized to zero by the compiler. Once all necessary modules have been assigned main storage locations, the loader adjusts all address constants to their proper values.

Rather than explain this process in any more detail, I have described a sample input to the loader in Figure 6.1 and the resulting output in Figure 6.2. By studying Figures 6.1 and 6.2 you should be able to gather enough information to understand the design problem. In designing the loader, we assume that it executes on some operating system containing main storage allocation functions and the necessary input/output functions to perform read, write, and search operations on the input and output files.

The first step in designing the loader is to define a top module having a function equivalent to the loader. This module is called LOAD-A-PROGRAM. The next step is to view this module as a problem to be solved and use STS decomposition to break it into smaller functions. Figure 6.3 shows that this problem can be structured by data flow into five processes. The major input stream is the stream of object modules. The major output stream is the loaded program (the memory map is a secondary output). By recognizing that an object module is a module with *relative* address constants and that a loaded program is a set of modules with *absolute* address constants, the points of highest abstraction are easily found and are indicated by asterisks. The problem has now been decomposed into three functions and the module structure is started as shown in Figure 6.3.

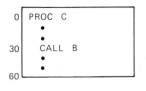

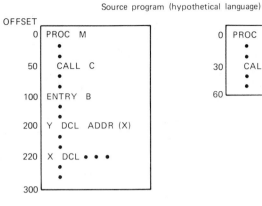

Source program (hypothetical language)

INFILE Contents

				Notes
ESD	M	MD	0000	
ESD	B	EP	0100	
ESD	C	ER	0000	
TXT			0300	
TXT	~~~ 000000 ~~~			Adcon at offset 54 to point to module C
TXT	~~~ 000220 ~~~			Adcon at offset 200 to point to X
RLD	0054	3		
RLD	0200	1		
END				
ESD	C	MD	0000	
ESD	B	ER	0000	
TXT			0060	
TXT	~~ 000000 ~~~			Adcon at offset 34 to point to entry B
RLD	0034	2		
END				

Figure 6.1   **Sample loader input.**

The remaining item to be defined at this level of the design is the module interfaces (the ones marked 1, 2, and 3). Starting with interface 3, we know that the output listing consists of the memory map (listing external symbols and their absolute addresses) and error messages. The input on interface 3 is now defined to be a list of error messages and ESTAB, a table containing external symbols, their types, and their absolute addresses. Note that we are not interested in defining precise data representations during the program structure design process (e.g., ESTAB could later be defined as a sequential list or a linked list). The output on interface 3 is some yet-to-be-defined error code.

OUTFILE Output

```
LOADER MEMORY MAP

MODULE/ENTRY PT.    LOCATION    TYPE

       M            100000      MOD
       B            100100      EP
       C            100300      MOD
```

Main storage output

Locations 100000-1002FF contain code for module M
    location 100054 contains 100300
    location 100200 contains 100220
Locations 100300-100360 contain code for module C
    location 100334 contains 100100

Figure 6.2 **Corresponding loader output.**

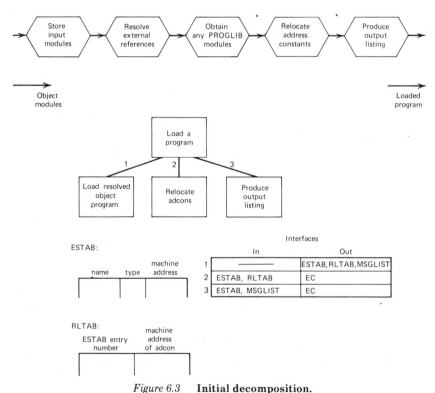

Figure 6.3 **Initial decomposition.**

102

The RELOCATE-ADCONS function needs two types of input: a description of the external symbols (particularly their absolute addresses) and a description of all address constants. Interface 2 contains two inputs: ESTAB and RLTAB, a table containing a pointer to each address constant and a pointer (or index) to the corresponding ESTAB entry. It is not necessary to pass the loaded object modules as a parameter because ESTAB points to the loaded modules. Interface 2 has one output, an error code. Interface 1 is now defined to have no inputs and three outputs: ESTAB, RLTAB, and a list of error messages for any errors encountered in the function.

The next step is to take the modules of Figure 6.3 and decompose them further. The logic of RELOCATE-ADCONS and PRODUCE-OUTPUT-LISTING is easily visualized, so they will not be further decomposed here. This leaves us with the LOAD-RESOLVED-OBJECT-PROGRAM module. The first task is to view this module as a problem to be solved and outline the problem structure as shown in Figure 6.4. The input stream is the set of object modules from INFILE and the output stream is a stored object program with all external references resolved. The input stream's point of highest abstraction occurs when all INFILE modules have been stored in memory and represented in ESTAB and RLTAB. The output stream only appears at the end-point of the problem structure. These two points break the problem into two functions, and two corresponding subordinate modules are defined.

Interface 4 has no inputs and returns three outputs: ESTAB, RLTAB, and a list of error messages. Interface 5 obviously needs ESTAB as an input. However, since the RESOLVE-EXTERNAL-REFERENCES module may have to load modules from PROGLIB, it

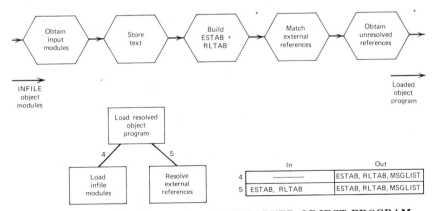

Figure 6.4   **Decomposition of LOAD-RESOLVED-OBJECT-PROGRAM.**

may have to add entries to both ESTAB and RLTAB, requiring them both as inputs and outputs.

Moving down the hierarchy, we can now attempt to decompose the LOAD-INFILE-MODULES module. Its problem structure is an iterative process as shown in Figure 6.5. The problem is simple enough so that decomposition is not necessary. However, because of a goal I have in mind (minimizing the number of modules that are aware of the representations of ESTAB and RLTAB), two functions are broken out as separate modules. Note that LOAD-INFILE-MODULES also calls the operating system for two functions: reading from INFILE and allocating blocks of main storage. ESTAB is an input on interface 6 and RLTAB is an input on interface 7, which ensures that the called modules are predictable and reentrant. One value of EC (error code) in interface 6 indicates an attempt to insert a duplicate name with type MD or EP into ESTAB.

We can now search for another module to decompose; we choose RESOLVE-EXTERNAL-REFERENCES from Figure 6.4. The input stream is the set (possibly empty) of unresolved references and the output stream is a complete object program. The points of highest abstraction and the resulting decomposition are indicated in Figure 6.6.

We are faced with an interesting tradeoff at this point. Modules LOAD-PROGLIB-MODULE and LOAD-INFILE-MODULES are similar in function, suggesting the alternative of generalizing the latter module to perform both functions. This is not an unreasonable tradeoff, but I chose not to use a single module for two reasons: the files have dif-

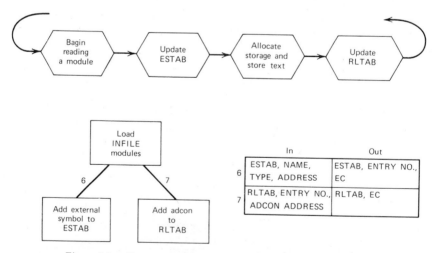

Figure 6.5   **Decomposition of LOAD-INFILE-MODULES.**

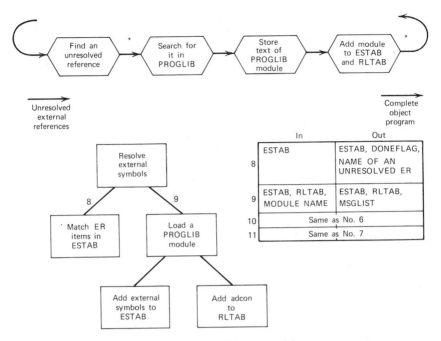

Figure 6.6   **Final decomposition.**

ferent file organizations, and using a single module would introduce control coupling (explicitly telling the module which file to read). Note, however, that I can use the subordinate modules of LOAD-INFILE-MODULES as shown.

Module MATCH-ER-ITEMS is quite simple. It scans ESTAB for unresolved names (indicated by a zero address field). When it encounters one it scans ESTAB looking for the same name of type MD or EP. If it finds one, it puts its address field into the address field for the unmatched name and then continues looking for other unmatched names. It returns when there are no symbols remaining unmatched (setting DONEFLAG) or when a name is encountered that cannot be matched (and returning the name as an output). Module RESOLVE-EXTERNAL-SYMBOLS is also quite simple; it iteratively calls MATCH-ER-ITEMS and LOAD-PROGLIB-MODULE until all symbols are matched or unmatched symbols cannot be located in PROGLIB. This is not the most efficient way to perform this function, but it is the simplest way. As Knuth [8] says, "Premature optimization is the root of all evil." After we have a working program, we can perform performance measurements and optimize the logic of one or

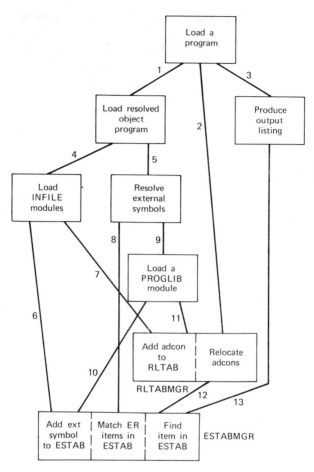

Figure 6.7   **The end result.**

Notes

1. LOAD-INFILE-MODULES uses operating system functions GET (from INFILE) and GETMAIN (to allocate storage).
2. LOAD-A-PROGLIB-MODULE uses system functions FIND and GET (from PROGLIB) and GETMAIN.
3. PRODUCE-OUTPUT-LISTING uses system function PUT (to OUTFILE).
4. ESTAB entry contains symbol name, type (MD, EP, or ER), and allocated machine address.
5. RLTAB entry contains number of corresponding ESTAB entry and the machine address of the address constant.

	In	Out
1	————————	ESTAB, RLTAB, MSGLIST
2	ESTAB, RLTAB	EC
3	ESTAB, MSGLIST	EC
4	————————	ESTAB, RLTAB, MSGLIST
5	ESTAB, RLTAB	ESTAB, RLTAB, MSGLIST
6	ESTAB, NAME, TYPE, ADDRESS	ESTAB, ENTRY NO., EC
7	RLTAB, ENTRY NO., ADCON ADDRESS	RLTAB, EC
8	ESTAB	ESTAB, DONE FLAG, NAME OF UNRES. ER
9	ESTAB, RLTAB, MODULE NAME	ESTAB, RLTAB, MSGLIST
10	SAME AS	NO. 6
11	SAME AS	NO. 7
12	ESTAB, ENTRY NO.	NAME, TYPE, ADDRESS, EC
13	SAME AS	NO. 12

more modules if warranted. (These points are mentioned only for the reader's understanding of the loader; we are not really interested in module logic at this time).

In scanning the current state of the design, I can find no other modules that need further decomposition. Hence we could call the design complete at this point. However, I still have the objective in mind that I mentioned earlier of minimizing the number of modules that know the attributes and representation of ESTAB and RLTAB. I can accomplish this by combining modules into informational-strength modules as shown in Figure 6.7. To isolate all knowledge of ESTAB into one module, I need to create a new function (entry point) named FIND-ITEM-IN-ESTAB, called by RELOCATE-ADCONS and PRODUCE-OUTPUT-LISTING as shown. Note that although other modules pass ESTAB and RLTAB as parameters, only the two informational-strength modules ESTABMGR and RLTABMGR are aware of the "insides" of the tables. For instance, only ESTABMGR knows the format of the ESTAB entries, whether ESTAB is a sequential table or a list, and whether ESTAB entries are sorted or unsorted.

In the final design in Figure 6.7 we have achieved several desirable results:

1. Six modules have functional strength; the other two have informational strength.
2. Each module is small and its logic is easily grasped.
3. Knowledge of ESTAB and RLTAB is hidden within single modules.
4. Only two modules are aware of the format of compiler-produced object modules.
5. Except for these two modules (which are stamp coupled), the only form of module coupling is data coupling.
6. All input/output operations to each file occur only within a single module.

Just as a reminder, an actual loader would contain one additional detail: it would either initiate execution of the loaded program or return the entry-point address of the loaded program to its caller.

VERIFICATION

Three steps can be taken to find flaws or errors in the program structure design: an n-plus-and-minus-one review, a static review, and a walk-through. The n-plus-and-minus-one review is a formal reading of the design documentation by the $n-1$ designers (authors of the system architecture and external specification), who look for translation mistakes, and by the $n+1$ designers (producers of the module external design), who check for feasibility, understandability, and compatibility with the programming language to be used and the underlying host system.

The static review is an evaluation of the design by a second party based on the guidelines discussed earlier in this chapter. The reviewer should check the design by considering such questions as: Do all modules have functional or informational strength? If not, why not? Are all modules strictly data coupled? Are all modules predictable? Is the decomposition complete (e.g., can you visualize the logic of each module)? Has the data access of each module been minimized?

The third verification step is the walk-through, similar to the walk-through methods discussed for the prior design processes. Paper test cases are designed (e.g., Figures 6.1 and 6.2 can be used as a test case for the loader) and each test case is stepped through the module structure while keeping track of the system state. In doing this, assume that the logic of each module is correct (that each module performs its function correctly). Look for flaws in the structure such as missing functions, incomplete interfaces, and incorrect results. Use enough test cases to ensure that each module is invoked at least once. Also, include test cases for invalid inputs (e.g., an object module with no ESD records) and boundary conditions (e.g., an object module with no external references and an object module with no address constants).

REFERENCES

1. B. H. Liskov, "A Design Methodology for Reliable Software Systems," *Proceedings of the 1972 Fall Joint Computer Conference.* Montvale, N.J.: AFIPS Press, 1972, pp. 191-199.

2. G. J. Myers, *Reliable Software Through Composite Design.* New York: Petrocelli/Charter, 1975.

3. D. L. Parnas, "On the Criteria to be Used in Decomposing Systems into Modules," *Communications of the ACM,* **15** (2), 1053-1058 (1972).

4. W. Wulf and M. Shaw, "Global Variable Considered Harmful," *SIGPLAN Notices,* **8** (2), 28-34 (1973).

5. M. J. Spier, "A Critical Look at the State of our Science," *Operating Systems Review,* **8** (2), 9-15 (1974).

6. J. B. Goodenough and D. T. Ross, "The Effect of Software Structure on Reliability, Modifiability, Reusability, Efficiency: A Preliminary Analysis," Report R-2099, SofTech Corp., Waltham, Mass., 1973.

7. R. C. Holt, "Structure of Computer Programs: A Survey," *Proceedings of the IEEE,* **63** (6), 879-893 (1975).

8. D. E. Knuth, "Structured Programming with GO TO Statements," *Computing Surveys,* **6** (4), 261-301 (1974).

9. Composite design is closely allied with the methodology called "structured design," the main differences being terminology and notation. Structured design is discussed in E. Yourdon and L. L. Constantine, *Structured Design.* New York: Yourdon, 1975.

CHAPTER 7

Design Practices

Chapter 3 stated that in considering the four basic categories of reliability techniques, fault-avoidance techniques have the highest payoff. However, in designing most software products, one must never make the assumption that the product will be error free. This is the premise of fault-detection, fault-correction, and fault-tolerant techniques: that the product will not be error free and therefore the product must be designed so that it operates predictably in the event of an error. These errors may take the form of software errors, user errors, or hardware failures.

PASSIVE FAULT DETECTION

If we make the assumption that the software product will have errors, obviously the first measure to be taken is the detection of errors. Moreover, if additional measures are necessary, such as means to circumvent or correct errors, we must first have a way of detecting errors.

Fault-detection measures can be grouped into two subcategories: *passive* attempts at detecting error symptoms during the execution of a software function, and *active* attempts by the software product to search itself periodically for indications of errors. Passive detection is discussed in this section and active detection is discussed in the following section.

Fault-detection measures can be applied to several structural levels of the software product. In this chapter we apply the measures at the subsystem or component level, that is, establishing measures to detect symptoms of errors that are passed from one component to another and to detect errors within a particular component. You should recognize that these measures can also be applied to individual modules within a component.

In developing detection measures we can begin by basing them on the following concepts:

1. *Mutual suspicion.* Each component will assume that all other components contain errors. When a component receives any data from another component or from a source outside of the system, the component will assume that the data may be incorrect and will attempt to find flaws in the data.
2. *Immediate detection.* Errors should be detected as soon after their occurrence as possible. Not only does this limit the extent of their damage, but it also greatly simplifies the task of debugging.
3. *Redundancy.* All fault-detection measures are based on some form of explicit or implicit redundancy.

The particular detection measures in a component are highly dependent on the particular application of the software product. However, the following list can be used for ideas:

1. Check the attributes of each input data item. If the input must be numeric or alphabetic, check it. If the input must be a positive number, check its sign. If it must have a certain length, check it.
2. Apply "dog tags" [1] to tables, records, and control blocks and use the dog tags to check the validity of input data. A dog tag is some self-identifying field in a record. For instance, in the loader example of Chapter 6 each ESD record was self-identifying because the characters "ESD" are physically contained in each record. A component that is supposed to receive ESD records as input would check the actual input for this dog tag.
3. Check the value of the input against known limits. For instance, if an input item is a main storage address, check its validity. Always check an address or pointer field for a zero value and assume it is incorrect if it is zero. If the input is a table of probabilities, check all entries for values zero through one.
4. Check all multivalued data for valid values. If an input field is a district code representing one of ten districts, never assume that if

the field is not district 1, district 2, . . ., or district 9, then it must be district 10.

5. If there are any explicit redundancies in the input data, check them for consistency.

6. Where there are no explicit redundancies in the input data, add some. If your system contains a critical table, consider adding a check-sum entry to the table. Whenever a software function updates the table, it must sum the fields (modulo some number) and place the sum in the check-sum entry. A component using the table can then perform the same operation to see if the table was inadvertently modified.

7. Compare the input data for consistency with any internal data. If an operating system receives an input parameter telling it to free a particular block of storage, it should first ensure that the particular block is, in fact, currently allocated.

If fault-detection functions are implemented, it is important to adopt a consistent strategy throughout the entire system (i.e., applying the concept of conceptual integrity discussed in Chapter 4 to fault detection). The action taken after detecting a software error (e.g., returning error codes) should be uniform for all components in the system. This leads to the difficult question of what action to take when an error is detected. The best action is immediately to terminate the program or, in the case of an operating system, place the CPU in a suspended state. From the point of view of giving a human debugger, for example a system programmer, the best opportunity to diagnose the error, immediate termination after the detection of an error is the best strategy. Of course, in many systems this strategy may not be practical (e.g., suspending system operation may be intolerable). In this event the practice of *error recording* can be used. A description of the error symptoms and a snapshot of the system state are recorded on an external file and the system then attempts to continue operation. This file can then be later examined by service personnel. This practice is used in IBM's OS/VS2 MVS operating system. Each component contains a *functional recovery routine,* a routine that intercepts all abnormal terminations and program interrupts in the component and records data about the error on an external file.

Whenever possible, choose immediate suspension of the program over error recording (or it may be possible to provide an option to allow the system to run in either mode). The difference between the two is similar to attempting to diagnose an intermittent squeal in your car. If you drive with an automotive mechanic in your back seat, he can examine the car in its current state when the squeal occurs. If you opt for error recording (making a tape recording of the squeal), the job of diagnosing the problem will be much more difficult.

Example: The PRIME System

The PRIME system is a virtual-memory multiprocessing system developed at the University of California at Berkeley [2]. A simplified view of the system is shown in Figure 7.1. One processor in the system is designated as the control processor and contains the central control monitor (CCM), a control program that allocates memory pages and disk space, assigns programs to the other processors (problem processors), and routes all interprocess messages. The extended control monitor (ECM) is a microcoded control program that resides in each processor, controlling process dispatching, input/output operations, and send/receive operations.

Data security is a primary goal of the system. To achieve this goal, the PRIME system goes one step farther than most secure systems: in addition to ensuring that the system is secure under normal conditions, the objective is to maintain security even in the presence of a single software error or hardware failure. Fault-detection measures represent the primary method of achieving this objective.

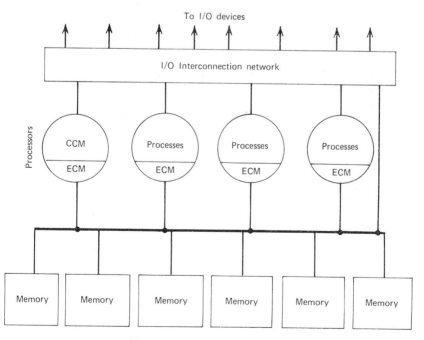

Figure 7.1   **The PRIME System.**

During the design of the PRIME system, all single operating system decisions were identified that, if made incorrectly, would potentially expose the data of one user to another user or user program. Fault-detection measures for each of these decisions were implemented. Many of the measures involve a combination hardware–software solution. For instance, whenever a terminal is allocated to a user process, the CCM stores a user process identifier in a register in the terminal. Whenever an ECM sends data to a terminal, the terminal compares the stored identifier with an identifier in the data. This ensures that no single hardware failure or software error will cause data to be printed at the wrong terminal.

The PRIME system contains a send/receive mechanism that allows one user process to send a message to another user process. In doing this, the originating process gives its ECM the message and an identifier of the destination process. The ECM adds the identifier of the originating process and gives the message to the CCM. The CCM passes the message to the ECM on the processor containing the destination process, and this ECM finally gives the message to the destination user process. Three fault-detection checks are made during this sequence. The CCM checks to see that the ECM added the correct identifier of the originating process; the CCM can do this because it knows what user process is scheduled on the processor. The destination ECM checks to see that the CCM routed the message to the correct processor; the ECM does this by comparing the process identifier in the message to the identifiers of the processes currently scheduled on this processor. The third check is to ensure that the message was unchanged in transit. The originating ECM generates a check-sum for the message and passes it with the message. The destination ECM computes the check-sum of the received message and compares the two check-sums.

As an example of another check, the CCM allocates free pages of memory to user processes by keeping a list of free pages. When an ECM no longer needs a page, it sets a tag in the page and then tells the CCM to add it to its free list. When a page is allocated, the ECM checks the tag in the page to ensure that the page is a free page. This redundancy can be used to detect errors because the free list is maintained by the CCM and the tags are set by the other processors.

ACTIVE FAULT DETECTION

Passive fault detection cannot detect all errors, because it only locates errors when symptoms of the errors are passed to the checking functions. Other checks for error symptoms can be made by designing software functions that actively search the system for indications of errors. Such measures are called *active fault-detection measures*.

Active fault-detection measures are usually embodied in a *detection monitor*: a parallel process that periodically scans through the system's data with the purpose of detecting errors. Large software systems that manage resources often have a class of software errors that result in the loss of resources over long periods of operation. For instance, the storage management function of an operating system has the function of "loaning" blocks of storage to user programs and to other parts of the operating system. Errors in these other parts of the system occasionally result in failures to return storage back to the storage manager, resulting in a slow deterioration of the system.

The detection monitor can be implemented as a periodic task (e.g., it is scheduled every hour) or as a low-priority task that is scheduled when the system would have entered a wait state. Again, the specific checks made by the monitor are dependent on the nature of the system, but the following examples should give some ideas. The monitor can scan main storage to detect storage blocks that are not allocated to any current program but yet are not on the system's list of available storage. It can check for unusual conditions such as processes that have not been scheduled in some reasonable time limit. The monitor can look for transactions that have seemed to disappear within the system, input/output operations that remain uncompleted for an unusually long time, disk storage that is neither marked as allocated nor on some free-list, and strange conditions in data files.

In extreme situations it may also be desirable to have the monitor perform diagnostic tests of the system. The monitor might call certain system functions, comparing their output with predefined expected output and checking their execution times for reasonableness. The monitor might also submit "dummy" or "ghost" transactions or jobs to the system to periodically ensure that the system is at least minimally operable.

Example: TRW Subverter Detector Program

The IBM Resource Security System is an experimental modification to the OS/360 operating system to study the problems of secure systems. In using the Resource Security System, the TRW Corporation developed a monitor that executes at preset time intervals and attempts to find indications that a user program has subverted the security of the system [3].

The monitor performs a large number of checks on system conditions. Many of these checks are peculiar to the internal logic of OS/360 and therefore are not of general interest. However, to give a few examples of some of the checks, the monitor determines if all of OS/360's control information about the user tasks is contained in protected storage. The monitor checks to see that all user programs are executing in problem-state mode and that all user storage is fetch-protected with the proper storage-protection key. The monitor checks all pending input/output operations for proper queuing, ensures that the entry points for all interrupts are the proper OS/360 entry points, and ensures that all supervisor storage has the proper storage protection. The system operator is immediately notified if any discrepancy is found.

FAULT CORRECTION AND TOLERANCE

Providing we have the means of detecting software errors, the next step is probably along the lines of providing software functions to attempt to correct the errors. Actually, the term "fault-correction" when applied to software means correcting the *damage* resulting from an error rather than the error itself. As has already been seen in Chapter 3, fault-correction in hardware devices (e.g., automatically switching to a spare device) is a viable technique, but attempting actually to fix a software error is impossible without human involvement. The best that can be done with software fault correction is undoing the resultant damage from an error. The best that can be done with fault tolerance is overlooking the damage or isolating it to only one part of the system.

Although correction/tolerance has had limited success in a few systems, it is best to avoid it in most situations. The number of potential errors in a large system is so high as to be, for practical purposes, infinite. In designing correction/tolerance functions, we are forced to predict a *few* types of errors in order to implement functions that will respond to the damage from these few errors. At best, our system will correct a tiny percentage of its potential faults. In addition, these functions are quite complex, which means that they cause the system to initially have a higher number of errors. Furthermore, these functions will undoubtedly have errors themselves. Finally, if one correction/tolerance function *does* work, it will tend to mask the error (make the error less noticeable), meaning that it may never be fixed by service personnel, which is an undesirable effect.

On top of these problems there is one remaining argument against fault correction and tolerance. Since it is necessary to predict in advance a few potential errors, one would generally be better off by focusing design and testing efforts in eliminating these errors in the first place.

Example: Bell Telephone Traffic Service Position System

The Bell System's TSPS is an example of fault-correction and tolerant methods [4]. The system performs the function of telephone line switching and has a stringent availability requirement: system down-time cannot exceed two hours in 40 years. In TSPS a total system crash is a serious event, while an occasional error such as breaking a phone connection is an acceptable event. (Note that in many systems this relationship is reversed. For instance, in a bank check-processing system, a system crash is less serious than a data error.)

TSPS uses passive and active fault detection followed by fault-correction measures to reduce system failures. The strategy is to detect certain types of errors as quickly as possible because these errors, if left undetected, will quickly propagate their effects through the system, leading to eventual system failure. In correcting the damage from these errors, losing some data is acceptable as long as the system can be kept operational.

Facilities in the telephone network are represented by tables in main storage, stored in a variety of linked linear lists. For instance, the list in Figure 7.2 could represent all of the network connections in the active state. There is a considerable amount of redundancy in the list. For instance, each block has a dog tag, the last block can be located in two ways, and the state field in each block in this list should be set to "active." The monitor (called an *audit program* in TSPS) periodically scans the lists. If a discrepancy is found such as the NEXT field of some block pointing to a wrong address (detected by an improper dog tag at that address), the list is truncated after the last valid block and the L-bit (lost bit) in each valid block is set to one. Another part of the monitor periodically makes a sequential scan of all facility blocks. If a block's L-bit is zero (implying it is "lost"), the block is added to the proper list of idle facilities of its type. This action may result in broken phone connections, but it keeps the total system operational.

Many facilities also have a "timeout" bit in their corresponding blocks. The monitor uses this bit to determine if a facility has been occupied for an abnormal period of time. If it has, further checks are made and the facility may be unconditionally transferred to an idle

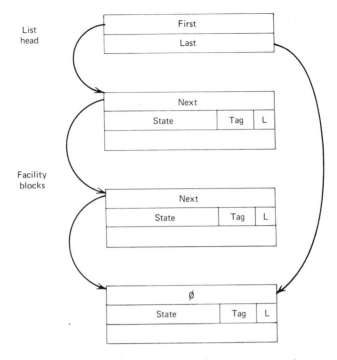

Figure 7.2   **Linear list of facilities (resources).**

status. If the monitor finds the system in a completely scrambled state, it has the capability to initiate a full system restart. The monitor also records all detected error conditions for later debugging.

The fault-correction mechanisms in TSPS make an awesome number of corrections each day. TSPS installations average beween 10 and 100 actual corrections per day after three years of operation, and an automatic system restart about once every two months.

ERROR ISOLATION

In a large computing system, isolation among programs is a key factor in ensuring that a failure in one user program does not lead to failures in other user programs or to total system failure. Guidelines for isolating errors are listed below. Although the term "operating system" is used in many of the guidelines, the guidelines are applicable to any program, such as an operating system, teleprocessing monitor, or file management subsystem, that performs functions on behalf of a set of other programs.

1. An application program must not be able to reference or modify another application program nor the data of another program.

2. An application program must not be able to reference or modify the operating system code nor any data within the operating system. Communication between two programs (or between a program and the operating system) is permitted only through well-defined interfaces and only when *both* programs agree to the communication.

3. Application programs and data must be protected from the operating system to the extent that an error in the operating system cannot result in an accidental modification of an application program or its data.

4. The operating system must protect all application programs and data from accidental modification by system operators and service personnel.

5. Application programs must not be able to stop the system nor induce the operating system to modify another application program or its data.

6. When an application program calls the operating system to perform a function, all parameters should be validity-checked. Furthermore, the application program should not be able to alter these parameters between the times of checking and actual use by the operating system.

7. The operating system's operation should be unaffected by any system data that is directly accessible to application programs. For instance, OS/360 stores certain storage management control blocks in main storage areas that are accessible by application programs. An error in an application program that causes this storage to be accidentally modified can result in the eventual failure of the system.

8. Application programs should not be able to bypass the operating system and directly use the hardware resources controlled by the operating system. Application programs should not be able to directly invoke functions within the operating system that are intended for use only by other parts of the operating system.

9. Functions in the operating system should be isolated from one another so that an error in one function does not result in the modification of other functions or their data.

10. If the operating system detects an error within itself, it should attempt to isolate this error as affecting a particular application program and, at worst, terminate only the affected application program.

11. Application programs should have the option of processing their own errors when the operating system detects an error in the application program, as opposed to the operating system unconditionally terminating the application program.

The implementation of many of these guidelines has implications for the architecture of the underlying system hardware. A few of these implications are discussed in Chapter 16.

The reader may recognize that most of these guidelines are also guidelines for security in operating systems. In fact, most of these were abstracted from Stepczyk [5], which is an excellent discussion of operating system security requirements and a survey of techniques to achieve the requirements. This confirms a statement in Chapter 4: security and reliability objectives are usually compatible. This relationship has also been confirmed in applying the experimental IBM Resource Security System to OS/360, which resulted in a system of increased reliability [3]. Because of the increased isolation in this system, previously undetected errors were discovered in system components (e.g., compilers) and application programs, and the frequency of accidental system failures due to application program errors was significantly reduced.

HANDLING HARDWARE FAILURES

In optimizing total system reliability, one must be concerned with more than software errors (although software reliability is the largest concern in system reliability). Other errors of concern are erroneous inputs to the system (user errors). The fault-detection measures discussed earlier can be applied to user errors, along with the guidelines for external design in Chapter 4.

The remaining errors of interest are hardware failures. Many hardware failures are handled by the hardware itself through the use of error-correcting codes, fault correction (e.g., switching to spare components), and fault tolerance (e.g., voting). Some failures, however, cannot be handled alone by the hardware and require assistance from software. Such errors are not discussed in this book, but for the sake of completeness, a list of functions often required in software systems to handle hardware failures appears below.

1. *Operation retry.* A large number of hardware failures are intermittent (e.g., power surges, noise in telecommunication lines, fluctuations in mechanical motion). It is always wise to retry the

failing operation (e.g., a machine instruction or I/O operation) several times before taking some other action.

2. *Memory refresh.* If a detected intermittent hardware failure causes an incorrect modification of part of main storage, and that area of main storage contains static data such as object code, the error can often be remedied by reloading the particular area of storage.

3. *Dynamic reconfiguration.* If a hardware subsystem such as a CPU, I/O channel, main storage unit, or I/O device fails, the system can often remain operational by dynamically removing the failing unit from the pool of system resources.

4. *File recovery.* Data base systems normally provide data redundancy by keeping an identical on-line copy of the data base on separate I/O devices, by keeping a journal of all alterations to the data base, or by periodically making off-line copies of the entire data base. Recovery programs can then reconstruct the data base in the event of a catastrophic I/O failure.

5. *Checkpoint/restart.* A *checkpoint* is a periodic copy that is made of the state of an application program or an entire system. If a hardware failure occurs, such as an I/O error, memory error, or power failure, the program can be restarted from its previous checkpoint.

6. *Power-failure warning.* Several computing systems, particularly those with volatile semiconductor memories, provide an interrupt to warn the software system of a pending power failure. This gives the software system the opportunity to take a checkpoint or to move any critical data to secondary storage.

7. *Error recording.* Any hardware failures that are circumvented should be recorded on an external file to give service personnel clues to the gradual deterioration of hardware devices.

Anyone with a need for more information on software processing of hardware failures can get a thorough education by studying practices in current operating systems, data management systems, and teleprocessing programs. These practices are also discussed in many textbooks, a few of which are listed in the references [6–10].

REFERENCES

1. B. Randell, "Operating Systems: The Problems of Performance and Reliability," *Proceedings of the 1971 IFIP Congress.* Amsterdam: North-Holland, 1971, pp. I100–I109.

2. R. S. Fabry, "Dynamic Verification of Operating System Decisions," *Communications of the ACM,* **16** (11), 659–668 (1973).

3. P. L. Pinchuk, "TRW Evaluation of a Secure Operating System," *Data Security and Data Processing, Volume 6, Evaluation and Installation Experiences: Resource Security System,* G320–1376, IBM Corp., White Plains, N.Y., 1974, pp. 39–121.

4. J. R. Connet, E. J. Pasternak, and B. D. Wagner, "Software Defenses in Real-Time Control Systems," *Digest of the 1972 International Symposium on Fault-Tolerant Computing.* New York: IEEE, 1972, pp. 94–99.

5. F. M. Stepczyk, "Requirements for Secure Operating Systems," *Data Security and Data Processing, Volume 5, Study Results: TRW Systems, Inc.,* G320–1375, IBM Corp., White Plains, N.Y., 1974, pp. 75–205.

6. R. W. Watson, *Timesharing System Design Concepts.* New York: McGraw-Hill, 1970.

7. J. Martin, *Systems Analysis for Data Transmission.* Englewood Cliffs, N.J.: Prentice-Hall, 1972.

8. B. Beizer, *The Architecture and Engineering of Digital Computer Complexes, Volume 2.* New York: Plenum, 1971.

9. E. Yourdon, *Design of On-Line Computer Systems.* Englewood Cliffs, N.J.: Prentice-Hall, 1972.

10. *IBM Systems Journal,* **6** (2), 1967 (special issue on the IBM 9020 air-traffic control system).

CHAPTER 8

Module Design
and Coding

The last processes in the design cycle are the steps of designing and coding each module. These processes are *module external design*, the design of the interfaces to each module, and *module logic design*, a set of steps including data definition, algorithm selection, logic design, and coding. To many people these processes are the essence of programming; however, after reading the first seven chapters of this book and the following 11 chapters, it should be apparent that these two processes are only a small part of the total software development cycle.

Principles and practices for module design and coding are discussed in this chapter. Certain topics that traditionally might fall within this chapter have been placed elsewhere. For instance, because of its importance, programming style is covered in a separate chapter (Chapter 9). Organizational issues such as programming teams and programming librarians are discussed in the chapter on management techniques (Chapter 14). Techniques such as top-down development and bottom-up development are discussed in Chapter 10 because of their close relationship to testing.

MODULE EXTERNAL DESIGN

The first step in designing a module is defining its external characteristics. This information is expressed in a *module external specification,* which contains all information needed by modules that call this module *and nothing more.* In particular, a module external specification must contain no information about the logic or internal data representations of the module. In addition, the specification should never contain any reference to the calling modules or to the contexts in which this module is used.

The module external specification should contain the following six types of information:

1. *Module name.* This defines the name used to invoke the module. For a module with multiple entry points, this name is the entry name (there is a separate specification for each entry point).
2. *Function.* This is a definition of the function or functions performed by the module. This item should *not* describe the module's logic or contexts (see Chapter 6 for a definition of function).
3. *Parameter list.* This defines the number and order of parameters passed to the module.
4. *Input.* This is a precise description of all input parameters to the module. It includes a definition of the format, size, attributes, units (e.g., nautical miles), and valid domains of all input data.
5. *Output.* This is a precise description of all output data returned by the module. It should include a definition of the format, size, attributes, units, and valid ranges of all outputs. This description should relate the outputs to the inputs in a cause-and-effect manner, that is, which outputs are generated from which inputs. The output generated by the module when the input is invalid must also be defined. For a module to be considered *completely specified,* its behavior under all input circumstances must be stated.
6. *External effects.* This is a description of any actions taken external to the program or system when this module is invoked. Examples of external effects are printing a report, reading a command, reading a transaction file, and writing an error message. The external effects of a module include any external effects of subordinate modules. For instance, if module A calls module B and B prints a report, then this external effect would appear in the module external specifications for both modules A and B.

It is important to separate a module's external specification from other documentation, such as a description of the module's logic, because module logic can be changed without affecting calling modules, but a change to a module's external specification normally leads to changes in calling modules.

The module external specification can take many physical forms as long as the six categories listed above are included. The preferred form is to place the specification in comment statements at the beginning of the source code for the module (or, in the case of multiple-entry-point modules, at the location of each entry point). The specification for one of the entry points in the ESTABMGR module for the loader designed in Chapter 6 is illustrated in Figure 8.1. Note that the format of ESTAB (the table of external symbols) is not described in the specification even though ESTAB is both an input and output. This is because of the original design objective of this module in Chapter 6: to hide all knowledge of the structure of ESTAB. Hence the calling module only

```
/*****************************************************************/
/*                                                             */
/* EXTERNAL SPECIFICATION FOR MATCHES                          */
/*                                                             */
/* FUNCTION: MATCH ALL EXTERNAL REFERENCE ITEMS IN ESTAB.      */
/*           IF ONE IS ENCOUNTERED THAT CANNOT BE MATCHED,     */
/*           RETURN ITS NAME.                                  */
/*                                                             */
/* PARAMETER LIST: CALL MATCHES (ESTAB,UNRESNAME,MATCHCODE)    */
/*                                                             */
/* INPUT:   ESTAB      POINTER     POINTER TO ESTABLE          */
/*                                                             */
/* OUTPUT:  ESTAB      POINTER     POINTER TO UPDATED ESTABLE  */
/*          UNRESNAME  CHAR(8)     NAME OF AN UNMATCHED        */
/*                                 EXTERNAL REFERENCE          */
/*          MATCHCODE  FIXED BIN(15)  RETURN CODE (0, 1, OR 2) */
/*                                                             */
/*          CAUSE/EFFECT RELATIONSHIP:                         */
/*                                                             */
/*          ANY UNMATCHED (NULL ADDRESS FIELD) EXTERNAL        */
/*          REFERENCES ARE MATCHED WITH A MATCHING MD OR       */
/*          EP ITEM BY TRANSFERRING THE ADDRESS OF THE MD OR   */
/*          EP ENTRY TO THE ER ENTRY UNTIL AN ER CANNOT BE     */
/*          MATCHED.                                           */
/*          -IF ALL ER'S CAN BE MATCHED, MATCHCODE=0 AND       */
/*             UNRESNAME IS UNCHANGED.                         */
/*          -IF AN ER CANNOT BE MATCHED, MATCHCODE=1 AND       */
/*             UNRESNAME = NAME OF ER ITEM                     */
/*          -IF AN ERROR OCCURS (INVALID ESTABLE), MATCH-      */
/*             CODE=2 AND UNRESNAME IS UNCHANGED               */
/*                                                             */
/* EXTERNAL EFFECTS: NONE                                      */
/*****************************************************************/
```

Figure 8.1   **Module external specification.**

gives this module a pointer variable called ESTAB, and the format of the table is not discussed as part of the module interface.

MODULE LOGIC DESIGN

The final process in the lengthy sequence of software design processes is the design and coding of the internal logic of each module. All too often, the concept of careful planning is tossed aside at this point and the programmer develops the module in a more or less haphazard manner. However, the module design process can, and should, be carefully planned. The following 11 steps outline a disciplined approach to module design:

1. *Select the language.* Language selection is usually dictated by contractual requirements or organizational standards. Although language selection is listed here, the programming language must be selected *early* in the project since it has a number of implications on project planning (e.g., programmer education and needs for compilers and test tools).

2. *Design module external specifications.* This is the process of defining the external characteristics of each module as discussed in the previous section.

3. *Verify module external specifications.* The specification for each module should be verified by comparing it with the interface information from the program structure design and by making sure that it is reviewed by the programmers of all modules that call this module.

4. *Select algorithm and data structures.* A vital step in the logic design process is the selection of an algorithm and the corresponding data structures. Few algorithms today are invented for the first time; a vast number of algorithms have already been invented, and chances are that one or more algorithms already exist that can fit the designer's needs. Rather than waste one's time reinventing algorithms and data structures, it is best to search for known solutions. For non-numerical algorithms (e.g., most types of data manipulation), the best place to start is Knuth's book on fundamental algorithms [1] and the subsequent volumes in his series. For numerical algorithms, start with the *Collected Algorithms from CACM* published by the Association for Computing Machinery. Other sources of both types of algorithms include texts, technical papers, and existing programs.

Generally the designer can find several functionally equivalent algorithms and data structures and must select from among them. Because many modern computing systems have multilevel program storages (normal main memory, virtual memory, and high-speed storage buffers), the trend for the efficiency-minded programmer is back toward the simplest algorithms and data structures (e.g., in a system with a multilevel storage, a binary search algorithm might not be appreciably faster than the simpler sequential search). This is one example where efficiency and reliability are becoming compatible objectives!

5. *Write first and last statements.* The next step is to write the PROCEDURE and END statements for the module (or their equivalents, depending on your programming language). If the module has multiple entry points, the ENTRY statements are also written at this time. Note that the traditional task of flowcharting has been skipped here; the reason for this will be discussed later.

6. *Declare all interface data.* The next step is to write the program statements that define or declare all variables in the module interface.

7. *Declare remaining data.* Write the program statements that define or declare all other variables to be used in the module. Because it is difficult to predict in advance every variable needed, this step is often overlapped with the following step.

8. *Refine the code.* The next step is an iterative one involving successive refinements of the module's logic, starting with an abstract definition of the logic and ending with the code for the module. This step uses the techniques of *step-wise refinement* and *structured programming,* which are discussed in the next section.

9. *Polish the code.* The module's code is now "polished" for clarity. Additional comments are added to answer any anticipated questions that a reader of the code might have. The points of programming style from Chapter 9 are reviewed to ensure that the module is as understandable as possible.

10. *Verify the code.* The module is manually verified for correctness. Procedures for this are discussed in a later section in this chapter.

11. *Compile the module.* The last step is the compilation of the module. This step marks the transition from design to testing; the compilation step is actually the start of software testing.

To further illustrate these points, I will use them to develop the ESTABMGR module. For step 1 it is assumed that the PL/I language has been selected. It is also assumed that steps 2 and 3 have been completed (the module external specification for one of the entry points is shown in Figure 8.1).

To perform step 4 for ESTABMGR, the most important considera-tion is the structure of ESTAB, the table containing the external symbols and their type and absolute address. The alternatives are sequential, linked, or hash-table allocation. Because there is no need to insert entries into the middle of ESTAB or to delete entries, linked allo-cation is not needed. Because the table will be processed sequentially as well as by direct look-up, a hash-table organization is undesirable. This leaves only the sequential allocation alternative. Hence ESTAB will be represented by a one-dimensional array (vector) of nodes where each node has three fields: name, type, and address. A remaining question might be whether to store the entries in ordered (sorted) form. Because the table is updated frequently, I chose to leave it unordered and to use a simple sequential search. (Note, however, that I made several edu-cated guesses. These decisions might be reviewed at a later time if effi-ciency tuning is necessary. The loader's design allows the structure of ESTAB to be altered by changing only a single module.)

Step 5 requires establishing the three-entry-point structure of ESTABMGR. I will let the PROCEDURE statement represent the MATCHES (match external references in ESTAB) function and two ENTRY statements represent the ADDTOES (add an external symbol to ESTAB) function and the FINDES (find an external symbol in ESTAB) function. I will use PL/I BEGIN blocks to surround the code for each function to isolate variable names. The module's structure is shown in Figure 8.2.

For step 6 I have to declare all interface data. As mentioned in the previous section, the ESTAB parameter is simply a pointer to the table. Since the table is a module-wide data structure, I will declare the struc-ture now. Rather than developing the entire module at this point, I will just develop a third of it: the MATCHES function. Figure 8.3 shows the definition of the external symbol table, the parameters for MATCHES, and a variable called NULL, a PL/I built-in function that I will need later for checking null (unset) address fields.

Step 7 involves the definition of any local variables in the MATCHES function. I recognize that I will need two counters for searching ESTAB, so I add the following within the BEGIN block MATCH_ER_ITEMS_IN_ESTAB:

```
DECLARE
    I FIXED BINARY (15), /* INDEX FOR SEARCHING FOR
                            AN UNMATCHED NAME */
    J FIXED BINARY (15); /* INDEX FOR SEARCHING FOR
                            A MATCHING NAME */
```

```
/* MODULE ESTABMGR (EXTERNAL SYMBOL TABLE MANAGER)        */
/*                                                        */
/* THIS IS AN INFORMATIONAL STRENGTH MODULE WITH 3 ENTRY  */
/* POINTS:                                                */
/*                                                        */
/* MATCHES (MATCH EXTERNAL REFERENCES IN ESTAB)           */
/* ADDTOES (ADD AN EXTERNAL SYMBOL TO ESTAB)              */
/* FINDES  (FIND AN EXTERNAL SYMBOL IN ESTAB)             */
/*                                                        */
/* THE DESIGN OBJECTIVE OF THIS MODULE IS TO HIDE ALL KNOW-*/
/* LEDGE OF ESTAB.  ALTHOUGH ESTAB IS AN INPUT AND OUTPUT */
/* OF THIS MODULE, THE INTENT IS THAT NO OTHER MODULES HAVE*/
/* ANY KNOWLEDGE OF THE STRUCTURE OF ESTAB.  HENCE THIS   */
/* IS AT WORST DATA COUPLED TO ANY OTHER MODULE.          */
/*                                                        */
/* STRUCTURE NOTES: EACH OF THE 3 FUNCTIONS ARE ENCLOSED IN*/
/*                  BEGIN BLOCKS TO ISOLATE NAMES.  MODULE-*/
/*                  WIDE DATA DEFINITIONS (ESTAB) ARE PLACED*/
/*                  OUTSIDE OF THE BEGIN BLOCKS.  ONE OF THE*/
/*                  FUNCTIONS (MATCHES) IS REPRESENTED BY  */
/*                  THE PROCEDURE STATEMENT.  THE OTHER TWO*/
/*                  FUNCTIONS ARE REPRESENTED BY ENTRY     */
/*                  STATEMENTS.                            */
/*********************************************************/
MATCHES: PROCEDURE (ESTAB,UNRESNAME,MATCHCODE);
     module-wide data declarations and
     parameter declarations
MATCH_ER_ITEMS_IN_ESTAB: BEGIN;
     local declares for MATCHES function
     code for MATCHES function
END;

ADDTOES: ENTRY (ESTAB,ESNAME,ESTYPE,ESADDR,ENTRYNUM,ADDCODE);
ADD_EXTSYM_TO_ESTAB: BEGIN;
     local declares for ADDTOES function
     code for ADDTOES function
END;

FINDES: ENTRY (ESTAB,ENTRYNUM,ESNAME,ESTYPE,ESADDR,FINDCODE);
FIND_EXTSYM_IN_ESTAB: BEGIN;
     local declares for FINDES function
     code for FINDES function
END;
END;
```

Figure 8.2   **Structure of the ESTABMGR module.**

Rather than completing the remaining four steps now, I will postpone them until we have had a chance to review a few additional topics.

STRUCTURED PROGRAMMING AND STEP-WISE REFINEMENT

The concept called structured programming has had such an impact on software development that it will probably be recorded in history as one of the great steps forward in programming technology (along with the subroutine concept and the high-level language concept). However, although there is a general vague agreement about the definition of

```
/*      MODULE-WIDE DATA DEFINITIONS                        */
/*                                                          */
DECLARE ESTAB  POINTER;
%DECLARE TABSIZE FIXED;
%TABSIZE=2000;          /* NO. OF POSSIBLE ESTAB ENTRIES    */
DECLARE 1 TABLE BASED(ESTAB),
          2 HEADER,
            3 TAG   CHAR(4),              /* DOG TAG ESTB */
            3 SIZE BINARY FIXED (15),  /* NO. OF CURRENT ENTRIES */
          2 BODY (TABSIZE),              /* ARRAY OF ENTRIES */
            3 NAME CHAR(8),
            3 TYPE CHAR(2),
            3 ADDRESS POINTER;
DECLARE                                  /* TYPE VALUES */
          MODULE  CHAR(2) STATIC INIT ('MD'),
          ENTRYPT CHAR(2) STATIC INIT ('EP'),
          EXTREF  CHAR(2) STATIC INIT ('ER');
DECLARE NULL BUILTIN;  /*FUNCTION RETURNS VALUE OF EMPTY POINTER*/
DECLARE MATCHCODE FIXED BINARY (15); /*MATCHES RETURN CODE*/
DECLARE UNRESNAME CHAR(8);  /* OUTPUT FROM MATCHES FUNCTION */
```

Figure 8.3   **Data definitions.**

structured programming, there is no specific widely accepted definition. Because of this, no rigorous definition of structured programming is presented here nor is a full discussion of the subject presented; there are already whole texts devoted to the subject [2, 3]. Instead, the basic properties of structured programs are discussed, as well as several fine points that are often overlooked.

Although the elements of structured programming have slowly evolved since the early 1960s, the concept first received wide attention in 1968 with the publication of Dijkstra's famous note [4]. Dijkstra pointed out that there should be a close correspondence between program text and its execution flow (a program should be able to be read from top to bottom) and that careless use of jump (GO TO) statements interferes with this correspondence. Because of this, structured programming is often referred to as "GO TO-less" programming. However, there have always been examples of programs that are nicely indented with no GO TO statements, yet are completely obscure, and other programs that contained GO TO statements and yet are perfectly understandable. Hence the presence or absence of GO TO statements is a poor measure of a good program, and Knuth illustrates many examples of this [5].

My favorite definition of structured programming is *the attitude of writing code with the intent of communicating with people instead of machines.* To accomplish this, the basic elements of a structured program are:

1.   The code is constructed from sequences of the three basic elements: sequential statements, DO loops, and IFTHENELSE statements.

2. Use of the GO TO statement is avoided wherever possible. In particular, the worst type of GO TO is one that branches to a previous statement in the program listing.
3. The code is written in an acceptable style (refer to Chapter 9).
4. The code is properly indented on the listing so that breaks in execution sequence can be easily followed (e.g., a DO statement can be easily matched with the statement ending the loop, corresponding THEN clauses and ELSE clauses can be matched, and so on).
5. There is only one point of entry and one point of exit in the code for each module. Note that informational-strength modules do not violate this because the code for each entry point is physically and logically separated.
6. The code is physically segmented on the listing to enhance readability. The executable statements for a module should fit on a single page of the listing.
7. The code represents a simple and straightforward solution to the problem.

These seven points illustrate the goals of structured programming: writing a program with minimal complexity, promoting clarity of thought by the programmer, and enhancing the readability of the program.

Structured Programming Constructs

Structured programs are constructed from sets of the five basic building blocks shown in Figure 8.4. One often hears of *three* building blocks because most programming languages have only one of the two forms of DO loops and do not contain the CASE construct.

The most important thing to understand about these three building blocks is that they are recursively defined. That is, the squares in Figure 8.4 represent nested building blocks; any one of the building blocks is used in place of the squares. For instance, the sequence block could contain an IFTHENELSE block followed by a DOWHILE block, and a DOWHILE block could contain a DOWHILE block. A square can also represent any single sequential statement (e.g., an assignment statement). There are people with the impression that these constructs prohibit CALL and RETURN statements. This impression is incorrect; CALL and RETURN statements are viewed as sequential statements.

The degree to which structured programming can be achieved is, of course, dependent on the programming language used. There is a significant amount of research in progress to invent the "best" programming language for structured programs. Of the widely used languages,

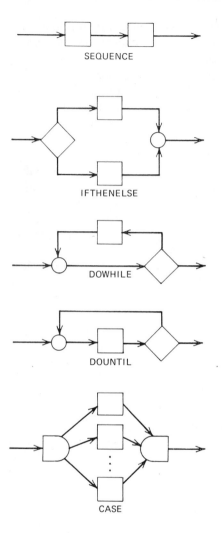

Figure 8.4   **The five structured programming constructs.**

PL/I, PL/C, PASCAL, and ALGOL are most suited for structured programming. Structured programming can also be used with the COBOL, FORTRAN, and BASIC languages, although with more diffi-culty and a few undesirable results. In COBOL the nesting of IFTHENELSE statements within IFTHENELSE statements does not behave according to the structure implied in Figure 8.4. Only the last statement in a COBOL sentence can be an IF statement, meaning that GO TO or PERFORM statements are occasionally needed. The COBOL PERFORM statement can be used as a DOWHILE construct. However, the PERFORM statement is actually a subroutine call, meaning that the code for the loop must be physically separated from the PERFORM statement. These two problems detract from the top-down readability property of a structured program.

Structured programming in FORTRAN and BASIC is even more difficult because they lack the IFTHENELSE, DOWHILE, DOUNTIL, and CASE constructs. This forces the designer to use the GO TO statement. However, Charmonman and Wagener [6] show how to make a FORTRAN program appear to be structured by simulating the IFTHENELSE and CASE constructs with a combination of indenting and comment statements. Figure 8.5 illustrates a FORTRAN IFTHENELSE construct. The code within the box has the appearances of a proper IF construct, and the code outside of the box adds the necessary detail to make the construct a valid FORTRAN program. Structured FORTRAN (or COBOL) code can be achieved in another fashion by using one of the many available language preprocessors. The preprocessors extend the language by adding the standard structured programming constructs.

Structured programming in two other popular languages, assembly languages and APL, is close to impossible. Although macro statements have been invented to simulate the basic structured programming constructs, most assembly language programs that use these macros could not in any way be termed "structured." The mere fact of using assembly language indicates that the program is being written primarily in machine terms, not for human comprehension, thus violating the fundamental property of structured programs. The APL language, an excellent language in many respects, is not compatible with structured programming. The basic constructs are not present in the APL language, indentation of statements is not allowed, and the language encourages obscure coding.

The reader interested in further exploration of the relationships

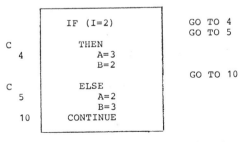

```
                    IF (I=2)              GO TO 4
                                          GO TO 5
        C             THEN
           4            A=3
                        B=2
                                          GO TO 10
        C             ELSE
           5            A=2
                        B=3
          10        CONTINUE
```

Figure 8.5   **Structured FORTRAN code.**

between languages and structured programming is encouraged to read Chapter 15.

Things to Avoid

Because the concept of structured programming is still evolving, several ideas relating to structured programming that have been suggested in the past actually have a negative effect on reliability and should be avoided. One of these is the so-called *Ashcroft–Manna technique*. This technique was named after the authors of a paper discussing a method of taking any program and converting it into an equivalent program without GO TOs [7]. Although the method is of theoretical interest, it should never be used in practice. It is vital to think in terms of the basic constructs when one is beginning to design the logic, as opposed to initially creating an unstructured program and then converting it into a structured program.

The attitude about GO TO statements should be to avoid using GO TOs wherever possible, but not at the expense of making the program more obscure. As Knuth [5] points out, the GO TO statement may be more desirable in certain situations than any other alternatives. Using GO TOs to escape from DO loops, to exit to the end of the module, to exit from a PL/I ON-unit to the end of the module, or to avoid excessive nesting of IFTHENELSE statements is often desirable as long as the branch is to a *subsequent* (lower) point in the source code, thus preserving the top-down readability property of structured programs.

Structured programming guidelines often suggest repeating an identical sequence of code in one or more places in the module as a way of eliminating certain GO TO statements. In this case the cure is worse than the disease; duplication of logic sharply increases the opportunities for error when changing the module in the future.

Step-Wise Refinement

Structured programming as it has been presented so far is a property or measure of the final code of the program. One key element must be added: a methodology or thought process that one uses to design a module's logic so that the outcome is a structured program. The thought process to be discussed is called *step-wise refinement*, a process originally conceived by Dijkstra [8] and later improved by Wirth [9, 10].

Step-wise refinement is a simple process involving an initial expression of the module's logic as statements in a hypothetical "very high-level" language, and then the subsequent refinement of each statement into lower-level language statements until finally one reaches the level of the programming language. Throughout the process the logic is always expressed in the basic constructs of structured programming.

To illustrate the process I will use it to design the logic of the MATCHES function. The initial refinement is:

```
DO I = 1 TO SIZE WHILE (don't encounter an item that
                        can't be matched);
   IF (encounter an unmatched item)
      THEN search for a matching external symbol;
           IF (find a match)
              THEN mark unmatched item;
              ELSE output its name;
      ELSE;
END;
```

Obviously, this initial refinement is expressed in a language that is considerably "higher" than my programming language (PL/I). The next step is to refine this code. I can use the output parameter MATCHCODE to represent the states of "currently have no unmatched item" (MATCHCODE=0) and "currently have an unmatched item" (MATCHCODE=1), since this is consistent with the final returned values of MATCHCODE. To do this I refine the code to:

```
MATCHCODE = 0;
DO I = 1 TO SIZE WHILE (MATCHCODE = 0);
   IF (encounter an unmatched item)
      THEN DO;
           MATCHCODE = 1;
           search for a matching external symbol;
           IF (find a match)
              THEN MATCHCODE = 0;
                   mark unmatched item;
              ELSE output its name;
           END;
      ELSE;
END;
```

For the third refinement I refine "encounter an unmatched item" to BODY (I). ADDRESS=NULL (in PL/I, NULL represents an unset pointer value). The next step is to refine the inside loop of searching for a matching external symbol and then marking it or returning the unmatched name. This inner loop refines to:

```
DO J=1 TO SIZE WHILE(MATCHCODE= 1);
    IF (find a match)
        THEN DO;
                MATCHCODE=0;
                BODY(I).ADDRESS=BODY(J).ADDRESS;
            END;
        ELSE;
END;
IF (MATCHCODE= 1) THEN UNRESNAME=BODY(I).NAME;
                    ELSE;
```

The fifth and final step is to refine "find a match." A match is indicated by a table entry with an identical name and a type of MODULE or ENTRYPT. This final refinement is shown in Figure 8.6.

The code for the MATCHES function is not quite finished; it will be completed in the next section. Also, the efficiency-minded reader has probably spotted a few potential efficiency improvements. However, to keep the example simple, efficiency improvements will be avoided.

The advantage of step-wise refinement is that it gives the designer a way of organizing his thoughts. The alternative, attempting to write the final code (or a flowchart) for the module in a single step, is much more difficult and more subject to error. The refinement steps for the MATCHES function do not represent an academic or theoretical discussion; they represent precisely the way I designed the code for

```
MATCHCODE=0;
DO I=1 TO SIZE WHILE (MATCHCODE=0);
    IF(BODY(I).ADDRESS=NULL)    /*UNMATCHED NAME?*/
        THEN DO;
                MATCHCODE=1;
                DO J=1 TO SIZE WHILE (MATCHCODE=1);
                    IF((BODY(I).NAME=BODY(J).NAME) &
                        ((BODY(J).TYPE=MODULE) |
                        (BODY(J).TYPE=ENTRYPT)))
                        THEN DO;
                                MATCHCODE=0;
                                BODY(I).ADDRESS=BODY(J).ADDRESS;
                            END;
                        ELSE;
                END;
                IF(MATCHCODE=1) THEN UNRESNAME=BODY(I).NAME;
                                    ELSE;
            END;
        ELSE;
END;
```

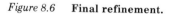

Figure 8.6   **Final refinement.**

MATCHES. In other words, I wrote five different versions of MATCHES, the first one being an abstract representation of the logic and the last one being the PL/I code shown in Figure 8.6.

A problem in doing this is that all the refinements except for the final one are apparently discarded at this point. This seems a waste because these steps illustrate the various abstractions of the logic and the designer's thought process. Rather than discarding all of this work, the initial refinement can be placed in comment statements at the beginning of the source code.

Should the ELSE Go Too?

If the GO TO statement is avoided completely, many structured programs take on the appearance of a maze of deeply nested IFTHENELSE statements. These programs are often as complicated as their "unstructured" counterparts. In examining a statement in the middle of a deeply nested IF, it is often quite difficult to determine the exact conditions under which the statement is executed. These conditions might be spread among many prior IF statements and these IF statements might be a considerable distance from the statement in question.

Bloom [11] makes a good case for the desirability of avoiding nested IFs and the ELSE clause. It is easy to show that the ELSE clause is usually unnecessary, for the ELSE is equivalent to stating IF (¬condition) THEN. (The only time that an ELSE is necessary is the rare situation where the THEN clause alters one of the variables in the IF condition.) For instance, the following block of code,

```
IF(cond1) THEN DO
            stmt1
            IF(cond2) THEN stmt2
                  ELSE DO
                        IF(cond3) THEN stmt3
                              ELSE stmt4

      ELSE stmt5
```

could be coded as

```
IF(cond1) THEN stmt1
IF(cond1 & cond2) THEN stmt2
IF(cond1 &¬cond2 & cond3) THEN stmt3
IF(cond1 &¬cond2 &¬cond3) THEN stmt4
IF(¬cond1) THEN stmt5
```

Admittedly, this approach has two drawbacks stemming from the duplication of condition tests (e.g., *cond1* is tested in five statements). If a condition must be changed, all occurrences of it must be changed (but at least they should be easier to spot). Repeating the tests of a condition adds some execution inefficiencies, but in most cases this is probably insignificant.

DEFENSIVE PROGRAMMING

The concepts of fault-detection discussed in Chapter 7 can also be applied at the level of individual modules; application of these concepts at the module level is often called *defensive programming*. Defensive programming is similar to the automotive technique of defensive driving, which is the attitude of being wary of the actions of other drivers (or, in programming terms, being wary of the actions of other modules).

Defensive programming is based on the important premise that the worst thing a module can do is accept incorrect input and then return an incorrect but believable output. To solve this problem, checks are placed at the beginning of the module to test the input data for proper attributes, proper domain, completeness, and reasonableness. An important consideration in choosing the proper checks is to review the module's code for all assumptions that it makes about the input data, and then consider checking the input data against these assumptions each time the module is called.

Defensive programming requires careful thought because, if carried to extremes, it can actually be undesirable. If every conceivable check is made on the input data, the defensive code may be so complex (and thus subject to error) that it has a negative, not positive, effect on reliability (and also on efficiency). To consider how much defensive code is warranted, first study the module's logic for assumptions it makes about the input data and then make a list of all possible checks that could be made. For each item in the list, consider the ease or difficulty of making the check, the probability that that input item might be incorrect, and the consequences of not making the check. The remaining step is to make the difficult tradeoff of determining the minimum amount of defensive code that will yield the maximum detection benefit.

To illustrate this process, consider the MATCHES function. The sole input is ESTAB, a pointer to the external symbol table. My list of possible checks for incorrect situations (and I do not claim to have identified them all) is:

1. ESTAB is not a pointer variable.

2. ESTAB is an unset pointer.
3. ESTAB is a valid pointer but does not point to an external symbol table.
4. The SIZE field (number of current entries) in the table is incorrect.
5. A table entry has an invalid type.
6. A module or entry-point table entry has a null address.
7. A module or entry-point table entry has an incorrect address.

All of the checks are feasible except 1 and 7 (I will assume the compiler-generated code will detect 1; it is impossible for MATCHES to check 7). The probability of each of the seven errors seems to be approximately equal and also quite low. The consequences of 2, 3, and 4 are severe since they would cause a program interruption or an incorrect output. Situations 5 and 6 actually have no effect on the MATCHES function (the code indicates that if a module entry has a null address, MATCHES would match it against itself, thus ignoring it). I decided to write defensive code for situations 2, 3, and 4. For 2 I check for a null pointer. For 3 I determine if the area pointed to has the valid dog tag ESTB. For 4 I check SIZE for a value greater than zero and less than or equal to the maximum size (there are no easy ways to determine if the table has fewer or more actual entries than SIZE indicates). The added defensive code is shown in Figure 8.7. Note that the code, data declarations, and specifications for the ADDTOES and FINDES entry points have been omitted.

HIGH-LEVEL LANGUAGES

The programming language used has a considerable effect on software reliability; in general, the "higher" the level of language, the fewer the errors. The case against coding in machine language (I use the terms machine language and assembly language synonymously because they are essentially the same) is so strong that I cannot conceive of a valid reason for anyone coding anything in machine language except for two minor situations: the initial compiler for a new computing system may need to be bootstrapped in machine language, and a tiny kernel of every operating system usually must be coded in machine language (not for efficiency but because certain architectural features peculiar to a machine such as its interrupt mechanism will not be reflected in its programming languages). A third exception obviously occurs when the only language available in your computing system is a machine language.

The case against machine language is so strong that it is one of the

```
/* MODULE ESTABMGR (EXTERNAL SYMBOL TABLE MANAGER)              */
/*                                                              */
/* THIS IS AN INFORMATIONAL STRENGTH MODULE WITH 3 ENTRY        */
/* POINTS:                                                      */
/*                                                              */
/* MATCHES (MATCH EXTERNAL REFERENCES IN ESTAB)                 */
/* ADDTOES (ADD AN EXTERNAL SYMBOL TO ESTAB)                    */
/* FINDES  (FIND AN EXTERNAL SYMBOL IN ESTAB)                   */
/*                                                              */
/* THE DESIGN OBJECTIVE OF THIS MODULE IS TO HIDE ALL KNOW-     */
/* LEDGE OF ESTAB.  ALTHOUGH ESTAB IS AN INPUT AND OUTPUT       */
/* OF THIS MODULE, THE INTENT IS THAT NO OTHER MODULES HAVE     */
/* ANY KNOWLEDGE OF THE STRUCTURE OF ESTAB.  HENCE THIS         */
/* IS AT WORST DATA COUPLED TO ANY OTHER MODULE.                */
/*                                                              */
/* STRUCTURE NOTES: EACH OF THE 3 FUNCTIONS ARE ENCLOSED IN     */
/*                  BEGIN BLOCKS TO ISOLATE NAMES.  MODULE-     */
/*                  WIDE DATA DEFINITIONS (ESTAB) ARE PLACED    */
/*                  OUTSIDE OF THE BEGIN BLOCKS.  ONE OF THE    */
/*                  FUNCTIONS (MATCHES) IS REPRESENTED BY       */
/*                  THE PROCEDURE STATEMENT.  THE OTHER TWO     */
/*                  FUNCTIONS ARE REPRESENTED BY ENTRY          */
/*                  STATEMENTS.                                 */
/****************************************************************/
MATCHES: PROCEDURE (ESTAB,UNRESNAME,MATCHCODE);
/*                                                              */
/*       MODULE-WIDE DATA DEFINITIONS                           */
/*                                                              */
DECLARE ESTAB  POINTER;
%DECLARE TABSIZE FIXED;
%TABSIZE=2000;              /* NO. OF POSSIBLE ESTAB ENTRIES    */
DECLARE 1 TABLE BASED(ESTAB),
          2 HEADER,
            3 TAG  CHAR(4),           /* DOG TAG ESTB */
            3 SIZE BINARY FIXED (15), /* NO. OF CURRENT ENTRIES */
          2 BODY (TABSIZE),           /* ARRAY OF ENTRIES */
            3 NAME CHAR(8),
            3 TYPE CHAR(2),
            3 ADDRESS POINTER;
DECLARE                               /* TYPE VALUES */
        MODULE  CHAR(2) STATIC INIT ('MD'),
        ENTRYPT CHAR(2) STATIC INIT ('EP'),
        EXTREF  CHAR(2) STATIC INIT ('ER');
DECLARE NULL BUILTIN;  /*FUNCTION RETURNS VALUE OF EMPTY POINTER*/
DECLARE MATCHCODE FIXED BINARY (15); /*MATCHES RETURN CODE*/
DECLARE UNRESNAME CHAR(8);  /* OUTPUT FROM MATCHES FUNCTION */
/*                                                              */
```

Figure 8.7   **Completed code for MATCHES.**

few conclusive arguments that can be made in the computer field. If a programmer is using a machine language, he spends most of his time not problem-solving but fumbling with the details of the machine. High-level languages eliminate several levels of software errors by hiding the machine idiosyncrasies and allowing any given function to be expressed in fewer statements. Programs in high-level languages are more understandable, easier to change, somewhat self-documenting, and enhance the compatibility and portability of programs. High-level language pro-

```
MATCH_ER_ITEMS_IN_ESTAB: BEGIN;
/*                                                                     */
/*********************************************************************/
/*                                                                     */
/* EXTERNAL SPECIFICATION FOR MATCHES                                  */
/*                                                                     */
/* FUNCTION: MATCH ALL EXTERNAL REFERENCE ITEMS IN ESTAB.              */
/*           IF ONE IS ENCOUNTERED THAT CANNOT BE MATCHED,             */
/*           RETURN ITS NAME.                                          */
/*                                                                     */
/* PARAMETER LIST: CALL MATCHES (ESTAB,UNRESNAME,MATCHCODE)            */
/*                                                                     */
/* INPUT:  ESTAB     POINTER    POINTER TO ESTABLE                     */
/*                                                                     */
/* OUTPUT: ESTAB     POINTER    POINTER TO UPDATED ESTABLE             */
/*         UNRESNAME CHAR(8)     NAME OF AN UNMATCHED                   */
/*                               EXTERNAL REFERENCE                     */
/*         MATCHCODE FIXED BIN(15)   RETURN CODE (0, 1, OR 2)          */
/*                                                                     */
/*         CAUSE/EFFECT RELATIONSHIP:                                  */
/*                                                                     */
/*             ANY UNMATCHED (NULL ADDRESS FIELD) EXTERNAL             */
/*             REFERENCES ARE MATCHED WITH A MATCHING MD OR            */
/*             EP ITEM BY TRANSFERRING THE ADDRESS OF THE MD OR        */
/*             EP ENTRY TO THE ER ENTRY UNTIL AN ER CANNOT BE          */
/*             MATCHED.                                                */
/*             -IF ALL ER'S CAN BE MATCHED, MATCHCODE=0 AND            */
/*              UNRESNAME IS UNCHANGED.                                */
/*             -IF AN ER CANNOT BE MATCHED, MATCHCODE=1 AND            */
/*              UNRESNAME = NAME OF ER ITEM                            */
/*             -IF AN ERROR OCCURS (INVALID ESTABLE), MATCH-           */
/*              CODE=2 AND UNRESNAME IS UNCHANGED                      */
/*                                                                     */
/* EXTERNAL EFFECTS: NONE                                              */
/*********************************************************************/
/* MATCHES LOGIC INFORMATION                                           */
/*                                                                     */
/* MODULES CALLED: NONE                                                */
/*                                                                     */
/* INITIAL REFINEMENT:                                                 */
/*                                                                     */
/*     DO I=1 TO SIZE WHILE(DON'T ENCOUNTER AN ITEM THAT              */
/*                          CAN'T BE MATCHED)                          */
/*        IF (ENCOUNTER AN UNMATCHED ITEM)                             */
/*           THEN SEARCH FOR A MATCHING EXTERNAL SYMBOL                */
/*                IF (FIND A MATCH)                                    */
/*                   THEN MARK UNMATCHED ITEM                          */
/*                   ELSE OUTPUT ITS NAME                              */
/*           ELSE                                                      */
/*     END                                                             */
/*********************************************************************/
```

Figure 8.7   (Continued)

grams cost less because, although programmers tend to code at a fixed rate regardless of the language, a high-level language statement is functionally superior to a machine language statement [12, 13].

The biggest advantage of high-level languages is their ability to express and manipulate complex data structures. The experienced

```
/*  LOCAL DECLARES        */
DECLARE
        I FIXED BINARY (15),  /*  INDEX FOR SEARCHING FOR AN
                                  UNMATCHED NAME */
        J FIXED BINARY (15);  /*  INDEX FOR SEARCHING FOR A
                                  MATCHING NAME  */
    /*                                                      */
MATCHCODE=2;
IF(ESTAB¬=NULL)                        /*NULL IS UNSET POINTER*/
    THEN
        IF((TAG='ESTB')&(SIZE>0)&(SIZE¬>TABSIZE))
        THEN
            DO;
                MATCHCODE=0;
                DO I=1 TO SIZE WHILE (MATCHCODE=0);
                    IF(BODY(I).ADDRESS=NULL)    /*UNMATCHED NAME?*/
                        THEN DO;
                                MATCHCODE=1;
                                DO J=1 TO SIZE WHILE (MATCHCODE=1);
                                    IF((BODY(I).NAME=BODY(J).NAME)&
                                        ((BODY(J).TYPE=MODULE) |
                                        (BODY(J).TYPE=ENTRYPT)))
                                        THEN DO;
                                                MATCHCODE=0;
                                                BODY(I).ADDRESS=BODY(J).ADDRESS;
                                            END;
                                        ELSE;
                                END;
                                IF(MATCHCODE=1) THEN UNRESNAME=BODY(I).NAME;
                                                ELSE;
                            END;
                        ELSE;
                END;
            END;
        ELSE;
    ELSE;
RETURN;
END;
END;
```

Figure 8.7   (*Continued*)

programmer will recognize that manipulation of data, not the manipulation of machine details, is what programming is all about. The question of efficiency is generally an insignificant consideration. One should recognize that efficiency is achieved through the intelligent selection of algorithms and data structures, not through the microefficiencies achieved by simply using a machine language. Furthermore, current optimizing compilers generate machine code that is remarkably efficient.

Confirmation of these points comes from the Multics system, a large operating system that was implemented in PL/I as a cooperative project among Bell Laboratories, General Electric, and MIT [12]. Only 5% of the system is written in machine language. This number would have been even lower except that the PL/I compiler was not available at the start of the project.

There is really no excuse today in the majority of programming projects for using a machine language. If I were a data processing manager, I would walk into my computing center and physically discard all assemblers. Computer manufacturers can help in this regard by adopting a policy of not providing assemblers for their systems (certain manufacturers already have this policy for some of their systems). The teaching of assembly languages in computer science programs should be deemphasized, except possibly to supplement computer architecture and compiler courses.

ATTITUDE

In the midst of all the technical ideas we can discuss for software reliability, there is an important and often overlooked factor: the programmer's attitude. Two particular aspects of attitude or psychology are of interest here: the attitude of the programmer toward his product and the way in which he approaches the compilation process.

The programmer's attitude toward his product is related to the principles of *egoless programming* and *cognitive dissonance* as explained by Weinberg [14]. Cognitive dissonance is the psychological principle that guides a person when his self-image is threatened. A programmer who sees his program as an extension of himself and who subconsciously equates defects in his program to defects in himself will have his behavior altered by cognitive dissonance.

"A programmer who truly sees his program as an extension of his own ego is not going to be trying to find all the errors in that program. On the contrary, he is going to be trying to prove that the program is correct—even if this means the oversight of errors which are monstrous to another eye. . . . the human eye has an almost infinite capacity for not seeing what it does not want to see." [14]

The escape from this situation is called egoless programming. Rather than being secretive and defensive toward his program, the programmer adopts the opposite attitude: his code is really a product of the entire project and he openly asks other programmers to read his code and constructively criticize it. When someone finds an error in his code, the programmer of course should not feel good about making a mistake, but his attitude is, "Wow, *we* found an error in *our* product! Good thing we found it now and not later! Let's learn from this mistake and also see if we can find another." A programmer who finds an error in another programmer's code does not respond with, "Look at your stupid mistake"; instead the response is more like "How interesting! I wonder if I made the same mistake in the module I wrote." Notice the fine point concerning cognitive dissonance in the previous sentence: I used the phrase "the module I wrote" instead of "my module."

The second important programmer attitude is one of precision. No other discipline requires the same degree of precision that programming does. A surgeon surely does not worry about making an incision so precise that it separates particular cells in the body. Programming has no concept of a *tolerance* such as the digital engineer saying, "I will represent the binary value 1 by five volts plus or minus one volt"; each piece of a program is right or wrong with no middle ground. An important attitude of precision is connected with the process of compiling a program. One often hears the remark, "Rather than wasting my time perfecting my module, I'll run it through the compiler and let the computer do the work." Letting the computer do the work is, of course, the justification for the entire data processing business. However, when "work" is equated with "programming," I have to draw the line, because computers are quite stupid in their knowledge of programming.

The attitude of experimenting with the compiler or compiling a hastily coded module to "see what happens" is a poor attitude because it conflicts with the requirement for precision. My feeling is that the professional programmer should expect his program to compile correctly the first time he compiles it. He should do his utmost to eliminate all syntax errors, and also have someone else read his code, before he compiles it. There are four rather convincing arguments for this:

1. One reason for syntax errors is that the programmer has misunderstood the language syntax. If you misunderstand one or more points of syntax, chances are that you also misunderstand points of semantics. However, the compiler will detect very few of your semantic errors.
2. A second reason for syntax errors is carelessness. The same argument holds here. If you are careless with the syntax, you are probably also careless with the semantics.
3. No compiler of which I am aware will detect every syntax error. The more syntax errors that are made, the higher the chances are that a syntax error will be undetected and thus lead to a logic error.
4. Haste makes waste. I have noticed an interesting turning point that occurs whenever a module is compiled for the first time: a type of self-induced pressure on the programmer increases suddenly and rapidly. Before the compilation the programmer generally spends a considerable amount of time thinking about each change or improvement. After he compiles the module for the first time, there

is considerable pressure to make changes as quickly as possible in order to "make it work" or "make it compile." Changes made under this pressure are more error prone.

DOCUMENTATION

Documentation has always been a sore point in programming because of the widespread belief that programmers hate to document. The truth is that no one enjoys documenting solely for the sake of documentation, but where documentation is an integral part of the programming process it is willingly accepted and produced. Ever since Chapter 4 we have been producing a rather thorough set of documentation although this has not been strongly emphasized. From Chapter 4 we have the product and project objectives and the external specifications. From Chapter 5 we have the definition of the system architecture. Chapter 6 gave us the program structure diagram and this chapter so far has produced the module external specifications and the source code itself. Excluding consideration of user publications because they are often produced by a separate group of professional writers, the question then is whether we need anything else.

The answer is that we do not need any additional documentation describing the program. In particular, the flowchart or any of its alternatives are quite unnecessary.

The type of documentation apparently missing is documentation describing module logic, for example, the flowchart. The flowchart was never mentioned in any discussion of the logic design process so obviously it is not a necessary part of design. Not only is the flowchart unnecessary, but it is also undesirable for several reasons. Flowcharts are not compatible with the idea of step-wise refinement. The key to step-wise refinement is a set of small refinement steps where, during each step, the logic design is brought a little closer to the eventual programming language. This could be done by using the flowchart, but the constant redrawing of the flowchart at each step would be cumbersome. Furthermore, one large translation step would still remain: converting the flowchart into source code. Also, although the basic structured programming constructs are shown in flowchart form in Figure 8.4, the flowchart is not consistent with structured programming; flowcharts are highly GO TO oriented.

If not the flowchart, then what else? Actually, we already have an acceptable alternative: the code! Since we already have the code, why not let it serve as the logic documentation? Looking back at Figure

8.7, it is evident that the code for MATCHES, along with the module external specification and the initial refinement, forms a sufficient and highly desirable set of documentation for the MATCHES function. Additional documentation such as a flowchart would be undesirable because it would be redundant with the code. Redundancy in any type of documentation should be avoided because it increases the chances of conflicts. Furthermore, unless care is taken to update the documentation (which is more difficult if the logic documentation is physically separated from the code), redundant documentation often becomes totally useless after the code is modified a few times.

Other alternatives to the flowchart, such as decision tables, narrative descriptions, and HIPO (hierarchy plus input-process-output) charts [15] have been used at times. Program logic HIPO charts consist of three blocks: a process block in the center showing the module's logic in narrative form, and surrounding blocks showing the input data used and output data produced. Although the HIPO chart is superior to the flowchart because it shows data flow as well as control flow, HIPO charts are not needed for the same reasons that flowcharts are not needed.

The module external specification and the source code form the primary module documentation. They are supplemented by a small amount of logic information and source code comments. In Figure 8.7 notice the block comment containing logic information for MATCHES; this contains the initial refinement and a list of modules called (note that module documentation should never mention the calling modules). A list of modification hints can also be placed with the logic information.

The last type of documentation is comments on the source code. All data declarations should be commented since understanding the data is the key to understanding a program. The executable statements in the module should be commented only sparsely if at all. If the program meets the definition of a structured program, comments on the executable statements should be unnecessary. In fact, an abundance of comments detracts from the readability of the code. A reasonable guideline is to read the code and try to anticipate questions that another reader might have. Comments are then generated to answer these questions. In any case, comments should never duplicate the code by describing logic; when used, comments should be viewed as notes to the reader.

STANDARDS

The subject of standards is another sore point with programmers because of the feeling that standards stifle creativity. Actually, well-selected standards do just the opposite; they establish guidelines for the many mundane decisions that must be made during a project so that a programmer's creativity can be applied to the *important* decisions (the problem solution). Standards also have a positive effect on reliability because they ensure that certain aspects of the programming job are done in a uniform way, thus preventing certain inconsistencies among programmers.

No programming standards should be viewed as absolute rules never to be broken. The purpose of a standard is to establish guidelines for certain aspects of the job, so that any proposed deviation can be publicly scrutinized to determine if it is justified. It would be pointless to attempt to list a set of standards since most organizations have evolved a set of standards applicable to their particular environment. However, to give an idea of what aspects of programming are included, most standards establish guidelines for methodologies to be used, documentation formats, compiler options, code indentation conventions, commenting, and features of the programming language that should be avoided.

VERIFICATION

The last step in the module design process is verification of the module logic. The type of verification discussed here is human verification, that is, verification before actually executing the code on a computer. Part III is devoted to the subject of testing, that is, verification of logic by execution on a computer.

Verification is based on various forms of *code reading*. Although different forms of code reading have been practiced for many years, it was not until Weinberg's book [14] that the industry realized the value of this practice.

Verification can take two forms: *static code reading* and *dynamic code reading*. These forms are complementary and both should be used. Static code reading is the process of taking the source code of a module and simply reading it from top to bottom as one would read a book. This is usually done in a meeting of three or four people, one of whom has the job of a moderator, that is, a person who keeps the meeting moving along productive lines. The purpose of the meeting is to find errors in the module, but not to correct any errors found. The correction of errors takes place after the meeting.

It is difficult to list specific items to check during the session because people using this technique quickly build up a mental checklist of common errors. Fagan carries this one step farther and recommends employing professional "code inspectors" and formally keeping track of the kinds of errors found in order to improve subsequent sessions [16]. To give a partial checklist, some common items to be checked are the completeness and accuracy of the module documentation and the readability of the code. The decision conditions in each IF and DO statement should be carefully checked. For instance, common errors occur in confusing "greater than or equal," "greater than," "less than," "not less than or equal," "at least," and so on. Complex logical tests involving *and* and *or* operators should be checked to ensure that the operations will be applied in the proper sequence. Each loop should be checked to determine that it can terminate. Iterative DO loops with constant (wired-in) upper limits should be viewed with suspicion. If you see a statement such as

```
DO I = 1 TO N WHILE(FOUND);
```

the two conditions of the loop never being executed (FOUND is initially true or N is less than 1) and the loop falling through (I reaches N before FOUND is true) should be examined carefully. Look for "off-by-one" problems in array subscripts and in loops (executing the loop one iteration too few or too many). Arguments passed to and from this module should be checked for correct order, format, units, and attributes.

The second verification technique is the *walk-through,* similar in concept to the design walk-throughs discussed in previous chapters. Again, a meeting of a few people is established with a moderator leading the meeting. Rather than simply reading the code, a few representative test cases are drafted and the execution flow through the module is traced. The state of the module (i.e., values of variables) is tracked during the procedure. The test cases should be simple and few in number to avoid making the process tedious, but the test cases must cover invalid and boundary input conditions. A good choice for a person to draft the paper test cases is a programmer of any module calling this module.

During the walk-through the programmer will be called on to explain parts of the module logic. His explanations often illustrate additional errors when he has based his logic on one or more questionable assumptions.

During each of these two processes a list is maintained of all problems found (problems can include poor programming practices as well as errors). The programmer later takes this list and makes the necessary corrections. A limit is usually established such that if the number of problems exceeds the limit, the module must pass through the process again after the corrections are made.

Because of the programmer's general attitude toward the compiler, the verification sessions should occur before the first compilation of the module. However, a third type of code reading should occur after the compilation: information produced by the compiler should be checked. For instance, most PL/I compilers produce a precise analysis of the attributes of each variable name in the module. This listing should be checked carefully to ensure that the compiler correctly interpreted the data declaration intentions.

Despite the advantages of code reading, the concept is occasionally downgraded because of the feeling that "computer testing" is cheaper. A study at Bell Laboratories [17] has indicated that this impression is false. The average detection cost of bugs found by code reading was $10.62; the average detection cost of bugs found in normal testing activities was $251.60 ($196.70 of this was computer time). Of course, it might be thought that the human-detected bugs were the simple ones and the computer-detected bugs were the more difficult bugs. However, an analysis of the errors refuted this argument. Furthermore, code reading has an additional but intangible benefit of programmer education.

A remaining and more sophisticated form of code reading is the concept of mathematically proving a program's correctness by stating and proving theorems about the program. Since this idea is mostly still in the research stage, it appears in a separate chapter, Chapter 17.

REFERENCES

1. D. E. Knuth, *The Art of Computer Programming, Volume 1, Fundamental Algorithms.* Reading, Mass.: Addison-Wesley, 1968.

2. O. J. Dahl, E. W. Dijkstra, and C. A. R. Hoare, *Structured Programming.* London: Academic Press, 1972.

3. C. L. McGowan and J. R. Kelly, *Top-Down Structured Programming Techniques.* New York: Petrocelli/Charter, 1975.

4. E. W. Dijkstra, "Go To Statement Considered Harmful," *Communications of the ACM,* **11** (3), 147–148 (1968).

5. D. E. Knuth, "Structured Programming with GO TO Statements," *Computing Surveys,* **6** (4), 261–301 (1974).

6. S. Charmonman and J. L. Wagener, "On Structured Programming in FORTRAN," *SIGNUM Newsletter,* **10** (1), 21–23 (1975).

7. E. Ashcroft and Z. Manna, "The Translation of 'GO TO' Programs to 'WHILE' Programs," *Proceedings of the 1971 IFIP Congress,* Booklet TA-2. Amsterdam: North-Holland, 1971, pp. 147–152.

8. E. W. Dijkstra, "A Constructive Approach to the Problem of Program Correctness," *BIT,* **8** (3), 174–186 (1968).

9. N. Wirth, "Program Development by Step-Wise Refinement," *Communications of the ACM*, **14** (4), 221–227 (1971).

10. N. Wirth, "On the Composition of Well-Structured Programs," *Computing Surveys*, **6** (4), 247–259 (1974).

11. A. M. Bloom, "The ELSE Must Go, Too," *DATAMATION*, **21** (5), 123–128 (1975).

12. F. J. Corbato, "PL/I as a Tool for System Programming," *DATAMATION*, **15** (5), 68–76 (1969).

13. G. J. Myers, "Estimating the Costs of a Programming System Development Project," TR 00.2316. IBM System Development Div., Poughkeepsie, N.Y., 1972.

14. G. M. Weinberg, *The Psychology of Computer Programming.* New York: Van Nostrand Reinhold, 1971.

15. *HIPO—A Design Aid and Documentation Technique*, GC20-1851. IBM Corp., White Plains, N.Y., 1974.

16. M. E. Fagan, "Design and Code Inspections and Process Control in the Development of Programs," TR 21.572. IBM System Development Div., Kingston, N.Y., 1974.

17. M. L. Shooman and M. I. Bolsky, "Types, Distribution, and Test and Correction Times for Programming Errors," *Proceedings of the 1975 International Conference on Reliable Software.* New York: IEEE, 1975, pp. 347–357.

CHAPTER 9

Programming Style

A remark occasionally made by programming managers is, "We used structured programming on our last project but we still had an excessive number of bugs and the maintenance programmers feel that the code is totally unreadable." Reactions such as this sometimes simply represent backlash to new concepts, but more frequently they represent a misinterpretation and oversimplification of the concepts of structured programming. As pointed out in Chapter 8, structured programming is a collection of many equally important ideas and techniques; focusing on any one of these techniques, such as simply avoiding the use of GO TO statements, at the neglect to the others leads to an unsuccessful project.

A key concept related to structured programming is programming style: the manner in which a programmer uses or abuses his programming language in the same sense that an author uses or abuses the English language. It is the goodness or badness of a program's style that is normally the underlying cause of such statements as, "I looked at a nicely indented program with no GO TO statements, but it was totally incomprehensible, yet I looked at another program that used several GO TO statements and it was perfectly understandable."

Programming style has a chapter of its own because of the importance of the subject. The observations and guidelines in this chapter are based on my personal experiences in reading programs, observations of colleagues, and ideas abstracted from Kernighan and Plauger's excellent book on programming style [1].

PROGRAM CLARITY

As I mentioned in Chapter 8, the programmer's goal must be writing source code for the primary audience of people instead of machines. Doing this requires focusing attention on the clarity, simplicity, and understandability of the code at the sacrifice of less important criteria such as brevity (number of key-strokes to initially write or type the program) and machine efficiency. The following guidelines have a significant effect on program clarity.

Use meaningful variable names. This single rule is the most important guideline in programming style. There is nothing worse than seeing a program with the set of variable names XX, XXX, XXXX, XY, EKK, EKKK, A, and AI, and then seeing an overabundance of comments within the program explaining the meaning and use of these names. The simple practice of using longer descriptive names significantly improves readability and minimizes the number of comments needed. Most variable names should be from 4 to 12 characters long. Extremely long names such as NO_OF_POINTS_IN_MILEAGE _GRAPHS are undesirable because they detract attention from the program flow and are subject to error.

The length used is dependent on restrictions in the programming language. FORTRAN severely restricts the length of names (six or less characters). Most PL/I implementations allow identifiers up to 31 characters long, but procedure names are restricted to seven characters or less, a severe restriction in attempting to give procedures meaningful names.

Even though the use of meaningful names is common sense, one occasionally sees recommendations to the contrary. For instance, I was shocked to read the following suggestion in a text published in 1974: If you want to minimize the compilation time of your FORTRAN program, don't use meaningful names. Instead, code a uniform distribution of one-character names, two-character names, and so on because this minimizes table searching time in some FORTRAN compilers!

Avoid similar names. Occasionally one sees a program that uses such variable names as VALUE and VALUES or the set of variables BRACA, BRACB, BRACC, and BRACD. This practice makes the program difficult to read and it also leads to coding errors. When selecting meaningful names, select names that are as dissimilar as possible.

If numerals are used in identifiers, place them only at the end. The numerals 0, 1, 2, and 5 are easily confused with the letters O, I, Z, and S. If numerals must be used in a variable name, the numerals should be placed at the end.

Never use language keywords as identifiers. Although the following FORTRAN and PL/I statements are syntactically correct, they will totally confuse the reader.

```
FORMAT(I6)=I
IF IF=THEN THEN THEN=ELSE;
ELSE ELSE=THEN;
```

Avoid temporary variables. Although most programs need a few temporary variables, never create any unnecessary ones. One often sees suggestions such as changing

$$X = A(I) + 1/A(I)$$

to

```
AI = A(I)
X  = AI + 1/AI
```

to save a subscript calculation, or changing

```
TOTAL = Y + A/B*C
VAR   = X + A/B*C
```

to

```
ABC   = A/B*C
TOTAL = Y + ABC
VAR   = X + ABC
```

to save a few arithmetic operations. Such suggestions should usually be ignored because they introduce unnecessary temporary variables. Temporary variables reduce readability by increasing the number of details with which a reader must deal. They also conflict with the purpose of the compiler-produced cross-reference (XREF) dictionary. The XREF is a valuable tool because it tells the reader which statement uses which identifier. Using temporary variables to save a few microseconds can totally destroy the intent of an XREF listing.

Use parentheses to avoid ambiguity. The order or precedence of arithmetic and logical operators in different programming languages is always a source of confusion. For instance, does $-A**2$ mean "square the negation of A" or "negate the square of A"? When there is any doubt, extra parentheses should be used to indicate the desired order of operations.

Most programmers are familiar with this guideline, but they overgeneralize it to the belief that extra parentheses never alter the meaning of a statement. Unfortunately, this rule is invalid in some programming languages, particularly in input/output and CALL statements. For instance, the following two PL/I statements are not semantically equivalent:

```
CALL  SUB(X,Y);
CALL  SUB((X),(Y));
```

The first one specifies the "call by location" argument-passing convention; the second specifies the "call by value" convention.

Be cautious when using constants as arguments. Most programmers are familiar with the following bug:

```
CALL SUB(X,2)
I = 2
WRITE  (6,101)  I
. . .
SUBROUTINE  SUB(S,J)
. . .
J = 3
RETURN
```

The value printed for I is 3, not 2, in many FORTRAN implementations because the subroutine alters the value of the constant 2.

Place only one statement on a line. Placing more than one statement on a physical line conflicts with the indentation conventions of structured programming. The classic case is the PL/I programmer who wrote $A=B=C$ on one line, thinking that the value of C would be assigned to both A and B. However, the statement is interpreted by the compiler as assigning the logical value 0 or 1 to A depending on whether or not B equals C. This is actually a fault of the PL/I language; the language uses the equal sign for two distinct operations: comparison and assignment.

Do not alter the value of the iteration variable within a loop. The practice of altering the DO loop iteration variable from within the loop makes the loop difficult to understand and makes it difficult to prove that it is not an "endless" loop.

Avoid statement labels. If the guidelines of structured programming are used, statement labels are unnecessary except as identifiers of such entities as BEGIN blocks, entry points, or ON-units in a PL/I program. A label should *never* be placed on a statement unless the program contains a branch to that label (the practice of some FORTRAN programmers of arbitrarily placing a statement number on every statement is completely confusing). If statement labels are needed, they should be meaningful and dissimilar.

USING THE LANGUAGE

A second important category in programming style is the way in which a programmer uses or misuses the features of the programming language. The general guideline is to understand and use all of the features of the language, but to steer clear of all poorly designed language features and implementation-dependent quirks.

Learn and use the straightforward features of the language. One occasionally sees a PL/I program containing a DO loop to initialize the elements of an array to zero. This is usually a sign of a lack of education in the language because the single statement $A=0$ would suffice. At other times programmers code DO loops to do such things as multiply an array by two and add it to another array when the simple statement $A=(B*2)+C$ again would suffice. COBOL has a SEARCH statement that usually eliminates the need for writing loops to search tables. The point is simply that a thorough education in the programming language is a good investment; it shortens programs and eliminates certain types of errors.

Learn and use the library and built-in functions. Many programmers are familiar with the scientific functions provided in a language (e.g., square root, sine, cosine, absolute value) but are less familiar with the useful nonscientific functions. Just to give an idea of the built-in functions in one language, PL/I contains over 80 built-in functions, including the traditional MAX and MIN functions (finding the largest- or smallest-valued variables in a group of variables), single array functions such as SUM and PROD (summing or multiplying all elements in an array), and array comparison functions such as ANY(A=B) (are any corresponding elements in arrays A and B equal?) and ALL(A=B) (are all corresponding elements in arrays A and B equal?). PL/I also has character-string functions such as INDEX(Z, 'DOG') (search string Z for the substring DOG), VERIFY (check a string to verify that every character in the string is a member of a second string), and TRANSLATE (replace particular characters in a string by the corresponding character in another string). The use of such language functions where applicable can enhance the program's readability and make it less prone to errors.

Avoid language tricks. Aspects of the language that will be obscure to the reader should be avoided. Such tricks as using the iteration variable of a DO loop after the loop has terminated and overlaying variables (assigning them the same storage space) to perform tricks such as the dangerous PL/I practice of performing arithmetic on pointer variables should be avoided.

Do not ignore warning messages. Some compilers, when they detect a tricky, questionable, or unintended use of the language, produce warning messages but allow the compilation to complete. These messages are important; they indicate that either the programmer is making a mistake or that a future reader of the program will be confused. The code should be changed so that it causes *no* warning messages to be generated.

Read the "pitfalls" section in your language manual. Many language reference manuals contain a chapter on common mistakes or blunders made in using the language. Save yourself some time by learning from the mistakes of others.

MICROEFFICIENCIES

By far the worst violations of good programming style are the many "coding improvements for efficiency" found in many textbooks, installation standards, and programmers' heads. Not only do these suggestions detract from readability and reliability, but they also have little, if any, effect on efficiency, hence the title "microefficiencies."

Anyone that has done any significant work on system performance knows that efficiency is achieved by careful consideration of data structures, algorithms, and resource usage, not by such trivia as eliminating a subscript calculation, changing an exponentiation to a multiplication, coding a program in machine language, or worrying about the quickest way to zero a register (I have many memos concerning the last point in my wastebasket).

To give an example of a successful approach to efficiency, a colleague of mine recently had an idea for improving the scheduling algorithms in IBM's TSS operating system. He applied his changes one night to the TSS system in use at the IBM Thomas J. Watson Research Center, and measurements since then have shown an improvement in system throughput by a factor of three, many times better than the typical 10% or 20% that most people set out to achieve. What makes this even more outstanding is the fact that the TSS system existed approximately six years before this change and that the TSS system at this location had been carefully tuned prior to the change. Also, his changes were not peculiar to this one installation; they have been installed and tested in other TSS installations with similar results.

As a second example of dealing with macroefficiencies instead of microefficiencies, I once had a job as a system programmer in a computing center that was about to install a new third-generation system. Another system programmer and I were given the job of taking the manufacturer's operating system and improving its performance. We devoted the first few months to developing and using a performance monitor to identify the bottlenecks in the system. After this analysis of the system was completed, we took such steps as improving the input/output buffering algorithms in the system's I/O software, reformatting the physical blocks in the system libraries to minimize disk rotational delay, and moving the physical locations of certain files in relation to one another to minimize seek time and balance channel utilization. After discovering that the system's printer now became the new bottleneck, we slightly altered the compilers and linkage editor to eliminate wasteful printing (e.g., the FORTRAN compiler printed several one-line pages in each job's listing). These steps, although they involved altering less than 1000 source statements in the system, increased system throughput by about four times!

These two examples illustrate the central ideas in performance improvement: measurement and optimization of *macroefficiencies*.

Both cases resulted in significant performance improvements without resorting to microefficiency measures.

Ignore all efficiency suggestions until the program is correct. One of the worst things a programmer can do is to worry about the speed of his program before he has the program functioning properly. A fast but incorrect program is useless; a slow but correct program is always of some, if not full, use. Weinberg [2] gives an amusing anecdote about a new program that was hopelessly unreliable because of its overly complex design. A new programmer was called in, saw a better approach, and produced a new reliable version of the program in two weeks. At an executive demonstration of the program the new programmer remarked that his program takes 10 seconds per input card. One of the original programmers then triumphantly replied, "But my program takes only one second per card." The classic reply of the new programmer was, "But your program doesn't work. If the program doesn't have to work, I can write one that takes one millisecond per card."

Let the compiler optimize. Many compilers used in production programming do a significant amount of code optimization, such as reducing subscript calculations, recognizing that expressions such as A**2 can be evaluated with one multiplication, removing constant expressions from DO loops, and placing frequently used variables in higher-speed registers. The programmer should not fight the compiler; the code should be written in a simple and straightfoward manner. Let the compiler worry about optimization.

Do not sacrifice readability for efficiency. Most suggestions for microefficiency improvements involve some type of trick, thus conflicting with the goal of readability. I recall reading a book full of efficiency suggestions and seeing the statement, "Most of the techniques that will make a program more efficient will not be detrimental to program readability," yet almost every suggestion in the book is contrary to the points made by Kernighan and Plauger [1].

Figure 9.1 shows a suggestion for coding a matrix multiplication loop from a paper on virtual storage coding techniques. The suggestion says that if the second version is used, paging will be reduced because the matrix· elements are referenced in the order that FORTRAN sequentially stores them. The "improved" version is definitely tricky and less understandable. In fact when I first examined it I was positive that it would not work. Furthermore, the originator of the suggestion failed to point out that the "improved" version could actually be *slower* under many conditions (e.g., if the matrices are not extremely large or if the system is lightly loaded so that sufficient real storage is available). The most remarkable feature of the "improved" version is that we can devise a simpler version that is faster! Write a DO loop to form the transpose of the second matrix, insert this loop in front of the original version in Figure 9.1, and change the expression B(K,J) to B(J,K).

As a second example, a report on coding hints for the IBM S/360 suggests that the quickest way to double the value in a register is to use the BXLE (branch on index less than or equal) machine instruction in a clever way. Not only did the report fail to say that this is completely obscure, but it also failed to point out that this only works for odd-numbered registers!

Never optimize unless you are forced to. Obviously, efficiency is not a totally insignificant issue. However, the programmer should never optimize just for the sake of optimization; he should optimize only when efficiency is important, and then only when he knows precisely what part of the program needs optimization.

Tackle efficiency through macroefficiencies. In a virtual memory system, efficiency can be significantly improved by using a method to physically order the modules within pages to minimize page faults and the program's working-set size [3]. This practice involves no coding

```
Initial version:

        DO 20 I = 1,M
        DO 20 J = 1,N
        SUM = 0
        DO 10 K = 1,L
   10   SUM = SUM + A(I,K) * B(K,J)
   20   C(I,J) = SUM


"Improved" version:

        M1 = 0
        I3 = -1
        DO 20 J = 1,N
        DO 20 I = 1,M
        SUM = 0
        I3 = -I3
        M1 = M1 + I3
        DO 10 K = 1,L
        SUM = SUM + A(I,M1) * B(M1,J)
   10   M1 = M1 + I3
   20   C(I,J) = SUM
```

Figure 9.1   **Matrix multiplication.**

changes to the program. Other macroefficiency measures include improving input/output operations and selecting optimal algorithms and data structures. For instance, some sorting and searching algorithms are hundreds of times faster than other equivalent algorithms. The programmer should avoid worrying about microefficiencies until all other avenues have been exhausted.

Tackle efficiency through measurement, not guesswork. Programmers have proven to be terrible guessers of the reasons for inefficiencies in programs. This is not a fault of programmers; the complex nature of programs and systems means that intuition about bottlenecks is almost always wrong. The best approach is to disregard most efficiency concerns during the initial development of the program. Once the program is working (and only if its efficiency is unsatisfactory), the programmer should measure it to find and improve the historical "five percent of the program that executes for 90 percent of the time." If the program was designed properly (meaning that it is highly adaptable), such after-the-fact improvements should be easy.

In complex systems the simplest algorithms are often the fastest. Many modern computers have three-level memories: a small high-speed buffer between the CPU and main memory, main memory itself, and virtual memories mapped onto secondary storage devices. In such systems *locality-of-reference,* the avoidance of rapid references to wide-ranging locations in the program and the data, is a key efficiency parameter. This means that the simple serial algorithms are often faster in this environment than their sophisticated and complicated alternatives.

COMMENTS

The best documentation for program logic is a simple and clean code structure using indentation and meaningful variable names, and following the other guidelines of programming style. If the code has these properties, a large number of comments in the code is unnecessary and, in fact, often undesirable. Comments have been known to *hinder* debugging because the debugger often believes the comments, resulting in his not examining the code close enough. Experienced debuggers often cover the comments with a sheet of paper when they are looking for an error in a module.

Avoid excessive comments. A large number of comments can hinder the code reader by detracting his attention from the code.

Whenever I see a module with a large number of comments I immediately have two thoughts: either the programmer wrote many comments because his logic is tricky or obscure, or the programmer was following some rule such as "at least 50% of all statements must have comments," which means that many of the comments will be meaningless. The programmer should be stingy with comments, using them only where absolutely necessary.

Comment to answer a reader's questions.   An effective technique is initially to write no code comments and then to read the code, putting oneself in a reader's or debugger's shoes. If it appears that a reader may have a question at a particular point, an informative comment to answer the question should be added.

Physically offset all code comments.   Comments should be physically offset to the right of the code on the listing so that a reader can examine the code without being interrupted by comments. In other words, comments in a program should be analogous to footnotes in a book.

Comment all variables.   The key to understanding a program is understanding its data. The data declaration statement for each variable should contain a comment explaining the meaning of the variable.

DATA DEFINITIONS

Because of the importance of data, a few rules about the definition and use of data are warranted.

Explicitly declare all variables.   Many languages allow the programmer to define variables implicitly by simply using the variables in executable statements. This "shortcut" was intended for amateur or casual programmers but not for the professional programmer. The professional programmer should explicitly define or declare all variables at the beginning of the module.

Declare the attributes of each variable.   Again, the language shortcuts of defaulting a variable's attributes if they are not explicitly stated should not be used. The default-selection process is often complicated, leading to errors if the programmer does not fully understand it. Furthermore, some compilers allow each computing installation to alter the compiler defaults, an extremely dangerous practice.

Avoid literal constants.   In examining a machine language program that purported to be a structured program because it used macro statements for the structured programming constructs, the first statement that caught my eye was:

$$MVC \quad DPSREP + 32(2), = X'0009'$$

This statement has three violations of good style (four including the fact that it was written in machine language). It addresses an absolute offset in the storage area DPSREP, it explicitly states the field length, and it contains the wired-in literal X'0009'.

Absolute constants should not be placed within the code except for commonly used values such as zero and one. Literal constants should be defined with a symbolic name and the name should then be used within the code. This allows a reader to examine the compiler's cross-reference listing to see where particular values are used.

An example of the wrong way to cure this problem is contained in a module in IBM's OS/360 system. The standard in machine language modules in OS/360 is to use symbolic names for general registers (e.g., saying R6 instead of 6) so that the cross-reference listing shows which statements use which registers. One programmer who used this convention decided to alter the register assignments after he had coded the module, so the module now contains statements such as:

$$R6 \quad EQU \quad 5$$
$$R7 \quad EQU \quad 4$$
$$R4 \quad EQU \quad 4$$

Needless to say, this made the module totally incomprehensible.

Never use multiple names for the same storage. Use of the FORTRAN EQUIVALENCE statement, COBOL REDEFINES clause, or PL/I DEFINED attribute, which give a variable alias names, is one of the most confusing things that can be done to a program.

Never use a variable for more than one purpose. A common programming practice to conserve a word of storage or save writing a DECLARE statement is to reuse a variable for different purposes. A programmer might say, "I'm done using variable TIME for the time calculation, so I'll use it as a temporary variable down here in my date calculation." This practice increases the chances of introducing an error when modifying a program.

Never use special values of a variable for special meanings. In defining subroutine parameters it is common to see comments such as,

"LINELEN represents the number of characters in the input line unless LINELEN is zero, which indicates that an I/O error occurred." This multiple use of a parameter often leads to ambiguous situations and makes certain modifications of the program difficult. To return an error code, a separate parameter should be defined.

Write table-driven modules. In writing a module that goes through a complex decision-making process on the input data, the decisions to be made should be described in tables instead of wiring the decisions throughout the code. This shortens and "generalizes" the code and makes modifications much simpler.

Be cautious in a binary computer. Binary machines have the property of representing floating-point numbers as *approximate* values. In such a computer 10.0 times 0.1 is rarely equal to 1.0. The programmer must beware of this property, particularly when trying to compare two floating-point numbers.

Be cautious of integer arithmetic. Care must be taken when multiplying or dividing integer values. If I is an integer variable, whether the expression 2*I/2 is equal to I depends on whether I has an even or odd value and whether the compiler generates the division or multiplication first.

Avoid mixed-mode operations. The programmer should avoid mixing variables with different types (e.g., binary, decimal, floating) or precisions in an expression; the compiler may do some surprising conversions. Such tricks as adding a character string to an integer variable should *never* be performed. Caution is necessary when using constant values, for the compiler might assign default attributes that may lead to surprising data conversions. For instance, the following PL/I DO loop

```
DCL I FIXED BIN(15), N FIXED DEC(5);
N= 10;
DO I = 1 TO N/2;
 . . .
END;
```

will never be executed because of the way the expression N/2 is converted to binary to compare it with I, which is defined as binary. Because of the way some compilers do the data conversion, the DO statement is semantically equivalent to

```
DO I= 1 TO 0;
```

PROGRAM STRUCTURE

The remaining guidelines of programming style fall into the category of program structure.

Avoid multiple-closure ENDs.   In PL/I it is a good practice to code a distinct END statement corresponding to each DO statement. This allows the compiler to diagnose certain errors and allows the reader more easily to understand the control flow. Multiple-closure (labeled) ENDs such as

END AMODULE;

should not be used because PL/I compilers assume that any missing ENDs should be automatically inserted at the point of the multiple-closure END.

Code an ELSE for each THEN.   A program should have an equal number of THEN and ELSE clauses in IF statements. Even if the programmer wants to do nothing for the ELSE condition, a null ELSE statement should be coded. This shows the reader that the ELSE condition has been considered and it also eases the job of following the control flow.

Note that this guideline should not be followed if the programmer adopts the suggestion from Chapter 8 of completely avoiding nested IF statements and the ELSE clause. The important thing to remember is to be consistent; if one ELSE clause is coded in a module, then *every* IF statement must have an ELSE clause.

Make exhaustive decisions.   In examining an input parameter whose expected values are 1, 2, or 3, the programmer should not write code that assumes it must be 3 if it is not 1 or 2.

Do not write self-modifying programs.   High-level languages have largely eliminated this practice. However, such constructs as PL/I label variables and the COBOL ALTER statement are methods of altering GO TO statements and should be avoided.

Be cautious with internal procedures.   If the programmer decides to use internal procedures in a language such as PL/I, he must be careful of the scoping rules that allow names in the "outer" procedures to be referenced in the internal procedure. Reread the section on module coupling in Chapter 6 and apply these rules to communication with internal procedures.

Use recursion where applicable.   The use of recursive modules is a simple way to tackle many complex computing problems. Learning to think recursively takes some work, but after one learns the concept the mystery surrounding it disappears. Recursion is desirable when processing any recursively defined data structure such as a bill-of-material tree, a list structure, or a graph or lattice, all having possibly unknown or variable lengths or depths. The reason recursion is so powerful is that it removes storage management burdens from the programmer and makes "backtracking" (e.g., going back up a tree and down another branch) a simple process.

However, recursion should not be used where simple iteration would suffice. For instance, the factorial function $(X! = X(X-1)!)$, a recursively defined mathematical function, is often used to illustrate recursive programming. However, since no backtracking occurs in computing the function, the simplest way to program a factorial function is with iteration (a DO loop) instead of a recursive subroutine.

There is a close relationship between programming style and programming language design, and because of this the reader is encouraged to examine Chapter 15. In addition, the books by Ledgard [4, 5] are additional sources of programming style suggestions and the study by Weissman [6] is one of the few experiments to statistically study the effects of programming style.

REFERENCES

1. B. W. Kernighan and P. J. Plauger, *The Elements of Programming Style.* New York: McGraw-Hill, 1974.
2. G. M. Weinberg, *The Psychology of Computer Programming.* New York: Van Nostrand Reinhold, 1971.
3. G. J. Myers, *Reliable Software Through Composite Design.* New York: Petrocelli/ Charter, 1975.
4. H. F. Ledgard, *Programming Proverbs.* Rochelle Park, N.J.: Hayden, 1975.
5. H. F. Ledgard, *Programming Proverbs for FORTRAN Programmers.* Rochelle Park, N.J.: Hayden, 1975.
6. L. M. Weissman, "A Methodology for Studying the Psychological Complexity of Computer Programs," CSRG-37. University of Toronto Computer Systems Research Group, Toronto, Canada, 1974.

Software Testing

CHAPTER 10

Testing Principles

Many programming organizations spend as much as 50% of their program development budgets on software testing, resulting in an annual world-wide expenditure of billions of dollars. Yet in spite of this huge investment, little is known about the subject of testing and most software products are unacceptably unreliable, even after "extensive" testing.

The most revealing aspect of testing is that most data processing people cannot even correctly define the word "testing"; in fact, this is the major reason for unsuccessful testing efforts. If any professional is asked to define the word testing, or if one examines the always-too-short "testing" chapter in any programming textbook, one usually encounters a definition such as, "Testing is the process of confirming that a program is correct. It is the demonstration that errors are not present." The main trouble with this definition is that it is totally wrong; in fact, it almost defines the antonym of testing. The reader with some programming experience probably already realizes that it is impossible to demonstrate that a program has no errors. Hence this definition describes testing as an impossible task, yet testing is often performed with at least some small degree of success, so the definition is logically incorrect. A proper definition of testing is,

Testing is the process of executing a program with the intention of finding errors.

Testing proves to be an unnatural process (which is why most people find it difficult) because it is a destructive process. The goal of the tester is to make the program fail. If his test case makes the program or system fail, then he is successful; if his test case does not make the program fail, then he is unsuccessful.

It is impossible to guarantee the absence of errors in a nontrivial program; the best that can be accomplished is to attempt to show the presence of errors. If a program behaves correctly under a large set of test cases, there is no justification for saying that the program has no errors; the only accurate statement one can make is that the program is not known not to work. Of course, if there is reason to believe that this set of test cases had a high probability of uncovering all possible errors, then the tests have established some confidence in the program's correctness.

This analysis of the definition of testing is more than a matter of playing with words. This subtle distinction in the definition of testing is the most important lesson to be learned about testing. Not only does the first definition describe an impossible task, but it has an undesirable influence on the programmer's attitude toward testing. If the tester's goal is to demonstrate that a program has no errors by executing a set of test cases that run correctly, his subconscious urges him to select those test cases that have a high probability of executing correctly, and his subconscious blocks any thoughts of running "devious" test cases with which he feels uncomfortable. Psychological experiments show that most people who set a goal (e.g., showing that no errors are present) will orient their activities to achieve this goal. Subconsciously, the tester will not permit himself to work against this goal by writing a test case to try to expose one of the remaining errors in the program. Since we all recognize that no program is perfectly designed and coded and therefore is plagued with a certain number of errors, the most productive use of testing is to find some of these errors. To do this and to avoid the psychological barrier that prevents us from working against a goal, the goal must be to find as many errors as possible. This fundamental lesson can be summarized as:

If your goal is to show the absence of errors, you won't discover many. If your goal is to show the presence of errors, you will discover a large percentage of them.

To some degree, testing is a difficult subject to discuss because, although testing has some bearing on software reliability, there is a limit to its value. Reliability cannot be tested into a program; a program's reliability is established by the correctness of the design stages. The best solution to unreliability is to leave out the errors initially. However, the probability of perfectly designing a large program is infinitesimal. The role of testing is to locate the remaining small number of errors in a well-designed program. Attempts to rely on testing to inject reliability into a poorly or carelessly designed program have proved to be fruitless.

A second reason that testing is a difficult subject is that little is known about it. If today we have 5% of the software design and coding knowledge that we will have in the year 2000, we know less than 1% of what should be known about testing. Furthermore, as illustrated in Figure 10.1, most of today's knowledge is clustered in the center of the software development processes. The base of knowledge in the areas of design, coding, and testing of individual modules is rather large, while

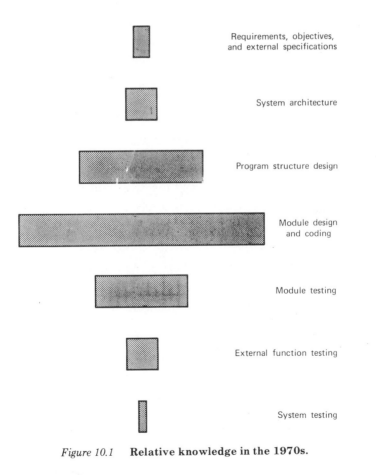

Requirements, objectives, and external specifications

System architecture

Program structure design

Module design and coding

Module testing

External function testing

System testing

Figure 10.1   **Relative knowledge in the 1970s.**

little is known about the early processes (requirements, objectives, and external design) and the later processes (e.g., system testing).

BASIC DEFINITIONS

Although testing can be structured into a number of distinct processes, words such as test, debug, proof, verification, and validation are often used interchangeably and unfortunately mean different things to different people. Although there are no standard industry-wide definitions of these terms, an attempt to create such definitions was made at a program testing symposium sponsored by the Association for Computing Machinery [1]. To begin sorting out the various forms of testing, the definitions are listed below, with slight expansions and a few additions.

Testing, as we have previously discussed, is the process of executing a program (or a part of a program) with the intention or goal of finding errors.

A *proof* is an attempt to find errors in a program without regard to the program's environment. Most proof techniques involve stating assertions about the program's behavior and then deriving and proving mathematical theorems about the program's correctness. Proofs can be considered a form of testing although they do not involve a direct execution of the program. Many researchers consider proofs to be an alternative to testing, a view that is largely incorrect and explored further in Chapter 17.

Verification is an attempt to find errors by executing a program in a test or simulated environment.

Validation is an attempt to find errors by executing a program in a given real environment.

Certification is an authoritative endorsement of the correctness of a program, analogous to the certification of electrical equipment by the Underwriters Laboratories. Testing for certification must be done against some predefined standard. At the time of writing this book a few certification efforts had been established such as the certification of COBOL compilers and mathematical subroutines by the United States National Bureau of Standards and Federal COBOL Compiler Testing Service [2, 3] and certification of mathematical software by the NATS project [4].

Debugging is not a form of testing. Although the words debugging and testing are often used interchangeably, they are distinct activities. Testing is the activity of finding errors; debugging is the activity of diagnosing the precise nature of a known error and then correcting the error. The two are related because the output of a testing activity (detected errors) is the input to a debugging activity.

These definitions represent one view of testing: the view of the testing environment. A second set of definitions listed below represents another view of testing: the types of errors that are expected to be found and the standard to which the program is being tested.

Module testing or *unit testing* is the verification of a single program module, usually in an isolated environment (i.e., isolated from all other modules). Module testing also occasionally includes mathematical proofs.

Integration testing is the verification of the interfaces among system parts (modules, components, and subsystems).

External function testing is the verification of the external system functions as stated in the external specifications.

System testing is the verification and/or validation of the system to its initial objectives. System testing is a verification process when it is done in a simulated environment; it is a validation process when it is performed in a live environment.

Acceptance testing is the validation of the system or program to the user requirements.

Installation testing is the validation of each particular installation of the system with the intent of pointing out any errors made while installing the system.

The relationships between these types of tests and the design documentation on which the tests are based are shown in Figure 10.2.

TESTING PHILOSOPHIES

Software testing encompasses a range of activities that are quite similar to the sequence of software development activities. These activities include establishing test objectives, designing test cases, writing test cases, testing test cases, executing the tests, and examining test

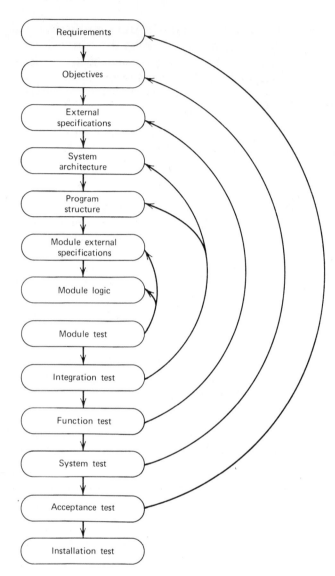

Figure 10.2   **The testing processes and their relationships to the design processes.**

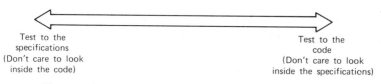

Test to the
specifications
(Don't care to look
inside the code)

Test to the
code
(Don't care to look
inside the specifications)

Figure 10.3   **Philosophy spectrum for test case design.**

results. Of these activities, test case design is the most crucial. In developing a philosophy or strategy for the design of test cases there is a spectrum of opinions as shown in Figure 10.3. In order to establish a strategy for test case design, it is worth examining the two philosophies at each extreme of the spectrum. It is also worth noting that many people in the field place their emphasis at one extreme or the other.

The person at the left end of the spectrum designs his (or her) test cases by examining the external specifications or interface specifications of the program or module he is testing. He views the program as a black-box. His attitude is, "I don't care what the code looks like, or whether I've executed every instruction or every path. As long as the code behaves precisely as stated in the specifications, I'm satisfied." His ultimate testing goal is to test every possible combination and value of input.

The person at the other end of the spectrum designs his test cases by examining the program logic. One criterion he starts with is designing enough test cases so that every instruction is executed at least once. If he is slightly more sophisticated, he designs his test cases so that every conditional branch instruction (e.g., IF statement) is exercised in every direction at least once. His ultimate goal is to test every execution path through the program logic. He designs his test cases with little or no regard to the specifications.

Neither extreme is a good strategy. However, the reader has probably observed that of these two extremes, the first one, treating the code as a black-box, is more desirable. Unfortunately this extreme suffers from the problem of being totally impossible. Consider attempting to test a trivial program that receives three input numbers and calculates their mean. Testing the program for every value of the input data would prove to be impossible. Even for a computer with relatively low numerical precision, the test cases would number in the billions. Even if we had enough computer power to run the test cases in a reasonable amount of time, we would need orders of magnitude more time to write and then verify each test. Programs such as real-time systems, operating systems, and data management programs that have "memories" across inputs are even worse. Not only would we have to test every input value, but we would have to test every sequential combination of the input data. Hence exhaustive testing of the inputs for virtually any program is impossible.

This discussion points out the second fundamental principle of testing: *testing is largely a problem in economics.* Since exhaustive input testing is impossible, we have to settle for something less. Each test case used should provide a maximum yield on our investment. Yield is measured by the probability that the test case will expose a previously undetected error. Investment is measured by the time and cost to produce, execute, and verify the test. Given that the investment is bounded by schedule and budget, the art of test case design is really the art of selecting those test cases with the highest yield. Furthermore, each test case should represent a *class* of inputs so that if the test case executes correctly, we have some confidence that a certain class of inputs will execute correctly. Doing this usually requires some knowledge of the logic and structure of the program, thus moving us toward the program logic end of the spectrum.

The Myth of Path Testing

Since the left extreme of the spectrum is infeasible, the next logical step is to explore the right extreme. This extreme with its goal of testing every execution path will prove to be even worse. Not only is the goal impossible (for the sake of argument I will use the word "impossible" to describe any activity that will take over 100 years), but even if it were possible it is still an insufficient test.

Figure 10.4 describes the execution flow of a small program module. Circles represent sequential segments of code and the edges represent transfers of control (because of DO and IF statements). The module consists of a DO loop that is executed anywhere from 0 to 10 times, followed by a two-way IF, followed by a second DO loop. Each loop contains a set of nested IF statements as shown. Assuming that each decision is completely independent from all others (admittedly a worst-case assumption), there are approximately 10^{18} unique paths through this module! As a basis for comparison, the estimated age of the universe is only about 4×10^{17} seconds. To illustrate an actual situation, executing all possible paths through the TITAN missile navigation and guidance software would take an estimated 60,000 hours of computer time [5]. Hence, even though the number of paths through a program is significantly lower than the number of input combinations, the number is still astronomical.

Just for the sake of argument suppose we built a computer that, by

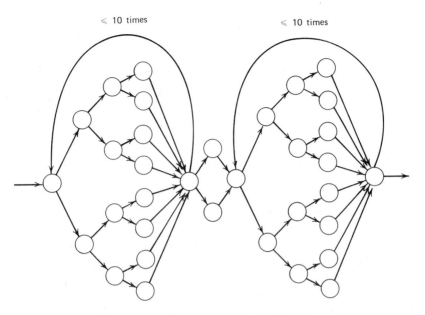

≤ 10 times   ≤ 10 times

Figure 10.4   **Flow graph of a small program.**

defying all known laws of physics, could execute all paths in Figure 10.4 in a matter of years. We are still faced with the even larger problem of writing and checking 10^{18} test cases. Again just for the sake of argument suppose we can also overcome this problem (I do not even speculate how). The question then is whether we have satisfactorily tested this module. The answer is a definite *no*.

The most obvious reason behind the answer is that executing every path is no guarantee that the program matches its specifications. If a programmer were asked to write a cube-root function and he wrote a square-root function, the program would be totally incorrect even though the programmer may have executed every path. A second and more realistic problem is missing paths. If the program incompletely implements the specification (e.g., a specified function such as a check for negative input to a square-root function was omitted), no amount of path testing would give information about the missing paths. A third subtle problem is one of *data sensitivities*. A path may execute correctly for certain input data values but not for other input values. To examine a trivial case, suppose the programmer is required to write a routine to determine if three integer numbers are equal to one another. He codes

IF (A+B+C)/3 = A

which works for most, but not all, values of A, B, and C (it fails only when B and C are equally greater than and less than A). If the programmer simply focused his attention on path testing, there is no reason to believe that he would detect this bug.

By this time the art of test case design probably looks bleak; in fact, it is rather bleak. We have seen that both extremes are unsatisfactory. In order to develop a reasonable and economical strategy, we use elements of both extremes, picking a point within the spectrum but somewhat toward the black-box end of the spectrum. Formulation of this strategy is begun in Chapter 11.

MODULE INTEGRATION

After the problems of test case design, the second most important testing consideration is the sequence used to merge all of the modules together to form the entire system or program. This consideration usually receives insufficient attention and is too often treated as an afterthought. However, this sequence is one of the most vital decisions to be made in a testing effort because it influences the form in which test cases are written, the types of test tools needed, the order in which modules are coded, and the thoroughness and economics of the testing effort. For these reasons the decision must be made on a project-wide basis and rather early in the project schedule.

There are a large number of possible approaches that can be used to sequence the testing of modules and the merging of modules into larger entities. Most of the approaches can be described as variations of one of six basic approaches, outlined in the next six sections. The section following these six sections compares these approaches in terms of their effects on software reliability.

BOTTOM-UP TESTING

In the bottom-up approach the program is merged and tested from the bottom to the top. The only modules that are module (unit) tested in isolation are the terminal modules (the modules that call no other modules). Once these modules are tested, a CALL to one of them should be as reliable as a built-up language function or an assignment statement. The next set of modules to be tested are the modules that directly call these tested modules. These higher-level modules are not tested in isolation; they are tested with the previously tested lower modules. This

process is repeated until the top is reached. At this point module test
and integration test for the program is complete.

Figure 10.5 shows the module structure of the loader that was
designed in Part 2. For brevity the modules have been labeled with
single letters. The loader is an unusual program in that it has only one
terminal module, module H. The first step is to test module H by itself.
Then modules C and G can be tested as parallel activities using the
tested module H. Next, modules D and F are tested, then E, then B,
and finally A. Because the testing sequence is closely related to the
program structure, a PERT chart can easily be drawn for planning purposes, as shown in Figure 10.6.

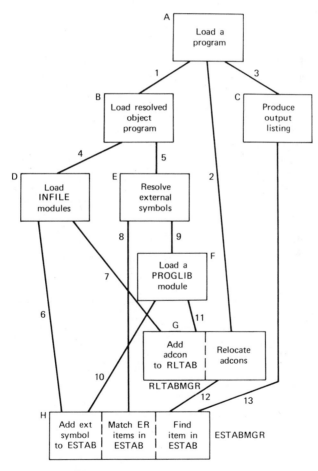

Figure 10.5   **The loader structure.**

Notes

1. LOAD-INFILE-MODULES uses operating system functions GET (from INFILE) and GETMAIN.
2. LOAD-A-PROGLIB-MODULE uses system functions FIND and GET (from PROGLIB) and GETMAIN.
3. PRODUCE-OUTPUT-LISTING uses system function PUT (to OUTFILE).
4. ESTAB entry contains symbol name, type (MD, EP, or ER), and allocated machine address.
5. RLTAB entry contains number of corresponding ESTAB entry and the machine address of the address constant.

	In	Out
1	————————	ESTAB, RLTAB, MSGLIST
2	ESTAB, RLTAB	EC
3	ESTAB, MSGLIST	EC
4	————————	ESTAB, RLTAB, MSGLIST
5	ESTAB, RLTAB	ESTAB, RLTAB, MSGLIST
6	ESTAB, NAME, TYPE, ADDRESS	ESTAB, ENTRY NO., EC
7	RLTAB, ENTRY NO., ADCON ADDRESS	RLTAB, EC
8	ESTAB	ESTAB, DONE FLAG, NAME OF UNRES. ER
9	ESTAB, RLTAB, MODULE NAME	ESTAB, RLTAB, MSGLIST
10	SAME AS	NO. 6
11	SAME AS	NO. 7
12	ESTAB, ENTRY NO.	NAME, TYPE, ADDRESS, EC
13	SAME AS	NO. 12

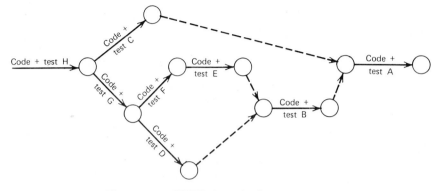

Figure 10.6   **PERT chart for bottom-up test.**

Bottom-up testing requires a *module driver* for each module: a method of feeding test case input to the interface of the module being tested. One solution is to write a small driving program for each module. The test cases are expressed as "wired-in" variables and data structures, and the driving program repeatedly calls the module being tested, passing it input data for each test case on each call. A more desirable solution is to use a module tester, which is a testing tool that lets one specify test cases in a special language, eliminating the task of writing driving programs. Chapter 11 mentions several module tester programs that are available in the marketplace.

TOP-DOWN TESTING

Top-down testing (also called top-down development [6]) is not the exact opposite of bottom-up testing, but it can initially be viewed as such. In the top-down approach the program is merged and tested from the top to the bottom. The only module that is unit tested in isolation is the top module in the program structure. After this module is tested, the modules directly called by this module are merged (e.g., link-edited) one by one with the top module and the combination is tested. This process is repeated until all modules have been combined and tested.

This approach immediately raises two questions: What happens when a module being tested calls a lower module (which currently does not exist), and how are test cases fed to the program? The answer to the first question is that *stub modules* are coded to simulate the functions of the missing modules. The phrase "just code a stub" is often seen in descriptions of this approach, but this is misleading because the task of writing a stub module is often difficult. A stub module is rarely as simple as a RETURN statement because the calling module usually expects output parameters from the called module. The usual approach is to wire-in a fixed output that is always returned from the stub. This approach sometimes fails because the calling module may expect the output of a CALL to be a function of the particular inputs. In some cases the stub module has to be rather sophisticated, approaching the module that it is attempting to simulate.

The second question, the form in which the test cases are written and how they are fed to the program, is an interesting consideration. If the top module contained all of the program's input and output operations, the answer would be simple: the test cases are written as external (user) inputs and are fed to the program through its input devices. However, this is rarely the case. In a well-designed program the physical input/output operations are performed at a low level in the structure because physical input/output is a low-level abstraction. To solve this problem in an economical way, rather than adding modules in a strictly top-down fashion (all the modules in one horizontal level, then the modules in the next level), the modules are added with the goal of *getting the program's physical input and output operations functioning as soon as possible.* Once this point is reached, top-down testing achieves a significant advantage: all further test cases can be in the form of user inputs.

The remaining test case question is: In what form are test cases written before we have reached this point in the program? The answer is that these test cases are imbedded within some of the stub modules. I will show how this is done for the loader program.

First, getting the input/output operations functioning is a key consideration in sequencing the integration of modules. In the loader program in Figure 10.5 the input is read by modules D and E and the output is produced by module C. The sequence starts by coding and testing module A. Module A is actually a small module; it simply calls three other modules sequentially and may also add one or more messages to the error message list if an error is detected in module G. To test module A, three stubs must be written. The stub for module B can simply return a predefined ESTAB, RLTAB, and message list. The stub for the address relocation entry in module G could simply contain a return statement, and the stub representing module C could print its input parameters. Since the error processing in module A must be tested, one or more stubs for the address relocation function are needed which, when called, return each error code. This points out a subtle disadvantage in using stub modules. Often, the testing of different conditions within the program requires stubs to return different sets of output data. If one of these stubs is called only once during the execution of the program, it may be necessary to produce different stubs for a single module and then vary the stubs used between each test execution (or, alternatively, have the stub read test data from an external file).

The next step in testing the loader is to move toward the input/output modules as quickly as possible. The stub for module C can be removed and replaced with the actual module C. Module C now requires a stub simulating the find-item function in module H. This stub could simply return a fixed set of output parameters, but this would prevent us from using the output listing produced in module C for checking the results of future test cases. Hence this stub should actually perform the function it is trying to simulate. Modules A and C and the stubs for B, G, and H are now tested together. Note that the test cases are actually the predefined outputs returned by stub B. Because B is called only once, it may be necessary to have many stubs representing module B to contain various versions of ESTAB, RLTAB, and message list to test module C.

The next step is to add module B. The stubs used to simulate module B are discarded and stubs for modules D and E are added. After this testing is completed the stub for module D is discarded and the real module D is coded and inserted. It is now necessary to add stubs for the entry points used in modules G and H. There appears to be no easy way to simulate these functions, so eventually these stubs may be forgotten and the actual modules may be used instead.

At this point the input/output operations are functioning, so test cases can be written in the form of records on INFILE (or, even easier, a compiler can be used to generate test cases). The loader now functions in a skeletal manner although it neither relocates address constants nor resolves any unresolved external references. The remaining steps involve integrating these remaining functions into the loader.

Top-down testing has some advantages and some disadvantages when compared to bottom-up testing. The most significant advantage is that it combines module testing, integration testing, and a small amount of external function testing. Related to this advantage is the advantage that test cases can be written as external inputs once the input/output modules are inserted. Top-down testing is also advantageous if the *feasibility* of the entire program is questionable or if there are major flaws in the program's design.

An advantage of top-down testing that is often mentioned is the absence of the need for module drivers; instead you "simply have to write stubs." As the reader may have guessed by now, this advantage is questionable.

Top-down testing also unfortunately has several disadvantages. A major disadvantage is that a module is rarely tested thoroughly right after it is integrated. For instance, thorough testing of certain modules may require extremely sophisticated stubs. The programmer often decides that rather than wasting a lot of time coding these sophisticated stubs, he will code simple stubs and only test a subset of the conditions in the module. He intends that later, when he removes the stubs, he will remember to return and finish testing the module in question. This plan is a definite disadvantage because these untested conditions are often forgotten.

A second subtle disadvantage of top-down testing is that it may lead to the belief that one can begin coding and testing the top of the program before the entire program is actually designed. This idea may initially sound economical, but usually the opposite is true. Most experienced designers recognize that program design is an iterative process. Rarely is the first design perfect. A normal experience in program structure design after the bottom levels have been designed is to go back and adjust the top of the program, either to make improvements or to correct errors, and even in some cases to scrap the design and start again because the designer suddenly sees a better approach. If the top of the program is already being coded and tested, there will be significant resistance to any structure improvements. In the long run these improvements usually save more than the few days or weeks that the designer initially thought he would save by beginning the coding too early.

MODIFIED TOP-DOWN TESTING

Top-down testing has another significant disadvantage in terms of thorough testing. Assume there is a large program and somewhere toward the bottom of the program is a module with the function of calculating the roots of a quadratic equation. Given input variables A, B, and C it solves the equation

$$AX^2 + BX + C = 0.$$

Anyone designing and coding this function should recognize that a quadratic equation can have complex as well as real roots. In order to completely implement this function, the outputs can be real or complex values (or, if there is no justification for the added expense of finding complex roots, the module must at least return an error code if the inputs will lead to complex roots). Let us suppose that the particular contexts in which this module is being used can never lead to complex roots (i.e., the calling modules never generate input parameters that would lead to complex roots). With strict top-down testing it may be impossible to test the module for complex roots (or to test the error condition). One could try to rationalize this away, saying that since it will never be given such an equation, no one cares whether it works for these cases. True, it may not matter right now, but it will matter in the future if someone tries to use the module in a new program or to modify the old program so that complex roots are possible.

This problem arises in many forms. Using top-down testing as defined in the previous section, it is often impossible to test certain logical conditions within the program such as error conditions or defensive programming checks. In the loader module that was designed and coded in Chapter 8, four defensive programming checks were placed at the beginning of the module. There is no way to test this defensive code using top-down testing because the code only functions when the module above it transmits invalid input (and it is fair to assume that since the designer decided to add these checks, he should also want to test them). Top-down testing also makes checking of specific logical conditions within a module either difficult or impossible when the program is only using that module in a limited context (implying that the module will never be passed its full range of input values). Even when testing of a condition is feasible, it is often difficult to determine what type of test case to write when the test case is entering the program at a point that is far removed from the condition.

The method called modified top-down testing solves these problems by requiring each module to be unit tested in isolation before it is integrated into the program. Although this method does solve these problems, it requires module drivers *and* stubs for each module.

BIG-BANG TESTING

Probably the most common approach to the integration of modules is the "big-bang" approach. In this method every module is first unit tested in isolation from every other module. After each module is tested all of the modules are integrated together at once.

Big-bang testing when compared to the other approaches has many disadvantages and few advantages. Stubs and module drivers are needed for every module. Modules are not integrated until late in the testing process, implying that serious module interface errors remain undetected for a long time.

To apply the big-bang approach to the loader, one would take all eight modules and unit test each module independently. The eight modules would then be link-edited together and testing would begin on the entire program. Note that in the bottom-up and top-down methods only a *single* module at any point in time is being integrated, so if an error suddenly occurs, the latest module added becomes the prime suspect. Debugging is more difficult in the big-bang approach.

The big-bang approach is not always undesirable. If the program is small (such as the loader program) and well designed, this approach may be feasible. For large programs, however, the big-bang approach is usually disastrous.

SANDWICH TESTING

Sandwich testing is a compromise between bottom-up and top-down testing. It attempts to extract the advantages of both methods while eliminating some of the disadvantages.

In sandwich testing one begins using top-down testing and bottom-up testing simultaneously, integrating the program from both the top and the bottom and eventually meeting somewhere in the middle. The point at which they converge in the middle depends on the particular program being tested. This point must be predetermined by examining the structure of the program. For instance, if the designer can view his system as containing levels of application-oriented modules, then levels of transaction-oriented modules, and then levels of primitive functions, he may decide to use top-down testing on the application levels (coding stubs for the transaction functions) and bottom-up testing on the primitive and transaction levels.

Sandwich testing is difficult to illustrate on a small program so the loader is not a helpful example. It is a reasonable approach for the integration of a large program such as an operating system or an application system.

Sandwich testing retains the bottom-up and top-down advantage of integrating modules together at an early point in the schedule. Because the top of the program is constructed early, one gains the top-down advantage of having an early skeletal working program. Because of the bottom-up construction of the lower levels of the program, the top-down testing problem of not being able to test specific conditions in the depths of the program is solved.

MODIFIED SANDWICH TESTING

Sandwich testing still has a problem in common with top-down testing, although to a smaller degree. This is the problem of not being able to thoroughly test particular modules within the program. The bottom-up portion of sandwich testing solves this problem for the lower levels of modules within the program, but the problem may still exist for modules in the lower half of the top part of the program. In modified sandwich testing, the lower levels are still tested in a strictly bottom-up fashion. However, the modules in the upper levels of the program are first unit tested in isolation before they are integrated using top-down testing. Therefore, modified sandwich testing is a compromise between bottom-up and modified top-down testing.

WHICH ONE IS BEST?

It is difficult to evaluate these six strategies to find the best one because the "best" approach varies from organization to organization and from program to program. In terms of software reliability, the six strategies can be evaluated by the eight criteria in Figure 10.7. The first category measures the time at which modules are integrated or combined together, recognizing that this is important in detecting module interface errors and invalid assumptions among modules. The second category measures the time at which an early skeletal working version of the program is constructed, recognizing that this might point out major design flaws. The third and fourth categories describe whether stubs are needed or whether module driver code or a testing tool is needed. The fifth category is a measure of the amount of parallel testing that can occur at the beginning or early stages of the testing effort. This is of interest because project resources (i.e., programmers) usually peak during the module design and coding phases. Therefore, it is important that the opportunity for parallel testing occur toward the beginning of the testing cycle rather than toward the end.

The sixth category measures the problem discussed earlier: the ability to test any particular path or condition within the program. The seventh category describes the difficulty of planning, tracking, and controlling the testing sequence, recognizing that testing efforts that are

	Bottom up	Top down	Modified top down	Big bang	Sandwich	Modified sandwich
Integration	Early	Early	Early	Late	Early	Early
Time to a basic working program	Late	Early	Early	Late	Early	Early
Module driver (code or tool) needed	Yes	No	Yes	Yes	In part	Yes
Stubs needed	No	Yes	Yes	Yes	In part	In part
Work parallelism at beginning	Medium	Low	Medium	High	Medium	High
Ability to test particular paths	Easy	Hard	Easy	Easy	Medium	Easy
Ability to plan and control the sequence	Easy	Hard	Hard	Easy	Hard	Hard
Machine inefficiencies			Judged as not significant			

Figure 10.7 **Qualitative comparison of the integration approaches.**

harder to plan and control lead to more frequent oversights and omissions. The last category measures machine time inefficiencies: the redundant execution of previously tested code. Occasionally, an objection is raised about top-down testing because testing of lower modules requires many redundant executions of the top modules. However this category is labeled as not significant. Although redundant executions may occur, there may also be many executions that appear to be redundant but actually generate slightly different conditions. These executions may turn up new errors, thus turning the disadvantage into an advantage. Since this effect is not well understood, we neglect it.

The next step is to evaluate the six approaches with respect to the eight criteria. As mentioned earlier this evaluation is dependent on the project. To provide a starting point for your own evaluation, a rough evaluation is presented. The first step is to weight each of the eight criteria in terms of their relative effect on reliable software. Early integration of modules, an early skeletal working program, and the ability to test particular conditions seem to be most important, so these are given a weight of three. The difficulty of producing stubs and the difficulty of planning and tracking the test sequence are also important, so they have a weight of two. The need for module driver code has a weight of one because of the availability of module testing tools. The criteria measuring work parallelism also has a weight of one because, although it may be important for other reasons, it does not have a strong effect on reliability. The eighth category was left unweighted.

Figure 10.8 shows the results of this evaluation. In each box the weight is either added, subtracted, or set to zero, depending on whether the approach indicates an advantage, disadvantage, or something in between. Modified sandwich testing and bottom-up testing appear to be the best approaches and big-bang testing appears to be the worst approach. If this evaluation seems close to your own situation then I recommend using modified sandwich testing for large systems or programs and using bottom-up testing for s nall or moderately sized programs.

TESTING AXIOMS

Before discussing the technical aspects of software testing any further, some vital axioms about testing should be discussed. The axioms listed in this section are a set of fundamental principles for testing. They do not represent a complete list; additional axioms are discussed where applicable in the remaining chapters of Part 3.

	Weight	Bottom up	Top down	Modified top down	Big bang	Sandwich	Modified sandwich
Integration	3	Early +	Early +	Early +	Late −	Early +	Early +
Time to a basic working program	3	Late −	Early +	Early +	Late −	Early +	Early +
Module driver (code or tool) needed	1	Yes −	No +	Yes −	Yes −	In part −	Yes −
Stubs needed	2	No +	Yes −	Yes −	Yes −	In part −	In part −
Work parallelism at beginning	1	Medium	Low −	Medium +	High +	Medium	High +
Ability to test particular paths	3	Easy +	Hard −	Easy +	Easy +	Medium −	Easy +
Ability to plan and control the sequence	2	Easy +	Hard −	Hard −	Easy +	Hard −	Hard −
Machine inefficiencies	0	Judged as not significant					
Total		+6	−1	+4	−3	+4	+7

Figure 10.8 A weighted comparison of the integration approaches.

A good test case is a test case that has a high probability of detecting an undiscovered error, not a test case that shows that the program works correctly.

This axiom is the fundamental principle of testing that I discussed at the beginning of the chapter. Since it is impossible and hence fruitless to attempt to show that a program has no errors, testing must be the process of trying to discover previously undetected errors within a program.

One of the most difficult problems in testing is knowing when to stop.

As discussed earlier, thorough testing (i.e., exhaustive testing of every input value) is impossible. The tester is then faced with an economic problem: choosing a finite number of test cases that maximize the yield (probability of detecting errors) for a given investment. There are too many testing efforts where many of the test cases written had an extremely low probability of finding new errors, yet obvious good test cases were overlooked. This problem is discussed further in the next few chapters.

It is impossible to test your own program.

No programmer should attempt to test his own program. This applies to all forms of testing, be it system testing, external function testing, or even unit testing. Many of the underlying reasons for this have already been discussed in Chapter 8 in discussing the value of code reading. Testing has to be an extremely destructive process, and there are deep psychological reasons that prevent a programmer from being destructive toward his own program. Additional pressures (e.g., tight schedules) on a single programmer or an entire project often prevent the programmer or the project from doing an adequate test. Furthermore, if a module contains errors due to some translation mistakes, the probability of the programmer's making the same translation mistakes (e.g., misinterpreting the specification) when designing test cases is high. Any misunderstandings the programmer has regarding other modules and their interfaces will also be reflected in the test cases.

Testing should always be done by an outside party who is somewhat detached from the program and the project. Rather than unit testing the modules oneself, the programmer should have the unit test cases designed (and maybe even executed and verified) by a programmer of one of the modules that calls the module to be tested. System testing should always be done by an independent group such as a separate quality-assurance department or a voluntary user group.

A necessary part of every test case is a description of the expected output or results.

One of the most common mistakes made in testing is to fail to predict the expected results from each test case *before* the test is executed. The expected results must be determined beforehand to eliminate the problem of "the eye seeing what it wants to see." To further minimize this problem, test cases should either be self-checking or the test tool being used should have the capability of automatically checking the test results.

Although this axiom is extremely important, there are circumstances such as the testing of mathematical software where a few slight exceptions are necessary. Mathematical software has the property that the outputs or results are approximations of the correct output. These approximations result from using finite computations to replace infinite mathematical processes, roundoff errors because of the finite precision of computer arithmetic and the inexact representation of numbers in a binary computer, and transmitted errors because of the finite precision of input data and constants. In many cases the correlation of errors becomes important. For instance, when a mathematical subroutine returns an array of numbers, it is important that the computed solution be an exact solution to a set of inputs that approximate the actual inputs. Hence in testing mathematical software, prediction of the precise output is much more difficult. A thorough discussion of these problems is beyond the scope of this book. For a survey of these problems and a bibliography see Cody [7].

Avoid nonreproducible or on-the-fly testing.

The use of on-line interactive systems is sometimes detrimental to good testing practices. To test a program in a batch-processing system, the programmer usually has to represent his test cases as a special driver program or as files of test data. All too often in an interactive environment the programmer performs "on-the-fly" testing by sitting at a terminal, setting up particular values in storage, and then executing his program to "see what happens." This is a sloppy and undesirable form of testing for several reasons. The major problem is that his test cases are transient; they disappear after the test has been executed. Whenever the program has to be retested (e.g., when correcting an error or making a modification), the test cases have to be developed all over again.

Testing is already expensive enough without causing this additional expense. Never use throw-away test cases (except on a throw-away program). Also, test cases should be documented sufficiently and stored in such a form to allow them to be reused by anyone.

Write test cases for invalid as well as valid input conditions.

Many programmers orient their test cases toward expected input conditions, forgetting about the consequences of unexpected or invalid input conditions. However, many errors that are suddenly discovered in operational programs are uncovered by some new unexpected action by the user of the program. Test cases representing unexpected or invalid inputs often have a higher error-detection yield than test cases for expected or valid input conditions.

Thoroughly inspect the results of each test.

Ingenious test cases are worthless if the test results are given only a cursory glance. Testing a program means more than just executing a sufficient number of test cases; it also means examining the results of each test. A common reply by programmers to a newly discovered error is, "Yes, I tested for that condition but somehow I didn't see *that* in the output."

As the number of detected errors in a piece of software increases, the probability of the existence of more undetected errors also increases.

This counter-intuitive phenomenon illustrated in Figure 10.9 implies that errors come in clusters. As the number of errors detected in a piece of software (e.g., module, subsystem, or user function) increases, the probability of the existence of additional undetected errors in that software also increases. Given two modules in which the tester has

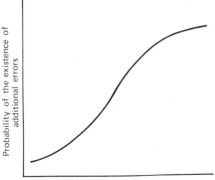

Probability of the existence of additional errors

No. of errors found to date

Figure 10.9   **Relationship between discovered and undiscovered errors.**

detected one and eight errors, the curve says that the module with eight known errors has a higher probability of having more.

This phenomenon has been observed in many systems, one example being IBM's OS/360 operating system. Understanding the relationship will help to refine testing efforts by applying feedback from the test execution process to the test case design process. If a particular part of the system appears to be highly error-prone during testing, additional testing efforts should be focused there. In other words, the testing yield on this part of the system will be higher than on other parts.

Assign your most creative programmers to testing.

Testing, particularly test case design, is the area of software development that demands the most creativity. Unfortunately, many organizations do not view testing this way. Testing is often viewed as mundane and undemanding work, leading to the staffing of testing organizations with primarily inexperienced or new programmers. However, testing experiences show that the opposite view is more accurate. Test case design demands even more creativity than software architecture and design. If I had a fixed number of highly creative programmers to assign on a project, I would assign at least half of them to testing jobs.

Ensure that testability is a key objective in your software design.

Although "testability" was not explicity discussed in Part II, the difficulty of testing a program is related to the program's design and structure. Although this relationship is not well understood, many of the design parameters (e.g., small highly independent modules and independent subsystems) discussed in Chapters 5 and 6 enhance the testability of a program.

The design of a system should be such that each module is integrated into the system only once.

A large number of problems in many large software systems stem from violations of this axiom. It is not uncommon in the testing cycle of a large system for particular modules to be reintegrated ten times or more. Each version of the module contains one small additional function needed by the current level of the system. Again, following the guidelines of Chapter 6 and having small modules that perform single functions alleviates this problem.

Never alter the program to make testing easier.

It is often tempting to alter a program to make testing easier. For instance, a programmer with a module containing a DO loop that has

100 iterations may alter the DO loop to iterate only 10 times to make testing easier. He may be testing, but he is testing the wrong program.

Testing, as almost every other activity, must start with objectives.

As mentioned earlier, the testing cycle is a microcosm of the entire software development cycle. Test cases must be designed, implemented, tested, and finally executed. Project-wide objectives should always be established for testing such as outlining goals for each particular type of testing (e.g., number of paths executed or conditional branches exercised) and the relative percentage of errors to be detected in each testing phase.

REFERENCES

1. W. C. Hetzel, "A Definitional Framework," in W. C. Hetzel, Ed., *Program Test Methods*. Englewood Cliffs, N.J.: Prentice-Hall, 1973, pp. 2–10.

2. G. N. Baird and M. M. Cook, "Experiences in COBOL Compiler Validation," *Proceedings of the 1974 National Computer Conference*. Montvale, N.J.: AFIPS Press, 1974, pp. 417–421.

3. W. L. Sadowski and D. W. Lozier, "A Unified Standards Approach to Algorithm Testing," in W. C. Hetzel, Ed., *Program Test Methods*. Englewood Cliffs, N.J.: Prentice-Hall, 1973, pp. 277–290.

4. J. M. Boyle, W. J. Cody, W. R. Cowell, B. S. Grabow, Y. Ikebe, C. B. Moler, and B. T. Smith, "NATS: A Collaborative Effort to Certify and Disseminate Mathematical Software," *Proceedings of the 1972 ACM Annual Conference*. New York: ACM, 1972, pp. 630–635.

5. R. H. Thayer, "Rome Air Development Center R & D Program in Computer Language Controls and Software Engineering Techniques," RADC-TR-74-80, Griffiss Air Force Base, Rome, N.Y., 1974.

6. R. C. McHenry, "Management Techniques for Top Down Structured Programming," FSC-73-0001, IBM Federal Systems Div., Gaithersburg, Md., 1973.

7. W. J. Cody, "The Evaluation of Mathematical Software," in W. C. Hetzel, Ed., *Program Test Methods*. Englewood Cliffs, N.J.: Prentice-Hall, 1973, pp. 121–133.

CHAPTER 11

Module Testing

In each of the six testing and integration approaches discussed in Chapter 10 the initial testing focus was on the individual software module. In the top-down approaches, each module to be tested is plugged into the bottom of the previously tested set of modules. In the bottom-up approaches, the new module is plugged onto the top of the previously tested set of modules. All of the approaches except the big-bang approach also provide integration testing (testing of module or component interfaces) as a side benefit.

The intent of the module or unit test is to find discrepancies between the module's logic and interfaces and its module external specification (the description of the module's function, inputs, outputs, and external effects). The step of compiling the module should also be considered as part of the module test since the compiler detects most syntax errors and a few semantic or logic errors.

TEST CASE DESIGN

To illustrate the difficulty of test case design I often assign the following homework problem at the beginning of courses on software reliability:

> I have a small program that reads three integer values representing the lengths of the sides of a

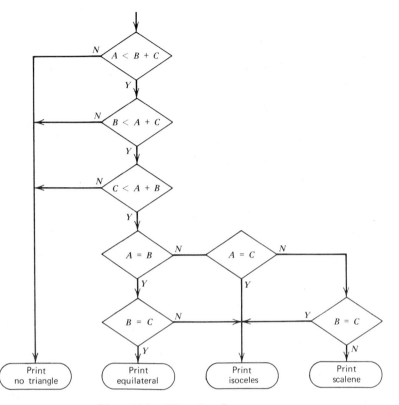

Figure 11.1   **The triangle program.**

triangle. The program examines the inputs and prints a message stating whether the triangle is scalene, isosceles, or equilateral. Write test cases to adequately test this program.

This program is a trivial program and most of the students are experienced data processing professionals, yet the results are always enlightening because most students do a poor job of testing the program. This is not meant as a criticism of the students; it simply illustrates the difficulties of designing good test cases even for a trivial program. Before reading any further you might want to try the problem yourself.

A good way to analyze the answers to the problem is to compare them with the logic of the program as shown in Figure 11.1. Notice the use of a flowchart, although Chapter 8 states that flowcharts are not an important part of program design. A flowchart is used here because flowcharts are useful in testing; flowcharts more clearly show the execution paths in the code than the source code itself does. This program has only eight unique execution paths, leading to a conclusion that at least eight test cases would be desirable.

The next step in analyzing the test cases is to hypothesize errors in the program to see how many students would have found the errors. An error could be hypothesized by removing one of the decisions in Figure 11.1 or by modifying a decision in some way. Figure 11.2 shows some typical logic errors and also the percentage of students that found each error.

Given the experience level of the students, the trivial nature of the program, and the fact that the exercise was done in a course on software reliability, one might expect the test cases to be rather complete, but Figure 11.2 shows that this was not the case. All students included tests for equilateral triangles, but a surprising percentage failed to test a scalene triangle. (The reason is that all students probably intended to test a scalene triangle, but they used inputs such as 1-2-4, which is not a triangle.) Although almost every student included at least one test

Hypothetical Bug	Percentage of students that would have detected the bug
Program doesn't check to see if input is a triangle	56
Program checks this but only by checking A<B+C	28
Program doesn't check for scalene	84
Program doesn't check for isosceles	95
Program checks for isosceles but only for A=B≠C	46
Program doesn't check for equilateral	100

Figure 11.2   Some test results for the triangle program.

case for an isosceles triangle, over half of the students failed to check the three input permutations that could lead to isosceles triangles (e.g., they tried 2-2-3 but not 2-3-2 and 3-2-2).

Notice that the program has to first check the input data to see if it even describes a valid triangle, for if the program were to print "scalene" for inputs 2-3-6, the program would be incorrect (sides of lengths 2-3-6 do not form a triangle). Fifty-six percent of the students checked for this with at least one test, but only 28% checked the three permutations.

Other results not shown in Figure 11.2 are also enlightening. Sixty-one percent of the students failed to state the expected result of each test case, which reduces their chances of spotting an error even if a test case encounters it. One student proposed over 1000 test cases, but he still failed to detect some of the hypothetical bugs. Seventy percent of the students had the good sense to try "garbage" input (e.g., character input), but only 37% explored the program's behavior when it receives less than three inputs.

To check your own skill at test case design, try writing test cases for a subroutine that finds the roots of a quadratic equation. Given inputs A, B, and C it finds the two values of X that solve the equation $AX^2 + BX + C = 0$. Compare your results with those at the end of the chapter.

The point of this discussion is to illustrate the difficulty of good test case design. Test case design is a creative and artistic process, but it also requires a highly destructive frame of mind. There are, however, a few simple rules that can be used to formulate a reasonable set of tests. These rules start by viewing the module as a black-box and using the module external specification to generate test cases (the black box extreme of the philosophy spectrum) and then later inspecting the insides of the module for supplemental test cases. The four steps are:

1. Using the module external specification, formulate a test case for each condition and option, the boundaries of all input domains and output ranges, and invalid conditions.
2. Inspect the code to ensure that all conditional branches will be executed in each direction. Add test cases to accomplish this where required.
3. Inspect the code to ensure that as many paths as feasible are covered with test cases. For instance, each DO loop should be covered with test cases for at least the paths reflecting zero iterations, one iteration, and the maximum number of iterations.

4. Inspect the code for any sensitivities to particular input values and add test cases where necessary.

The first test case design step involves viewing the module as a black-box and deriving test cases by manipulating the module's input data. This step requires a great deal of creativity (the remaining three steps are, in contrast, quite methodical). If the module accepts a small number of distinct input values (e.g., one of five transaction codes), develop a test case for each. If the module accepts a number of input parameters and each one has a small number of valid values, develop test cases for all combinations.

More creativity is required when the input data can take on a large number of values. A reasonable solution is to design test cases to exercise the module at the *boundaries* of its input domain. If an input parameter has a valid domain of -1.0 to $+1.0$, design test cases at these boundaries. In this situation a third test case supplying an input of 0.0 is also desirable to detect such errors as indexing or division by zero. If your computing system has *two* representations of zero, one for -0.0 and another for $+0.0$, supply both in test cases.

Many programs also have *functional boundaries*. A good deal of thought is often required to recognize these functional boundaries, but this thought usually pays off in high-yield test cases. Suppose one is about to test a module that performs an in-core sort of a list of input records. Functional boundaries occur when the input list is empty, when the input list contains only one record, when the input records are already sorted, and when all of the input records have equal values.

The output values returned by the module may span some fixed range (e.g., the integers 1 through 65535 or a character string of length 1 to 255). Ensure that you have test cases to exercise the module at the boundaries of its output ranges. Note that it is not always true that inputs at the boundaries of the input domain generate outputs at the boundaries of the output range.

The remaining consideration in the first step is test cases for invalid conditions. If the module being tested has been completely specified, its behavior should be known for invalid as well as valid inputs. Good invalid inputs to use in test cases are those that are one beyond the boundaries of the valid input domains.

To illustrate the first step test cases designed are for the MATCHES function in the loader designed in Part 2. Later on steps 2, 3, and 4 are used to supplement these test cases. Refer back to Figure 8.7 for the module external specification and code for MATCHES.

MATCHES receives one input (the pointer ESTAB to the external symbol table ESTABLE) and produces three outputs: the updated ESTABLE, a name of an unmatched external reference (UNRESNAME), and a return code (MATCHCODE). By examining the module external specification, one should arrive at the following test conditions:

1. Invalid ESTABLE.
2. An ESTABLE in which all external references can be matched.
3. An ESTABLE whose initial state contains no unmatched references.
4. An ESTABLE in which one or more external references can be matched before an unmatched name is encountered.
5. An ESTABLE in which an unmatched name is immediately encountered (meaning that no matches are performed).

For the boundary conditions we should try a single-entry ESTABLE and unmatched names of one and eight characters. Other boundary conditions include placing the unmatched entries and the corresponding matching entries as the first and last entries in ESTABLE. These conditions lead to the test case designs illustrated in Figure 11.3. Notice that the fifth test case covers several of the conditions and, in adherence to the axioms in Chapter 10, the expected outputs are listed.

The three remaining test case design steps involve an examination of the logic of the module. One basic criterion for a set of test cases is ensuring that they cause every instruction in the module to be executed at least once. This criterion is certainly necessary, but it is not the place to stop. A better criterion is to ensure that the tester has enough test cases so that every decision point in the module that leads to a multiway branch is executed in each direction at least once. This leads to an additional axiom for unit testing:

The minimum criteria for the unit test of any module is to execute all branches in all possible directions at least once.

The best way to start is to draw a flowchart or its equivalent of the module. To completely identify all unique branches it is necessary to account for the way the compiler will generate the object code for complex decisions. Figure 11.4 shows some examples of the proper way to view PL/I IF and DO statements when trying to identify all branch conditions.

Since we are only interested in the flow of execution through the program, an elaborate flowchart is unnecessary. A simpler way of analyzing branches is with a *flow diagram*: a directed graph that shows

Test case no.	Input	Expected output
1	ESTABLE all zeros.	MATCHCODE = 2 UNRESNAME unchanged
2	ESTB 001 A EP 00200	MATCHCODE = 0 UNRESNAME unchanged ESTABLE unchanged
3	ESTB 001 X ER null	MATCHCODE = 1 UNRESNAME = 'X' ESTABLE unchanged

4	ESTB 002
	ABCDEFGH ER null
	ABCDEFGH MD 44444
		MATCHCODE = 0
		UNRESNAME unchanged
		ESTABLE unchanged except
		  first entry addr field
		   = 44444

5	ESTB 006
	XX MD 00003
	Z ER null
	XX ER null
	XXXXXXXX ER null
	Z ER null
	Z EP 00022
		MATCHCODE = 1
		UNRESNAME = 'XXXXXXXX'
		ESTABLE unchanged except
		  second entry addr field
		   = 00022
		Third entry addr field
		   = 00003

Figure 11.3   **Initial test cases for MATCHES.**

the branching structure of the program. Each node (circle) in the graph represents a sequential segment of code (the sequences of statements that are only entered through the first statement and that fall between decision, or branch, points). The edges in the graph represent the execution flow connections between the code segments. A flow diagram for MATCHES is shown in Figure 11.5.

The flow diagram shows that there are 13 two-way branches. To determine if additional test cases are needed to exercise all 26 directions, a matrix is drawn and the current five test cases are plotted to

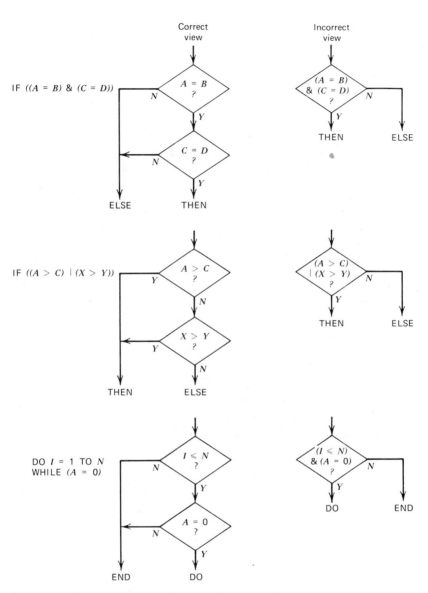

Figure 11.4 **Identifying paths in complex statements.**

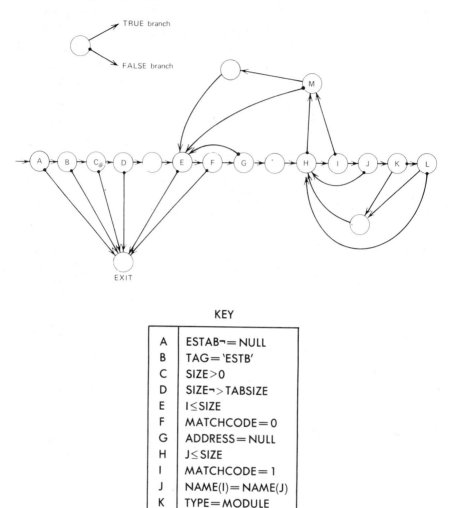

Figure 11.5   **Flow diagram for MATCHES.**

show which branches are executed. Note that since this involves walking each test case through the logic, the matrix could be developed during the code walk-through activity discussed in Chapter 8. The branch coverage matrix for MATCHES is shown in Figure 11.6.

Surprisingly (because this is not always the case), the matrix shows that only three branches have not been exercised. Three additional test cases must be added to cover these three conditions.

	Decision	Test cases				
		1	2	3	4	5
A	ESTAB¬=NULL	T	X	X	X	X	X
		F					
B	TAG='ESTB'	T		X	X	X	X
		F	X				
C	SIZE>0	T		X	X	X	X
		F					
D	SIZE¬>TABSIZE	T		X	X	X	X
		F					
E	I≤SIZE	T		X	X	X	X
		F		X	X	X	
F	MATCHCODE=0	T		X	X	X	X
		F					X
G	ADDRESS=NULL	T			X	X	X
		F		X		X	X
H	J≤SIZE	T			X	X	X
		F			X	X	X
I	MATCHCODE=1	T			X	X	X
		F					X
J	NAME(I)=NAME(J)	T			X	X	X
		F					X
K	TYPE=MODULE	T				X	X
		F			X	X	X
L	TYPE=ENTRYPT	T					X
		F			X	X	X
M	MATCHCODE=1	T			X		X
		F				X	X

Figure 11.6   **Branch coverage matrix.**

The third step is to examine the code to ensure that as many paths as possible are covered. MATCHES does not have a fixed number of paths; the number of paths it has is a function of the number, location, and content of the ESTABLE entries. Because of the two loops, MATCHES can have an astronomical number of paths, so attempting to test them all would be impossible. However, each loop should be inspected to see that it is executed at least zero, one, and the maximum number of times. By inspecting the two DO loops in MATCHES, the tester should see that it is impossible to execute the loops for zero iterations (SIZE is always greater than zero and the WHILE conditions are always initially true). The loops can be executed one time and the maximum (SIZE) number of times, but the existing test cases cover these conditions.

A further check can be made on logical expressions (e.g., an iterative DO loop with a WHILE clause or a complex IF test) to see that all possible logical combinations have been tested (e.g., a statement such as IF $((A=0)$ & $(B=4))$ has four combinations of conditions). Examination of the code for MATCHES shows that the current set of test cases satisfies this requirement.

The last design step is to inspect the logic for sensitivities to particular input values. Tests should also be added to try to force the module to overflow and underflow array boundaries and numerical limits.

MATCHES has a few data sensitivities that were mentioned in Chapter 8. If it encounters a module or entry-point entry with a null address field (a "never should occur" condition), it reacts by overlooking its null address and moves to the next entry. Also, MATCHES should not attempt to match an external reference that it already matched (i.e., having a non-null address field). Another test case is added to verify these conditions. Figure 11.7 shows the four test cases added as a result of examining the logic.

The steps for test case design may seem to be laborious, but no one has ever claimed that testing is easy. Following these steps will lead to a set of carefully designed test cases with a high error-detection yield. This process might take a few more hours than the haphazard process of selecting a few arbitrary test cases, but if it leads to the discovery of an occasional error or two then the extra time was well spent.

TEST EXECUTION

Once the test cases for the module have been designed, the next steps are the writing, testing, and execution of the test cases. As was

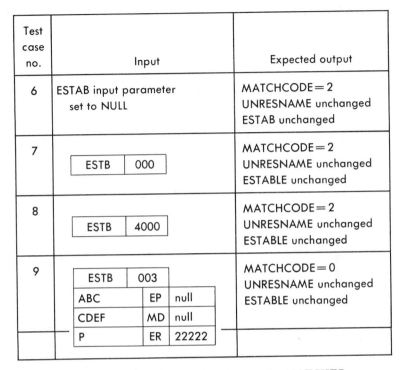

Test case no.	Input	Expected output
6	ESTAB input parameter set to NULL	MATCHCODE = 2 UNRESNAME unchanged ESTAB unchanged
7	ESTB 000	MATCHCODE = 2 UNRESNAME unchanged ESTABLE unchanged
8	ESTB 4000	MATCHCODE = 2 UNRESNAME unchanged ESTABLE unchanged
9	ESTB 003 ABC EP null CDEF MD null P ER 22222	MATCHCODE = 0 UNRESNAME unchanged ESTABLE unchanged

Figure 11.7   **Supplemental test cases for MATCHES.**

mentioned in Chapter 10, the physical form of the test cases depends on the module integration method. In the top-down methods the early test cases are written as unique sets of output data returned by stub modules, and the later test cases are written as external or user inputs. In the bottom-up methods or when testing a single module in isolation, the test cases take the form of a "module driver" program or test language statements to a module testing tool. In this section we assume that a module testing tool is not being used. The next section discusses these tools.

The process of writing test cases (as opposed to designing them) is quite straightforward and is only briefly presented. For instance, if a module driver program is needed, a small program is written to call the module being tested. Each test case is represented by a call to the module, passing it unique sets of input data. To ease the task of rerunning the tests in the future and to solve the problem of the "eye seeing what it wants to see," the tester should try to make the test cases self-checking. Rather than printing the output from each test, the output checking should be programmed into the driver program where possible; the driver program should simply report the success or failure of each test.

Ideally, test cases should be tested before they are actually used to test a program. Normally this is infeasible; the only way of checking the correctness of the test cases (other than by human inspection) is by actually executing the test cases against the program. However, one should keep in mind during the test that the test cases themselves may contain errors.

The critical part of test execution is the inspection of the output, either by using a program or doing it by eye. A common mistake is to spend many hours designing ingenious test cases, only to overlook errors because the test output only received a cursory glance. It is extremely important to study carefully the output of each test, looking for any sign of trouble. Again, it is vital to state the expected output before examining the actual output.

There are many types of errors that cannot be detected by just examining the module's outputs. These errors can be classified as erroneous side effects. A module might return the correct output parameters but also overwrite the input parameters, store some data in a random location in storage, or perform some other unwanted side effect. Certain computer architectures and programming languages reduce the probability of such errors, but some may go undetected and when they occur they are difficult to find. There are a few checks that can be made to detect certain side effects. If an input parameter is specified as being only an input (referenced but not altered), the tester should check to see that this is the case after each test. Figures 11.3 and 11.7 show that a number of data areas should be checked for the "unchanged" condition after each test of MATCHES. If possible, the tester should examine the storage immediately above and below each output area to detect "off-by-one" errors.

During the test, one must not forget the axioms in Chapter 10. Instead of testing the module that you coded, have the programmer of one of the calling modules test your module, or try the "buddy system" by swapping modules for unit testing with another programmer on the project. Avoid "on-the-fly" testing; never assume that a test case will be used only once. Never alter your program to make testing easier.

MODULE DRIVER TOOLS

Knowing that programming is a multibillion dollar industry, one would expect to find a high degree of automation such as a large variety of sophisticated program development tools to minimize the clerical and repetitive work that is part of every programmer's job. This is not the case; in fact, the programming industry is often accused of utilizing computers less than any other industry. This and the following sections describe a few steps in the right direction: programmed tools that aid the task of module testing. Some of the tools described are available in the marketplace; others are "in-house" developments. I have not attempted to provide a complete survey of all such tools, for such a survey would be immediately out of date. Instead, I have chosen a representative sample to give an idea of what has been accomplished.

Automated Unit Test (AUT) is a module driver tool that was developed for use within the IBM Corporation [1]. Its objectives are to ease the work involved in top-down and bottom-up testing methods by eliminating the need for driver programs and stubs, standardizing the form of unit test cases, making rerunning module tests (e.g., after a program modification) a trivial task, automating the verification of test case output, and being independent of the programming language used.

The major user interface is a language called MIL-S, which is used to describe the input data and expected output data for each test case. The programmer begins by encoding his test cases in the MIL-S language and storing this representation in a data base. To test the MATCHES module he would then type "AUT MATCHES" at the terminal, which causes AUT to select each MIL-S test case for MATCHES, compile the test case, and invoke the module. When the module completes execution, the expected output is compared to the actual output and any discrepancies are reported to the user.

MIL-S is a nonprocedural language for representing test cases. Test case 2 from Figure 11.3 would be represented by the following statements:

```
IN02        PARMLIST    ESTAB,UNRNAME,MCODE;
ESTAB       PTR         ESTABLE;
UNRNAME     DATA        (8) ('   ');
MCODE       DATA        (2) IGNORE;
ESTABLE     DATA        (4) ('ESTB');
SIZE        DATA        (2) ('1'D);
            DATA        (8) ('A');
            DATA        (2) ('EP');
            PTR         ESTABLE; TO GIVE ADDR FIELD
   *                    ANY NON-NULL VALUE
OUT02       COPY;
MCODE       DATA        (2) ('0'D); EXPECT NO UNMATCHED
   *                    ITEMS
```

The input and output sections of each test case are compiled separately to generate an input storage structure to pass to the module being tested and an expected output storage structure to use in verifying the actual output. The input section above should be self-explanatory (the word IGNORE states that the value of this item is not significant). The word COPY in the output section is a shortcut specifying that the MIL-S statements for the input section are to be copied into the output section before compilation. Any additional statements in the output section (in this case MCODE) replace the corresponding copied statements or are inserted if there is no corresponding statement. This is an easy way to include checking for unchanged input data as part of the output verification.

For this test case AUT will verify the following conditions after execution of the module:

1. The parameter list contains three parameters.
2. The first parameter is a pointer. This parameter points to a sequential storage structure with the characters ESTB in the first four bytes, the value 1 in the next two bytes, an A followed by seven blanks in the next eight bytes, the characters EP in the next two bytes, and the address of ESTABLE (representing any non-null address) in the last four bytes.
3. The second parameter is an eight-byte string of blanks (to verify that UNRNAME is unchanged).
4. The third parameter is a two-byte field with the value zero.

If any discrepancy is found, the user is notified of the precise data item in error and given its expected and actual values. Program check interruptions within the module being tested are trapped by AUT. An interesting design consideration in the AUT program is that AUT can itself program check when verifying the test output (e.g., when following an erroneous pointer variable). When this occurs, it is never seen by the user. AUT remembers what data area it was examining at the time of the program check, intercepts the program check, and reports that this area is in error.

When AUT is used for bottom-up testing, all modules below the module being tested in the program structure are automatically loaded when the AUT command is entered. For top-down testing, AUT provides a simulation facility to solve some of the difficulties in using stub modules. The MATCHES function calls no other modules, but suppose, for the sake of illustration, that MATCHES calls another module named INVERT. To simulate INVERT one could place the statement

INVERT CALL IN07;

within the input section of the test case for MATCHES. This statement directs AUT to perform the following actions. When MATCHES calls INVERT, AUT intercepts the call. It searches the data base for test case 07 for INVERT and compiles the test case (AUT is a recursive program). AUT determines if the input currently being passed by MATCHES to INVERT is identical to the input specified in INVERT's test case 07, and, if so, AUT sets up the corresponding output section as if INVERT had actually executed and then returns control to MATCHES. Not only does this eliminate the need for stubs, but it also allows one to specify a different simulation of the nonexistent module in each test case.

A tool with many similar concepts is the Module Testing System (MTS), marketed by Management Systems and Programming Limited. MTS will operate on most IBM 360/370 and ICL systems and can test modules written in assembly language, COBOL, PL/I, or FORTRAN.

MTS test cases are written in a language analogous to the MIL-S language in AUT. Language statements include a PARAMETER statement for defining data areas, a TEST statement for initiating a test execution, a PRINT COMPARE statement for verifying test results, and a SIMULATE statement for simulating the output of nonexistent modules. A test case for a module FINDMEAN that computes the mean of three numbers would appear as:

```
PARAMETER   X       6 CORE
PARAMETER   Y       6 CORE
PARAMETER   Z       6 CORE
PARAMETER   MEAN    6 CORE
X           D(6)       1230.0
Y           D(6)       2722.00
Z           D(6)       1502.00
EXP-MEAN    D(6)       1818.00
TEST        FINDMEAN X Y Z MEAN
PRINT COMPARE MEAN EXP-MEAN
```

A third module driver tool is TESTMASTER, which can be leased from Hoskyns Inc. and is oriented toward the testing of COBOL programs running on an IBM 360/370 system. Test cases are written in a COBOL-like language and submitted to a preprocessor, which converts the language to standard COBOL and compiles it. No automatic verification of the output is performed; the output of the test is a core dump that must be manually checked by the programmer.

STATIC FLOW ANALYSIS

Another area of module testing that can be automated is a static analysis of the source program (the word "static" implies that this analysis is done without actually executing the program). For instance, it should be possible to write a program that analyzes a module and draws its flow diagram (e.g., the diagram in Figure 11.5). This analysis program could also enumerate all possible paths through the module and analyze the module for error conditions such as using a data area before it is initialized.

One such tool is ASES (Automated Software Evaluation System) [2]. ASES analyzes the source program and represents it internally as a directed graph. From this graph ASES deduces certain structural characteristics of the program and reports them to the user. The report includes a list of all loops, a list of all statements that can never be executed, and a list of error-prone constructs such as branching to the middle of a DO loop.

An aid that is available for the testing of FORTRAN programs is RXVP, produced by General Research Corporation [3]. RXVP starts by developing and printing a directed graph of the program. It also produces a list of potential errors such as the use of a variable before it is assigned, inconsistencies between subroutine arguments and parameters, and denominators that can potentially become zero.

RUN-TIME TOOLS

The remaining set of module test tools are tools that interact with the program during its execution. Their primary purpose is to measure *test coverage*: the degree to which the test cases exercise the program's logic. Some tools simply monitor each subroutine to count the number of times it is called. Other tools indicate the number of times each source statement is executed. More sophisticated tools indicate whether each conditional branch is executed in all directions. Most of these tools obtain these statistics by inserting probes or traps at each branch point in the program being monitored.

The more sophisticated tools also keep *cumulative* statistics about the program in a data base or file. Although this is unnecessary for module testing because all test cases for a module are usually executed at one time, it is important for function and system testing when the testing process is spread over several weeks or months. The cumulative statistics allow one to determine what logic has not yet been exercised at various times in the testing process.

Two products that perform run-time monitoring are IBM's PL/I Checkout and Optimizing compilers. They contain a COUNT option that reports at the end of the execution on the number of times each statement was executed. Another product, Applied Data Research's MetaCOBOL, will report on the number of times each COBOL paragraph is executed. National Computing Industries' Series-J package produces a report showing all statements in a COBOL program that were not executed in a test run.

A more sophisticated aid for FORTRAN programs is PET (Program Evaluator and Tester) [4]. PET shows the number of times each statement was executed and, more importantly, it indicates how many times each conditional branch (e.g., an IF or computed GO TO statement) was executed in each direction. PET contains an unusual feature for debugging purposes: it monitors the results of all assignment statements and iteration variables in DO statements and prints the first, last, minimum, and maximum values of all variables.

The ASES tool mentioned earlier also performs run-time monitoring. Given a list of variables and their specified upper and lower bounds, ASES will monitor all changes to the variables and report all occurrences of a variable going outside of the bounds. TRW Corporation has developed a second aid called PACE (Product Assurance Confidence Evaluator) that counts the number of times each statement and subroutine is executed [5]. This counting is cumulative and maintained on a file.

The RXVP aid mentioned earlier also performs run-time monitoring. It reports on statement execution counts, the number of executions of each outcome of decision statements, and the minimum, maximum, and average values of each assignment statement result. RXVP supplies both cumulative statistics and statistics for each individual run.

A word of caution is in order for the reader who is considering developing his own testing aids. Many organizations attempt to develop their own testing aids and, although the concepts are often good, the aids are poorly accepted by programmers. The major problem plaguing most test tools is poor human factors. A designer in the position of developing a new test tool should pay particular care to its human factors design. The major human factors problem in testing aids is the production of too much printed output, resulting in the programmer's having to read through pages and pages of reports to locate the single result in which he is interested. For instance, most run-time monitors produce a listing of the source code with several added columns showing the execution count of each statement. This may be acceptable for module testing, but it is cumbersome when testing an entire program or system where one is more interested in knowing what has not been executed. Monitors that maintain cumulative statistics should be able to produce a concise report showing only those branch directions that have not been exercised.

QUADRATIC EQUATION TESTS

For the reader who tried to develop the test cases earlier in the chapter for the module that solves quadratic equations, the test cases developed by Gruenberger [6] are listed below.

1. $A=0$, $B=0$, $C=0$. In this case the equation becomes $0=0$ and cannot be solved for X. Did you try this test case to examine the module's behavior under this input?
2. $A=0$, $B=0$, $C=10$. This represents the equation $10=0$, which is not a valid equation. This is an interesting test of an invalid input condition.
3. $A=0$, $B=5$, $C=17$. This equation $(5X+17=0)$ is not a quadratic equation. How does the module handle it? It is also likely that this test may detect an attempt to divide by zero.
4. $A=6$, $B=1$, $C=2$. This is one of several normal cases that you should have checked. Did you remember to state the expected output for each test case?
5. $A=3$, $B=7$, $C=0$. Another "normal" test case. It checks the circumstance where one root is zero.
6. $A=3$, $B=2$, $C=5$. Did you recall that quadratic equations can have complex roots?
7. $A=7$, $B=0$, $C=0$. This is a test to see if the module can take the square root of zero.
8. Other useful test cases are ones that explore the arithmetic limits and precision of the module.

REFERENCES

1. C. A. Heuermann, G. J. Myers, and J. H. Winterton, "Automated Test and Verification," *IBM Technical Disclosure Bulletin*, **17** (7), 2030–2035 (1974).

2. R. E. Meeker and C. V. Ramamoorthy, "A Study in Software Reliability and Evaluation," Tech. Memo. No. 39, Electronics Research Center, University of Texas at Austin, Austin, Texas, 1973.

3. *RXVP User's Guide*, RM-1942, General Research Corp., Santa Barbara, Cal., 1975.

4. L. G. Stucki, "Automatic Generation of Self-Metric Software," *Record of the 1973 IEEE Symposium on Computer Software Reliability*. New York: IEEE, 1973, pp. 94–100.

5. J. R. Brown, A. J. DeSalvio, D. E. Heine, and J. G. Purdy, "Automated Software Quality Assurance," in W. C. Hetzel, Ed., *Program Test Methods*. Englewood Cliffs, N.J.: Prentice-Hall, 1973, pp. 181–203.

6. F. Gruenberger, "Program Testing and Validation," *DATAMATION*, **14** (7), 39–47 (1968).

CHAPTER 12

Function and
System Testing

After module testing has been performed and
the integration or interface testing that is an
inherent part of five of the six module integration approaches has been completed, the testing
process is only just beginning. The program or
system has yet to be tested against its external
specification (function testing), its objectives
(system testing), its requirements (acceptance
testing), and to determine whether it has been
installed properly (installation testing).

EXTERNAL FUNCTION TESTING

The purpose of the function test is to find
discrepancies between the program and its
external specification. The prerequisite for a
successful function test is a precise and
accurate external specification. If the external
specification is incomplete or ambiguous, then
the function test cannot but end up being the
same.

To design function test cases, the external
specification is usually segmented into individual external functions (e.g., each type of
input transaction or user command), and test
cases are derived by careful examination of
each function. In doing this, most of the module

test case design guidelines discussed in Chapter 11 can be applied to function testing. For instance, test cases should be developed for all input conditions and options and at the boundaries of all input domains and output ranges. Test cases should also probe the program's behavior at functional boundaries and for invalid or unexpected inputs. A methodology for test case design called *cause–effect graphing* is discussed in the next section.

Tools exist that automatically generate test cases, but they usually should be avoided. For instance, the IEBDG utility program [1] could be used to generate a stream of deposit transactions for a banking system with varying account numbers and dollar amounts. However, this type of "brute force" testing is not productive for several reasons: the test cases tend to have a low error-detection yield and the testing usually violates one of the fundamental axioms that dictates prediction of the expected results of each test case. Without predicting the expected output beforehand, the tester is unlikely to see errors that occur (except for the obvious ones such as program interruptions).

As was the case for unit test cases, function test cases should not be "throw-away" tests. Each test case should be documented (e.g., set-up instructions and expected results) and made self-checking where feasible. It is also a good idea to weight each test case in terms of its relative importance. This allows a small percentage of the test cases to be designated as *regression tests*: test cases that will always be run in the future after every modification and correction to the program.

Function testing is a *verification* process because it is usually performed in a test environment (as opposed to a live environment). In other words, function testing is usually performed on pieces of the system before the entire system has been constructed. For instance, certain input/output devices may not be available, requiring that special programs be written to simulate their operation, or particular software components may be incomplete or missing, requiring the use of simulation or "scaffolding" code.

The proper point on the philosophy spectrum (Figure 10.3) for function testing is toward the left-hand (black-box) side. Test cases should initially be derived from the external specification without regard to the program's internal structure or logic. However, the program should be monitored during function testing to determine the coverage of conditional branches.

The minimum criterion for function testing is to execute all branches at least once in each direction except for those branches representing defensive programming.

A run-time monitor that keeps cumulative coverage statistics should be used during the function test. If any branch directions are not exercised, the appropriate test cases must be added. This implies that conditions such as invalid inputs and input/output errors must be generated. The only exceptions are branch directions that are executed only in the presence of software errors (i.e., defensive programming checks). A reasonable strategy is to rely just on unit testing for the verification of defensive logic.

CAUSE–EFFECT GRAPHING

Cause–effect graphing [2, 3], a technique that resides on the left extreme of the philosophy spectrum, is a method for transforming a natural-language specification into a formal-language specification. This process produces a design of nonredundant high-yield test cases, as well as a side benefit of finding incomplete and ambiguous points in the original specification as mentioned in Chapter 4.

The technique involves analyzing the semantic content of the external specification and restating it as a logic relationship between inputs (causes) and outputs and transformations (effects) in a boolean graph called a *cause–effect graph*. The graph is annotated with any syntactical rules and environmental constraints and then converted to a limited-entry decision table. Each column in the decision table represents a test case to be written.

To describe the cause–effect graph technique its use is first illustrated on an example. The first step in the technique is segmenting the external specification into single functions whose combinatorial properties are to be tested. The specification fragment in Figure 12.1 will serve as the example. Note that the specification has been simplified slightly to make it "textbook" sized.

The second step is to analyze the specification to identify all explicit and implicit causes (input conditions) and effects (output actions). The best way to do this is to underline each cause and effect as it is encountered in reading the specification. Each cause and effect is given an arbitrary unique number. The causes and effects for this example are listed below:

Cause 1. The first nonblank character following the "C" and one or more blanks is a "/".

Cause 2. The command contains exactly two "/" characters.

Cause 3. String1 has length one.

3.4 The CHANGE Subcommand

The CHANGE subcommand is used to modify a character string in the "current line" of the file being edited.

3.4.1 Inputs

The syntax of the subcommand is:

C /string1/string2

String1 represents the character string you want to replace. It can be from 1 through 30 characters long and can contain any characters except "/". String2 represents the character string that is to replace string1. It can be from 0 through 30 characters long and can contain any characters except "/". If string2 is omitted (zero length), string1 is simply deleted.

At least one blank must follow the command name "C".

3.4.2 Outputs

The changed line is printed on the terminal if the command is successful. If the change cannot be made because string1 cannot be found in the current line, the message "NOT FOUND" is printed. If the command syntax is incorrect, the message "INVALID SYNTAX" is printed.

3.4.3 System Transformations

If the syntax is valid and string1 can be found in the current line, then string1 is removed from the line and string2 is inserted in its place. The line is expanded or contracted as necessary based on the length differences between string1 and string2. If the command syntax is invalid, or if string1 cannot be found in the current line, the line is not changed.

Figure 12.1 **Specification to be graphed.**

Cause 4. String1 has length 30.
Cause 5. String1 has length 2–29.
Cause 6. String2 has length zero.
Cause 7. String2 has length 30.
Cause 8. String2 has length 1–29.
Cause 9. The current line contains an occurrence of string1.

Effect 31. The changed line is typed.
Effect 32. The first occurrence of string1 in the current line is replaced by string2.

Effect 33.   NOT FOUND printed.
Effect 34.   INVALID SYNTAX printed.

This command can have an astronomical number of variations because string1 and string2 taken together have 30 × 31 valid combinations of lengths and each character in the strings can be one of about 80 terminal characters. Causes 3–8 represent a compromise; they imply that we are primarily interested in the length boundaries and that (hopefully) the command is insensitive to the actual characters in string1 and string2. Effect 32 shows that an ambiguity has already been discovered in the specification. The specification did not explicitly state what happens when multiple occurrences of string1 appear in the line. It should have stated that only the *first* occurrence of string1 in the line is changed.

The third step is to draw the cause–effect graph. The causes are drawn as nodes on the left side of a sheet of paper and the effects are drawn on the right side. The causes and effects are joined in a structure of logical relationships using the primitive relationships shown in Figure 12.2. Intermediate nodes are used where necessary to express more

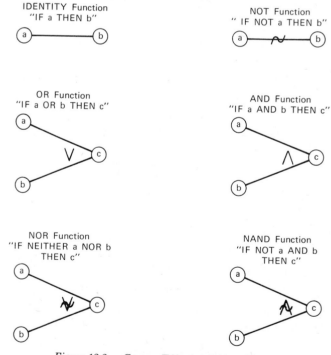

Figure 12.2   **Cause–Effect relationships.**

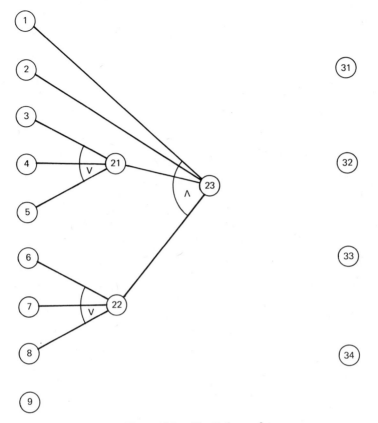

Figure 12.3   **Partial graph.**

complicated relationships (e.g., effect M is present under the condition: cause A AND (cause B OR cause C)). In boolean terms, causes and effects can have two states: zero (meaning suppressed or absent) and one (meaning invoked or present).

Figure 12.3 shows a partially completed form of the graph. The nine causes and four effects have been represented as nodes 1–9 and 31–34. Intermediate nodes 21 and 22 represent the conditions of syntactically valid string1 and string2 operands. Intermediate node 23 represents the condition of a syntactically valid command.

Figure 12.4 shows the completed graph. This graph represents a formal statement of the natural-language specification in Figure 12.1. During the process of completing the graph, specification errors are often discovered such as encountering a cause or combination of causes with no apparent effect or encountering an effect with no corresponding causes.

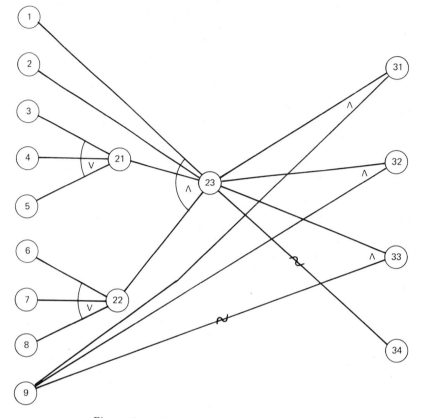

Figure 12.4   **Complete cause–effect graph.**

It is likely that in any graph certain combinations of causes and effects are impossible because of syntactical or environmental constraints. Such constraints should be added to the graph to eliminate impossible test conditions. Figure 12.5 describes additional primitive relationships that are added to the graph as needed. The *exclusive, inclusive, one-only-one,* and *requires* constraints are used to describe relationships among causes. The *masks* constraint is used to describe a relationship among effects where the presence of one effect forces the masking or suppression of another effect.

Figure 12.6 shows the final graph with all constraints added. Causes 3, 4, and 5 are mutually exclusive because string1 can have only one length in any single command. Causes 3, 4, and 5 are *not* described by the one-only-one constraint because the string1 length could be less than one or greater than 30. The same constraint applies to causes 6, 7, and 8.

The remaining step is to convert the graph into a limited-entry decision table. This is started by selecting an effect and writing down all combinations of causes that generate that effect and then also writing down the states of all other effects under those combinations of causes. The first nine columns in Figure 12.7 represent the combinations of causes that generate effect 31.

The next effect to be studied is effect 32. However, the graph shows that effect 32 is generated by the same conditions that generate effect 31, so effect 32 has already been accounted for.

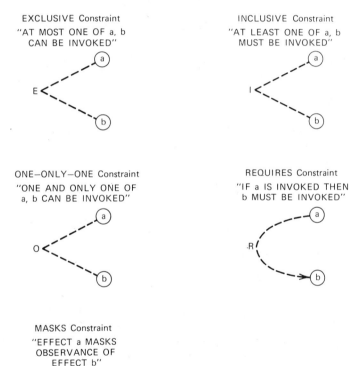

Figure 12.5   **Cause–effect constraints.**

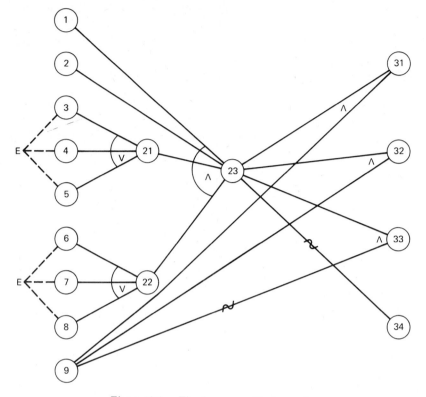

Figure 12.6   **Final cause–effect graph.**

Effect 33 can be generated by nine new combinations represented by columns 10–18. The last effect, effect 34, is present whenever intermediate node 23 is a "zero." This occurs if any of nodes 1, 2, 21, or 22 are zero. We could represent this by four columns where, in each column, one of the nodes 1, 2, 21, or 22 is set to zero and all other causes are set to a "don't care" state (i.e., their states are irrelevant). However, the yield of the test cases can be improved by *path sensitizing.* This principle states that when one of several causes can generate a single effect, the columns should be designed so that only one of these causes generates the effect. For instance, if we suppressed causes 1 and 2 simultaneously, we might not detect an error where the program is checking one condition but not the other. Hence columns 19–22 are arranged so that only the state of a single cause generates effect 34.

Figure 12.7 represents the test cause design. It describes the input

Causes / Effects	1	2	3	4	5	6	7	8	9	10	11	12	13	14	15	16	17	18	19	20	21	22
1	I	I	I	I	I	I	I	I	I	I	I	I	I	I	I	I	I	I	I	I	I	S
2	I	I	I	I	I	I	I	I	I	I	I	I	I	I	I	I	I	I	I	I	S	I
3	I	I	I	S	S	S	S	S	S	I	I	I	S	S	S	S	S	S	S	S	S	S
4	S	S	S	I	I	I	S	S	S	S	S	S	I	I	I	S	S	S	S	S	S	S
5	S	S	S	S	S	S	I	I	I	S	S	S	S	S	S	I	I	I	S	I	I	I
6	I	S	S	I	S	S	I	S	S	I	S	S	I	S	S	I	S	S	S	S	S	S
7	S	I	S	S	I	S	S	I	S	S	I	S	S	I	S	S	I	S	S	S	S	S
8	S	S	I	S	S	I	S	S	I	S	S	I	S	S	I	S	S	I	I	S	I	I
9	I	I	I	I	I	I	I	I	I	I	S	S	S	S	S	S	S	S	X	X	X	X
31	P	P	P	P	P	P	P	P	P	P	A	A	A	A	A	A	A	A	A	A	A	A
32	P	P	P	P	P	P	P	P	P	P	A	A	A	A	A	A	A	A	A	A	A	A
33	A	A	A	A	A	A	A	A	A	A	P	P	P	P	P	P	P	P	A	A	A	A
34	A	A	A	A	A	A	A	A	A	A	A	A	A	A	A	A	A	A	P	P	P	P

(Causes = rows 1–9; Effects = rows 31–34)

S: Suppressed
I: Invoked
X: Don't care
A: Absent
P: Present

Figure 12.7 **Decision table representation of the graph.**

conditions and expected output for each of 22 test cases. Notice that the process produces a number of test cases that is significantly less than the brute force approach of trying all combinations of causes. There are 512 combinations of causes (nine causes, each in one of two states) but this has been reduced to only 22 meaningful cases. If the tester did not use cause–effect graphing, he might start by identifying all 512 combinations and then cutting this number down to 20 or 30 because of time pressures. However, he probably does this in an ad hoc manner, meaning that his 20 or 30 tests represent a less than optimal subset. The advantage of the cause–effect approach is its identification of a limited number of high-yield test cases.

By applying some intuition to the decision table we could reduce this number further if necessary. Tests 10–18 define test cases for the condition of string1 not being found in the file's current line. Intuition might tell us that the program is insensitive to string2 (causes 6–8) in this situation. Hence a combination of the test cases such as cases 11, 12, 14, 15, 17, and 18 probably have a low error-detection yield and could be eliminated, reducing the number of test cases to 16. This type of economic tradeoff (corresponding to the axiom that part of the art of testing is knowing when to stop) is often needed when the cause–effect graph leads to a large number of potential test cases. In this event priorities should be set for each test case based on estimates of its detection yield, the cost to produce the test case, and the significance to the user of an error under this condition, and the test cases with a low priority can be discarded if economics must prevail.

Analysis of the Technique

Cause–effect graphing reinforces several of the testing axioms discussed in Chapters 10 and 11. Predicting the expected results of each test case is an inherent part of the technique. The absent state of effects encourages the tester to look for erroneous side effects. For instance, test cases 10–18 state that effect 32 should be checked for the absent state (i.e., that the current line was not altered) in addition to checking for the presence of the "NOT FOUND" message.

Cause–effect graphing does have a few shortcomings. It does not "invent" highly destructive test cases, so the test cases that it produces should be supplemented with additional test cases based on the tester's suspicions, intuition, and ingenuity. The tests in Figure 12.7 should be supplemented with test cases that include special characters such as tab and back-space characters in string1 and string2 and test cases that place the matching string at the very beginning and end of the current line. Cause–effect graphs can only express combinatorial relationships among causes. They cannot handle such situations as time delays, iterative functions, and feedback loops from effects to causes.

Several experimental programs have been developed within IBM to process cause–effect graphs so that the burden of analyzing the graph and producing the decision table is lifted from the programmers' shoulders [2]. These programs use electronic circuit design and graph minimization algorithms to produce an optimal set of test cases.

To summarize, cause–effect graphing is a rigorous way of transforming a natural-language specification into a more formal specification. It produces a test case design that is much more economical than any brute force or ad hoc method and has an additional benefit of locating ambiguities in the specification. People that have used it often feel that it is too difficult and time consuming, but to repeat the statement in Chapter 11, no one has ever claimed that testing is easy. Cause–effect graphing is hard work, but it is worth it.

SYSTEM INTEGRATION

For most projects the six approaches described in Chapter 10 are the only methods needed to construct a system from its parts (modules). However, there are unique types of projects where these six approaches are not sufficient. These projects may be characterized as projects involving the development of extremely large systems and projects where portions of the system are being developed in different geographical locations or by different subcontracting companies. These projects lead to a special set of logistical, planning, and control problems.

Build Planning

The integration process for such a project starts with a *build* or *integration plan*, detailing how, by whom, where, and when the system will be built from its individual components. The primary purpose of the build plan is to specify the process of incrementally piecing the system together. Each incremental version or level of the system is referred to as a *spin* (the term *driver* is often used, but it could be confused with the module drivers discussed in Chapter 11). Spin 0 denotes the "empty" version of the system on which all following spins are constructed. For a new application system spin 0 might simply contain the host operating system. If the objective of the project is to produce a new release of an operating system, spin 0 contains the previous release of the system. Spin N denotes the last spin: the completed system.

The build plan specifies, among other things, the number of spins and their schedules and functional content. Deciding on the number of spins is a key consideration in the process. At one extreme there is only one spin (analogous to the "big-bang" approach) and at the other extreme there may be a new spin constructed every day, where a spin differs from the previous spin by as little as the addition of one module. Evidence now points toward the latter case as being more desirable. The latter philosophy is known as *continuous integration.* Continuous integration implies that spins are constructed on a frequent basis, perhaps daily or at most weekly. Each spin differs from the previous spin by only a small amount, making debugging easier and allowing one to "back out" any new functions that are not behaving correctly.

As an example of the benefits of continuous integration, each release of IBM's huge OS/360 operating system was built with a few massive spins. Some releases were built with only one spin, meaning that literally thousands of modules were simultaneously hammered together. Other releases were built with four spins. The spins were built about two months apart and each spin contained hundreds or even thousands of added modules. Several significant problems became apparent with this approach. Each build was immense, leading to lost modules, logistical foul-ups, and the loss of many weeks in getting each spin just barely operational. Debugging was difficult because of the large amounts of code being mated together for the first time. Fixes to errors were delayed because the corrections were grouped together and applied to the system on infrequent intervals.

Continuous integration was introduced to OS in the first release of OS/VS2. Spins were constructed on almost a daily basis. The fact that this was the first release of OS to be completed ahead of schedule is largely attributed to the continuous integration concept.

The build plan is dependent on subdividing the system into *integration units.* An integration unit reflects the set of modules that a development organization will integrate into a particular spin. An integration unit is normally some system function that is larger than a single module but smaller than a subsystem. The major part of the build planning process is the identification and scheduling of the integration units. This planning effort requires significant technical and negotiating skills and is driven by the following factors:

1. The build plan is constrained to some degree by the resources and schedules of the development organizations.
2. The integration sequence should be arranged so that a skeletal working version of the system is constructed in an early spin.
3. The integration sequence should be arranged so that all critical functions are integrated in early spins.
4. Integration units will have *dependencies* on other integration units (e.g., the deposit transaction handler will be dependent on certain data base manager functions). The integration sequence must be arranged with these dependencies in mind.
5. In all but the final spin, pieces of the system are missing. These missing pieces often must be simulated by specially written programs called *scaffold code* (analogous to the concept of a *stub module*). The build plan must attempt to minimize the scaffold code needed.

The build plan should be specified so that each module in the system is integrated *only once* (except for corrections of errors). If this seems impossible, either something is wrong with the system design or else the identification of the integration units is incorrect. Because of its relationships to the plans and schedules of the development organizations, the build plan must be established at an early date, certainly before any coding begins.

Another key element of the build plan is some measurable *ship criterion,* such as stating that the quality of each integration unit must be such that no more than two errors per 1000 code statements will be discovered after the integration unit is integrated. This often raises some eyebrows because there is no way that the development organizations can measure this at the time of integration. Even so this does have a positive psychological effect. Because the development organizations know that they will be publicly measured to this criterion, it creates an atmosphere of healthy competition and has a positive effect on their design and testing activities.

Build Control

The remaining part of system integration is the process of actually constructing each spin. The key to this activity is *control.* The integration organization must know precisely what is contained in each level of the system. The only way to make any change to the system is through an integration unit or a formal error-correction process. All error corrections should take the form of source code replacements of an entire module. Other types of changes such as "superzaps" (object code patches) or "update cards" (source code patches) must be prohibited. Even the integration organization itself should be prohibited from changing the system. It an error is encountered the integration organization should remove the entire integration unit from the system if necessary and formally notify the development organization.

The integration organization has the responsibility of maintaining the current spin of the system in controlled libraries, approving all changes (which includes examining the source code of all fixes), building each spin, documenting the use and restrictions of each spin, and supplying each spin to the development organizations. The integration organization initially supplies spin 0 and then waits for all integration units planned for the next spin. It adds the integration units to the previous spin (thus creating the new spin), adds any necessary scaffold code, *regression tests* the new spin to ensure that the system has not regressed, and then distributes the new spin to the development groups. After the final spin has been created the system is ready for system testing.

Each development group is performing the following steps in synchronization with the integration group. The development group unit tests and integration tests the modules to be integrated in the next spin. It then installs these modules on its local copy of the previous spin and performs function testing. These modules are shipped to the integration group and the process is repeated for the next spin. When the last spin is available, the development group should rerun its function test cases in parallel with the system test.

One remaining consideration is ensuring that each development group discards its copy of the previous spin as soon as a new spin becomes available. This ensures that all organizations are using copies of the same and latest version of the system.

SYSTEM TESTING

System testing is probably the most misunderstood form of testing. What system testing is *not* is the testing of all functions of the completely integrated system; this type of testing is called function testing. System testing is the process of trying to find discrepancies between the system and its original objectives. The items involved in a system test are the system itself, the product objectives, and all documentation that will be supplied with the system. The external specification, which was a key part of function testing, plays only a minor role in system testing.

In Chapter 4 the importance of writing measurable objectives was stressed. Part of the rationale for this should have been obvious at that time: measurable objectives are necessary to provide guidance to the design processes. The remainder of the rationale should be apparent now. If the objectives are stated in such terms as that the system should be adequately fast, quite reliable, and reasonably secure, then there is no way that one can test the system to these objectives.

If you do not have written objectives for your product, or if your objectives are unmeasurable, then you cannot perform a system test.

System testing is a process of both verification and validation. System testing is a validation process when it is done in the end-users' actual environment or when it is done in an environment that is constructed to resemble the users' environment. However, this luxury is often unavailable for several reasons and in these cases system testing is a verification process (i.e., performed in a simulated or test environment). For instance, if the system is an onboard spacecraft computer or an antiballistic missile system, a live environment (launching a real spacecraft or firing a real missile at your system) is usually out of the question. In addition, as will be seen later, certain types of system tests are economically infeasible in a live environment and are best performed in a simulated environment.

System Test Case Design

Of the types of testing discussed so far, system testing requires the most creativity. Designing good system test cases requires even more ingenuity than that required to design the system. There are no easy guidelines such as conditional branch coverage or cause–effect graphing for system testing. However, the following 14 categories outline the kinds of tests that may be necessary:

1. *Load/stress* testing. A common failure of large systems is that they seem to function correctly under light or moderate loads, but they quickly come to a halt under the heavy loads and stresses of a live environment. Load and stress testing attempts to subject the system to extreme pressures such as attempting to simultaneously log-on 100 terminals to a time-sharing system, saturating a banking system with a heavy load of input transactions, or subjecting a process-control system to a barrage of emergency signals from all of its processes.
   One reason that load/stress testing is omitted (other than the

obvious logistical problems, which are discussed in a later section), is that the test personnel, although they admit the tests might be useful, have a feeling that these high-stress conditions will never occur in the real environment. This feeling is rarely correct. For instance, there *are* occasions where every user of a time-sharing system is trying to log-on at the same time (e.g., after the system has failed for a minute or two and has just been restored). Banking systems that support consumer terminals have peak loads at the beginning of shopping hours and during the lunch hour. Better stress testing of the Apollo software might have prevented the overload situation that occurred during the landing of Apollo 11.

2. *Volume testing.* While load/stress testing attempts to subject the system to heavy loads in a short time span, volume testing attempts to expose the system to massive amounts of data over a longer time period. If the system processes multivolume tape or disk files, volume testing feeds the system enough data to force it from one volume to another. A compiler would be fed a ridiculously large source program to compile. A text-formatting program would be fed a massive document to format. An operating system's job queue would be filled to capacity. The intent of volume testing is to show that the system or program cannot handle the amounts of data specified in the objectives.

3. *Configuration testing.* Many systems such as operating systems and file-management systems support a large variety of hardware and software configurations. This number is often too large to allow testing of every possible configuration. However, at the very least the maximum and minimum configurations should be tested. The system should be tested with every hardware device it supports and every other system or program with which it has to communicate. If the software system itself can be configured (i.e., the customer selects only certain parts or options of the system to install), then each software configuration must be tested.

4. *Compatibility testing.* Most systems that are developed are not completely new; they represent improvements to a previous version of the system or replacements for earlier outdated systems. In these cases the system probably has compatibility objectives stating that the user interface in the previous version must remain intact in the new system. For instance, a new release of an operating system might have objectives stating that the job control language, terminal language, and compiled application programs that were used in the past can be used without change on the new release. These compatibility objectives must be tested. As has been

repeatedly emphasized for all other forms of testing, the intent of compatibility testing is to expose incompatibilities.

5. *Security testing.* Because of the increasing concern for privacy in today's automated society, most systems have security objectives. For instance, an operating system must prevent all users and programs from spying on another user's data or programs. A management information system must prevent a junior executive from obtaining his superior's salary. The intent of security testing is to break the system's security. One technique is to hire a professional penetration team: a group of people with expertise in subverting system security measures.

6. *Storage testing.* Many systems have storage objectives stating the amounts of main and secondary storage used by the system under different conditions. Test cases should be written to attempt to prove that the system does not achieve these objectives.

7. *Performance testing.* Performance or efficiency objectives such as response times and throughput rates under a variety of workloads and configurations are an important part of most system designs. In relation to the other types of system testing, a lot is known about performance testing and there are entire books devoted to the subject [4].

8. *Installability testing.* Many systems unfortunately have complicated procedures for installation. For instance, there are firms that specialize in installing IBM's OS/360 for a fee. Testing the installation process of a system is vital, for one of the most discouraging situations a customer faces is not even being able to install the new system.

9. *Reliability/Availability testing.* A key part of the system test is the attempt to prove that the system does not meet its original reliability objectives such as mean-time-to-failure, goals for the number of errors, and functions for the detection, correction, and/or tolerance of software and/or hardware errors. Reliability testing is extremely difficult, yet efforts should be made to test as many of these objectives as possible. For instance, errors (both hardware and software) can be purposely injected into the system to test the detection, correction, and tolerance functions. Other types of reliability objectives are almost impossible to test. If the system has a 250-hour mean-time-to-failure objective, one has to operate the system for periods much greater than 250 hours to statistically establish that this objective has been met. Showing that the system will contain at its time of delivery more software errors than the stated objective is impossible, for if you could count the number of

remaining software errors, you could correct them. Chapter 18 discusses some primitive techniques that can be used to compare the system with these objectives.

10. *Recovery testing.* An important part of the objectives for such systems as operating systems or data base and data communications systems is a set of goals for system recovery functions such as recovering lost data in a data base or recovering from a telecommunications line failure. In many projects testing of these recovery functions is completely overlooked. System testing is the proper time to attempt to show that these functions do not work correctly.

11. *Serviceability testing.* In either the product or project objectives, goals should have been listed for the serviceability or maintainability characteristics of the system. All service aids in the system such as dump programs, trace programs, and diagnostic messages must be tested during the system test. Any internal logic publications should be examined from the service personnel's point of view to judge how quickly and accurately they can pinpoint the cause of an error given only some symptoms of the error. All maintenance procedures supplied with the system must also be tested.

12. *Publications testing.* Checking the accuracy of all user documentation is an important part of system testing. All system test cases should be derived using only the user documentation for source material. In particular, all examples shown in the user documentation should be checked for correctness.

13. *Human factors testing.* Although some checking of the usability or human factors of the system should be done during the system test, this category is not as important as the other categories because it is normally too late to correct any major human factors problems. This is one reason why the simulation methods discussed in Chapter 4 are important (i.e., to detect human factors problems during the external design process). Minor human factors problems can often be detected and corrected during the system test. For instance, system responses or messages may be poorly worded or a terminal command may require the user to repeatedly shift between upper- and lower-case characters.

14. *Procedure testing.* Most data processing systems are either components in larger systems involving human procedures, or they specify certain human procedures to be followed during the use of the system. All such procedures should be tested such as system operator procedures and procedures that a terminal user must follow under certain conditions.

All of these 14 categories are not applicable to every system test (e.g., when testing a single application program), but they still form a reasonable checklist of things to consider.

The basic rule in system testing is that "anything goes"; write highly destructive test cases, check the system at all of its operational boundaries, and write test cases representing user mistakes such as errors by the system operator. Performing a system test requires that the tester think like a customer or user, which implies a thorough understanding of how the system will be used. This raises the question of who should perform the system test, in particular, who should design the system test cases. System testing should definitely not be performed by programmers, nor by the organization responsible for developing the system. The system test group should be a separate organization containing a team of people including professional system test experts, a few eventual users of the system, the key analysts and designers of the system, and possibly a psychologist or two. It is important to include the original designers of the system. This does not violate the axiom stating that you cannot test your own system, because the system has passed through many hands since the original architect or designer specified the system. He is not really attempting to test his own system; he is attempting to find discrepancies between the final version of the system and what he originally intended perhaps one or two years ago. It is also desirable to obtain marketing or user input for the system testing effort describing the expected configurations and usage patterns of the system.

System testing is such a special and critical operation that in the future there may be companies whose sole business is performing system tests on systems developed by other companies. In fact, within the United States Air Force there is a recommendation that, if a software contractor does not appear to have the expertise to perform his own system test, a separate contract for system testing should be given to a separate company [5].

As mentioned earlier, the components of a system test are the initial objectives, the user documentation or publications, and the system itself. All system test cases should be written using the user publications (not the external specification) as source material. The external specification should only be used to resolve detected discrepancies between the system and its publications.

Because of their nature, system test cases rarely involve the invocation of a single system function. System test cases are often written as *scenarios* representing a large set of sequential operations by a user. For instance, a single test case might represent a terminal user logging on the system, issuing 10 or 20 commands in sequence, and then logging off the system. Because of their complexity, system test cases are composed of several parts: a *script,* the input data, and the expected output. The script tells the tester exactly what operations to perform in running the test case.

Performing the System Test

System testing is at the extreme left of the spectrum described in Chapter 10. System testing views the entire system as a black box; in particular, code coverage mapping is not of interest in a system test.

One technique used to obtain user involvement in the test is to perform a *field test.* For a field test a contract is written with one or a few user organizations to install the system in the users' locations. This is often advantageous to all parties; the development organization is notified of software errors it might not have detected itself, and the user organizations get a chance to learn and experiment with the system before it becomes officially available.

A second useful technique is to use the system internally for production work before it is officially delivered to others. This cannot be done in all circumstances (e.g., a software company probably has no use for a process-control system that monitors an oil refinery), but it can be done in many circumstances. For instance, a computer manufacturer can install a new operating system in production mode in all its internal computing centers before it delivers it, and a software company can use its own compilers, text-processing programs, payroll programs, and so on. One reason for the relative success of IBM's TSO (Time-Sharing Option) system was its use within IBM for application program development before it was shipped.

Use your own product in production mode before you expect others to use it.

A tendency in many system tests is to begin by running the simpler test cases and saving the complex tests until the end. This sequence is not recommended because system testing comes toward the very end of the development cycle, meaning that there is an elapsed time problem in debugging and correcting errors found during the test. Because the complex test cases often detect the errors that are more difficult to correct, reverse the sequence: begin with the most complex test cases and then taper down to the simpler tests.

Although the testing processes have been discussed sequentially, this does not imply that the processes must be implemented sequentially;

by necessity, large projects often overlap the testing processes. For instance, a system test organization can perform tests in many of the 14 categories before the entire system has been pieced together.

Figure 12.8 shows two relationships concerning errors corrections versus schedule time. The first relationship showing that the cost of correcting an error increases rapidly during the latter parts of the development cycle should be obvious to most readers. However, a second and less-known relationship also follows the same general curve. The probability of fixing a known error incorrectly also increases rapidly during the latter stages. This phenomenon is of interest because an incorrect fix to a problem often causes more harm than the original problem. This leads us to an important question: Is there ever a good reason to purposely not correct a software error?

Before answering the question, we consider a hypothetical situation to develop a better appreciation of the problem. Assume that every error can be ranked with a severity of one through ten based on its impact on the user (remember that the severity of an error and its size in terms of the number of code statements that have to be corrected are not directly related). Suppose that a correction to any error during system testing has a 0.2 probability of not fixing the error and a 0.3 probability of introducing a new error, and this new error has a random

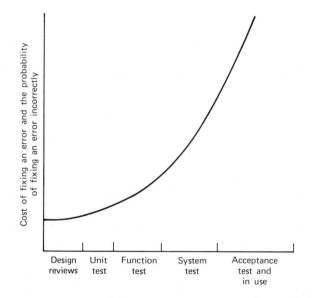

Figure 12.8   **Relationships between error corrections and time.**

severity from one to ten. This implies that we might be better off by consciously refusing to correct low-severity errors, because their corrections would make the system worse, not better.

This is a hard pill to swallow, particularly in a book about reliability. On one hand, the designer would like to say that he delivered his system with no known errors, but on the other hand one must recognize this phenomenon. The better structured the system is, of course, the less severe this phenomenon is, but there is no evidence showing that it disappears for well-structured systems.

This implies that a management decision must be made for every "minor" error detected during system testing and later forms of testing to determine whether to correct the error or to defer its correction to a future version of the system. The key to this decision is the ranking of the error by severity. A programmer's opinion of an error's severity often differs widely with the users' opinions. Any decision to defer the correction of an error must be based on a thorough understanding of the user environment.

FUNCTION AND SYSTEM TESTING TOOLS

In 1969 I had the good fortune to participate in a small project to produce a real-time operating system and application programs for a system that automates the testing of integrated circuits and performs on-line engineering experiments on electronic circuits. The system as shown in Figure 12.9 was to be connected to larger OS/360 multiprocessing system to allow the larger data reduction programs and their data to be transmitted to the OS system for more efficient processing.

Most of my assignment involved designing, coding, and testing all of

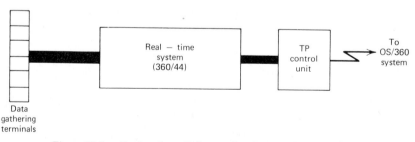

Figure 12.9   **Technology Information Processing System.**

the teleprocessing software for the operating system. In planning the test process I immediately encountered three questions:

1. How could the teleprocessing software be function-tested without the TP control unit (which had not yet been manufactured).
2. Since the OS/360 installation was wary of connecting this "newfangled" system to their system, how could the application programs that used the teleprocessing functions be tested without connecting the system to the OS/360 system?
3. After the two systems were interconnected, how could teleprocessing errors be detected and debugged?

Three tools were developed to solve these problems: a *device simulator*, a *terminal* or *remote system simulator*, and an *input/output monitor*. The device simulator simulated the interface characteristics of the TP control unit and was used to test the teleprocessing access method (low-level I/O software), including all of its error recovery routines. The simulator trapped the operating system's initiation of I/O operations and simulated interrupts from the control unit. Through control records the simulator could be directed to generate a particular I/O error on a particular type of I/O operation, and could be told whether the error should be permanent or transient, how much of a time delay to insert in its operation, and what data to return on read operations. Note that many of these conditions would have been difficult to test even if the hardware device was available.

A second simulator was written to function test the combination of the teleprocessing application programs and the access method. This simulator trapped all primitive I/O operations to the control unit and simulated the operation of the remote OS/360 system, including all line control operations and appropriate time delays. When data were sent to the OS system, the simulator returned the appropriate acknowledgements and captured the data for later examination. Periodically, the simulator would take the initiative and begin a conversation with the real-time system, sending it a stream of predefined data.

A third tool, an I/O monitor, was developed for use in system testing. The real-time system operator could start the monitor as a low-priority parallel task and point it at any I/O device. The monitor captures all data transferred to and from the device, all I/O channel programs, and a record of all interrupts, and stores this data in a ring of buffers. When no other tasks are active, the monitor transfers this data to a tape file. A utility program was also written to analyze the tape files.

During system testing the monitor was set to track the TP control unit. In the first week of system test, a situation was encountered where the communications between the two systems suddenly halted. An analysis of the trace tapes showed that both systems were trying to transmit data at the same time because of a misunderstanding in both systems of the line control conventions. Without the monitor, detection of this intermittent error might have taken weeks instead of hours.

The most common system test tool for testing interactive systems or applications is the *terminal simulator*. A typical terminal simulator configuration is shown in Figure 12.10. Instead of connecting the system being tested to actual terminal devices, the system is connected to a second system that simulates a large number of terminals by extracting test cases from a data base and feeding these test cases (terminal commands) in various patterns to the system under test through a number of telecommunication lines. This allows a variety of terminal configurations to be tested under heavy stress, load, and volume conditions without the logistical and economic problems inherent in the use of live terminals. The simulator usually records all communications during the test session on a log file.

One successful application of a terminal simulator was MUSE

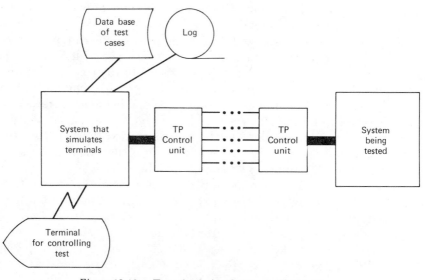

Figure 12.10   **Terminal simulator configuration.**

(Multi-User Environment Simulator), used in testing the Control Data 6000 Series TTY RESPOND time-sharing system [6]. MUSE feeds the RESPOND system a set of predefined commands, simulating the actions of up to 64 terminals. MUSE contains an interesting feature that allows it to alter its input depending on the responses from RESPOND. The sequence of commands issued can vary by placing "conditional branches" in the command stream whose directions are dependent on the responses received from the RESPOND system.

MUSE was primarily used to detect timing and saturation problems in the RESPOND system. A number of significant bugs were found during the test, such as an error that occurred only when a multiple of nine terminal users request the sort function and an error that appeared when the thirteenth request enters the disk I/O queue. The feeling was that these errors would not have been detected during system testing if the terminal simulator had not been used [6].

A large number of terminal simulators have been developed and tailored for specific projects. Representative of simulators designed for general use are IBM's DB/DC Driver System [7] and Mitre's remote terminal emulator [8].

Simulators play an important role in the function and system testing of interactive and real-time systems, but obviously a large amount of testing should be done in "live" environments. However, there are situations where simulation must be relied on for the entire system test. One example was the testing of the NORAD Command and Control System, a large complex real-time system at the heart of the North American Air Defense Command [9]. Simulation had to be relied upon since live testing could only occur by establishing actual war situations. Simulated messages were transmitted to the NORAD system representing a variety of incidents, some of which were full-scale attacks by aircraft and missiles in a variety of attack patterns. A vital part of the system test included testing the reactions of the human NORAD operators as well as testing the software and hardware system.

Simulation is also a vital part of the testing of aerospace systems, where a live system test could result in billion-dollar costs and even risk human lives. Simulation was used to test the flight computer software in the Saturn rocket, the launch vehicle for the Apollo spacecraft [10]. The flight computer performs the functions of prelaunch checkout, liftoff control, and guidance into earth orbit and lunar trajectory. It controls the engines and nozzles in the rocket by analyzing a wide variety of sensory inputs and ground communications. The simulation system "surrounds" the flight computer and allows a human flight analyst to execute test cases by entering a number of flight perturbations and sequencing failures and watching the flight computer's reactions.

In addition to the device simulation, terminal simulation, remote system simulation, and monitor tools discussed, one remaining useful test tool is the concept of a *virtual machine*. The virtual machine as implemented in IBM's VM/370 system provides a hypervisor that allows multiple software systems to execute on one physical machine, but each system thinks that it has sole access and control of a single dedicated physical machine. Virtual machines are useful for testing systems that directly access the physical resources of a machine (e.g., operating systems). For instance, the virtual machine concept allows an installation to run its production system in one virtual machine while testing a new version of the system in another virtual machine on the same physical machine.

TEST PLANNING AND CONTROL

Since this is not a book on project management techniques, only a few words have so far been devoted to planning, tracking, and controlling the programming process. However, since these considerations are of critical importance in the testing processes, a few words of advice are in order.

One of the most common mistakes made in software testing is to develop testing plans with the subconscious assumption that no errors will be encountered. Recall that the goal of testing is to find errors. Planning test resources (e.g., people, computer time, and schedule time) under the assumption that every test case will execute correctly the first time it is executed leads to two significant problems. First, it leads to gross underestimates of the resources needed. The fact that testing falls toward the end of the schedule compounds this problem further because massive readjustments of resources at this time are almost impossible. Second, if test personnel find themselves in this situation, their goal is often meeting the unreasonable schedule, forcing them to overlook errors and to use only the "easy" tests, omitting the highly destructive test cases.

As is the case for any complex undertaking, the *plan* is the vital component of the test process. The test plan must be developed well in advance of the start of testing, probably at the time that the system design is getting underway. The elements of a good test plan are:

1. *Objectives.*   A definition of the goals of each test phase.
2. *Responsibilities and schedules.*   A definition of who will perform

test case design, development, execution, and debugging for each test phase and the schedules of these activities.

3.   *Tools.*   A description of the needed test tools and how and when they will be obtained.

4.   *Computer time.*   A description of the amounts of computer time needed for each time period and how and when this will be obtained.

5.   *Configurations.*   A description of any special hardware configurations or devices needed, including ordering and installation schedules and responsibilities.

6.   *Test case libraries and standards.*   A definition of how test cases will be stored and standards for writing test cases.

7.   *Tracking procedures.*   A description of the method to be used for monitoring test progress.

8.   *Debugging process.*   A definition of the procedures needed to report and correct errors. This is discussed further in Chapter 13.

9.   *Success criteria.*   The criteria that will be measured to judge successful completion of each test phase.

10.   *Integration sequence.*   The integration or build plan as discussed earlier in this chapter. This must include descriptions of all scaffold code needed and responsibilities and schedules for producing it.

Of the items listed above, one of the most difficult is establishing success criteria. For example, a common criterion used in judging whether a system function can enter system test is to state that 100% of the function test cases must execute correctly. This criterion is weak because, although I refuse to believe that people are basically dishonest, it certainly does not encourage the function tester to write highly destructive test cases. To encourage the detection of as many errors as possible in the early testing phases, *negative* criteria, such as that function testing is not complete until the tester detects and corrects at least two errors per 1000 lines of code in the function, are preferable. This type of criterion reinforces the idea that the aim of testing is to find errors. Of course, this criterion presents a problem to the tester of an exceptionally error-free function, but in these situations the problem is manageable (wouldn't we all like to be faced with more problems like this?). It initially forces him to test harder and then, if he cannot meet the criterion, to negotiate with the system test group to convince them that he really could not find enough bugs. The criteria mentioned earlier, such as the function test criterion of exercising all branch directions at least once (except for defensive code), should also be used.

Test phase completion criteria must be stated in terms of the number of errors to be found, not in meaningless terms such as the percentage of test cases executed correctly.

The same principle can be applied to determining when system testing can be termed complete. System testing could be judged as finished at the later of the following two dates: the elapsed scheduled time has been reached or at least X number of errors have been detected during the test. Another useful measure is to plot the number of errors detected per unit time (e.g., per week). Rather than counting all errors as equal in the graph, they should be weighted by their severity. This graph allows a management decision to be made by analyzing the trend of the weighted error-detection rates.

In the discussion the phrase "the test case was successful" was avoided because it presents an interesting paradox. Managers tend to use the word "success" to describe a test case that executed without detecting an error. However, if testing is viewed as the process of finding errors, the word "success" might be taken as describing a test case that detected a new error.

In tracking the testing effort the tester must not forget the axiom in Chapter 10 that the more errors one detects in a section of the system, the higher the probability that there are additional undetected errors. Analyzing error data to determine error-prone modules or functions can give early feedback as to where to concentrate the remainder of the testing efforts.

Testing projects are always faced with another interesting paradox: on one hand one does not want to find too many errors, so that schedules can be met, and on the other hand one realizes that the objective of testing is to find as many errors as possible. This reinforces two necessary ideas discussed earlier: completion criteria must be stated in a negative sense (e.g., a testing phase is not complete until a predetermined number of errors are found), and testing should be performed by a separate organization that is shielded from the schedule pressures on the development organization.

ACCEPTANCE TESTING

Acceptance testing is a validation process that tests the system not to the external specification, not to the objectives, but to the initial requirements. Acceptance testing is an unusual type of testing because it is performed by the customer or user organization, not by the software development organization.

For *any* type of new software product, be it a contracted product from a software company, an agreement with an internal programming organization, installation of a new version of an operating system, or purchase of an off-the-shelf program product, the user organization must design and write a set of test cases with the intent of showing how the product does not meet the requirements. If these tests are "unsuccessful," then the product is formally accepted for use. Acceptance testing usually takes on any combination of three approaches: *benchmark testing* in which specially prepared test cases are executed, *pilot operation testing* where the product is installed on a limited or experimental basis, and *parallel operation testing* where the product is installed and operated in parallel with the previous system.

INSTALLATION TESTING

The remaining form of software testing is, as are all other types of testing, concerned with finding errors, but in this case not software errors. Many large software systems and programs have complicated installation procedures. The customer must select options, allocate files and libraries, have an appropriate hardware configuration available, and often mate this new product with other programs. The purpose of installation testing is to find any mistakes that were made during the installation process.

Installation tests should be designed and written by the software developer and shipped with the product and its documentation. The tests are run by either the customer or the software organization's service personnel after the product has been installed. Installation test cases check such things as the presence of all necessary files and hardware devices, the contents of the first record of each file, and whether all parts of the software product are present.

All programs should be shipped with a small number of test cases that detect installation errors.

REFERENCES

1. *OS/VS Utilities,* C35-0005, IBM Corp., White Plains, N.Y., 1974.
2. W. R. Elmendorf, "Cause-Effect Graphs in Functional Testing," TR-00.2487, IBM Systems Development Div., Poughkeepsie, N.Y., 1973.
3. W. R. Elmendorf, "Functional Analysis Using Cause-Effect Graphs," *Proceedings of SHARE XLIII.* New York: SHARE, 1974, pp. 567–577.

4. M. E. Drummond, Jr., *Evaluation and Measurement Techniques for Digital Computer Systems.* Englewood Cliffs, N.J.: Prentice-Hall, 1973.

5. M. Shelley, "Computer Software Reliability, Fact or Myth?," TR-MMER/RM-73-125, Hill Air Force Base, Utah, 1973.

6. E. W. Pullen and D. R. Shuttee, "MUSE: A Tool for Testing and Debugging a Multi-terminal Programming System," *Proceedings of the 1968 Spring Joint Computer Conference.* Washington: Thompson, 1968, pp. 491–502.

7. *The Data Base/Data Communication Driver System: Design Objectives,* GH20-4281, IBM Corp., White Plains, N.Y., 1974.

8. D. L. James, "Remote-Terminal Emulator (Design Verification Model)—Data Structures, Scenario Instructions, and Commands," MTR-2677, Mitre Corp., Bedford, Mass., 1974.

9. R. T. Stevens, "Testing the NORAD Command and Control System," *IEEE Transactions on Systems Science and Cybernetics,* **SSC-4** (1), 47–51 (1968).

10. J. H. Jacobs and T. J. Dillon, "Interactive Saturn Flight Program Simulator," *IBM Systems Journal,* **9** (2), 145–158 (1970).

CHAPTER **13**

Debugging

In spite of the recommendations in Part II, some software errors will always be created and the difficult task of debugging the software will be necessary. In fact, if one approaches the testing processes correctly, the goal is to find as many errors as possible. The fact that this chapter is unlucky number 13 is just an interesting coincidence.

Debugging is just what its name implies: it starts with some evidence or symptoms of a software error and is the process of locating and correcting the error. The reason that debugging is considered a difficult art is that somehow we all subconsciously assume that it is "something that other less-perfect people do." There is remarkably little instruction or research on the subject of debugging, yet the average programmer spends more time debugging than he does designing and coding. However, there are a few encouraging signs: there is a book partially devoted to the subject [1] and at least one university offers a course solely on the subject of debugging [2].

FINDING THE ERROR

The first step in debugging an error is to locate the error precisely. We might start with some symptom such as, "the last character is missing in every other record in the output file," and have to determine precisely which statement or statements in our 100,000 statement program are incorrect. The suggestion in many programming books to "scatter many print statements throughout the program to print intermediate results" is not an entirely bad suggestion, but it represents an haphazard approach and in any case should not be an initial method. Just as Polya's problem-solving technique [3] was adapted to design problems in Chapter 3, the technique is also applicable to debugging.

1. *Understand the problem.* Many programmers begin the debugging process in a haphazard manner by omitting the vital task of thoroughly analyzing the available data. The first step must be a careful examination of what the program did correctly and what the program did incorrectly, to develop one or more theories about the nature of the error. One of the most common causes of difficulty in debugging is overlooking a significant factor in the program's output. The output data should be examined to estimate its sufficiency to locate the error, for if it is insufficient the first step is to collect more data by writing and running additional test cases. An important consideration is examining the data for *contradictions* (e.g., the error only occurs on every other record), for these will lead to a more precise theory about the error or possibly indicate that there is more than one error.

   A useful approach to studying the error symptoms is Brown and Sampson's *The Method* [1]. The form shown in Figure 13.1 is used to organize and analyze the available data. The WHAT boxes describe the basic symptoms, the WHERE boxes describe the places where the symptoms are noticed, the WHEN boxes contain any clues concerning the time at which the symptoms do and do not occur, and the TO WHAT EXTENT boxes describe the scope of the symptoms. The IS and IS NOT columns are the crux of the technique, for they show the distinctions and contradictions that will lead to a theory.

   Let us suppose that an error is encountered while using the loader program designed in Part 2. The general symptom is that the last module loaded seems to encounter a program check interruption during its execution although the module appears correctly in the output listing. The first step is to probe the symptoms for enough clues to fill in each box in Figure 13.1. These clues are shown in Figure 13.2.

2. *Devise a plan.* The next step is to develop one or more theories about the error and to devise a plan to confirm these theories.

?	Is	Is not
What		
Where		
When		
To what extent		

Figure 13.1   **A form for analyzing error symptoms.**

Examination of Figure 13.2 leads to the theory that the last entry in the relocation table RLTAB is not being resolved (causing a wild branch in the corresponding CALL statement in the loaded program) and the error is probably in the RELOCATE ADCONS function in the RLTABMGR module.

3. *Carry out the plan.*   The plan is followed to attempt to prove the theory. If the plan involves several steps, the correctness of each step should be checked. To confirm the loader theory one might write a test case and take a snapshot of RLTAB and the loaded program at the completion of the RELOCATE ADCONS function.

4. *Review the solution.*   If it appears that the precise location of the error has been detected, a few checks are necessary before one attempts to correct the error. Analyze the suspected error to determine if it will cause these exact symptoms. Make sure that the entire error has been located and not just one part of the error. Check to see that a correction of this error will not cause another error.

A major cause of difficulties in debugging is *psychological set,* the situation where the mind sees what it expects to see and not necessarily what is really there [4]. For instance, this is the primary reason for failing to spot all typographical and spelling errors in a book. One way of

?	Is	Is not
What	Loaded program branches to an invalid instruction	Does not appear to be an error in the source logic of the loaded program
Where	Only occurs in the last module that was loaded	The listing (meaning that ESTAB is probably correct)
When	When a CALL statement is being executed in the last module	When any other CALL statement is executed
To what extent	Only seems to occur when the last module loaded contains a CALL statement	When the last module loaded doesn't contain any CALL statements

Figure 13.2   **Symptoms of the loader error.**

overcoming this is by being skeptical about everything you examine, particularly the comments and documentation. Experienced debuggers often physically cover the comments when examining a module, for comments often describe what the original programmer *thought* his code did. *Backtracking* (reading the program's code in a backwards manner) is another useful tactic because it gives you a different perspective of the logic.

Another problem in debugging is reaching a mental impasse where the error simply cannot be pinpointed. This means one of two things: either you are looking in the wrong place, which means you should study the symptoms again and develop another theory, or you are looking in the right places but your mind refuses to spot the error. If the latter seems to be the case, the best solution is to "sleep on it." Divert your attention to a different activity and let your subconscious work on the problem. Many programmers find that they solve their most difficult problems while taking a shower or driving to work!

When you do find and verify the error, do not forget the phenomenon shown in Figure 10.9, which says that the probability of additional errors in that part of the program is now higher. Examine the code in the vicinity of the error for additional mistakes. Study the error to determine if the same mistake was made in other parts of the program.

Research studies on debugging have primarily been focused on comparisons of debugging in a batch environment versus debugging in an interactive time-sharing environment, with most studies concluding that the interactive environment is more desirable [5]. A more recent study has shown that perhaps a third environment is best [6]. Experienced programmers were given complex FORTRAN programs (that they had never seen before) to debug. In some experiments they were told only that the program contains an error. In other cases they were also given the expected output and the actual output and in further experiments they were told which program statement contains the error. The bugs were usually located in a remarkably short time (and without any computer assistance) and the debugging-time differences among the different experiments were surprisingly small. One conclusion from the study was that perhaps the best way to debug is by simply reading and struggling with the program's logic, although this demands high degrees of motivation and concentration.

It is important to remember that many of the design techniques discussed in Part 2 are of benefit in the debugging process. Not only do techniques such as composite design, structured programming, and good programming style minimize the number of original errors, but they make debugging easier by making the program easier to understand. The defensive measures described in Chapters 7 and 8 also assist the debugging process by detecting symptoms shortly after the error is encountered, thus making pinpointing of the error easier.

MAKING THE CORRECTION

Once the precise location of the error has been determined, the next step is to correct the error. The biggest problem encountered in correcting an error is failing to fix the entire problem; a common mistake is to fix only a symptom of the error. Avoid making an "experimental" fix (e.g., "This looks like the spot; I'll try to change it this way and see what happens."); experimental fixes show that you are not yet qualified to debug this program because you do not understand it.

The most important thing to realize about fixing an error is that it reverts you back into the design stage. It is discouraging to see a project with a rigorous design process discard all of its rigor when fixes are made. Fixes should be treated at least as rigorously as the initial design of the program was treated. The documentation should be updated if necessary and the fix should pass through a code reading or walk-through process. No fix is so "minor" that it does not need to be tested. If the error was detected after the unit test process, add the unit test cases that were obviously missing in the original test and rerun all of the module's unit tests.

Because of their nature, fixes always have some negative effect on the program's structure and readability. The fact that fixes are made under heavy pressure also compounds this problem. Experience has shown that fixes have a high probability (usually from 20 to 50%) of introducing a *new* error into the program. This implies that debugging should be performed by the best programmers on the project and never relegated to inexperienced programmers.

Completely avoid the "superzap" approach of making corrections directly to the object code with intentions of later correcting the source code. Projects that allow this approach to be used always find themselves in deep trouble because the object code and source code can easily become unsynchronized. The extra time needed to correct and compile the source code is always a wise investment.

DEBUGGING TOOLS

The unfortunate state of most debugging tools is illustrated in a recent advertisement explaining why one should buy a new book on assembly language: "First, one of these days you're going to have to interpret diagnostic or compilation records produced by a higher level language. If you're not familiar with Basic Assembler Language, you're going to find this task next to impossible." Unfortunately, this statement gives a true picture of most debugging aids. It is inexcusable today for an operating system to print an octal or hexadecimal dump after detecting an error in a FORTRAN program, cruelly printing out floating-point variables in hexadecimal format (requiring the FORTRAN programmer to do a nontrivial conversion), representing the FORTRAN program as machine instructions and addresses instead of its original form, and overwhelming the programmer with an excess of irrelevant and meaningless data such as descriptions of the contents of the system's control blocks.

The main problem with most debugging tools is that they force the high-level language programmer to be an expert in machine language details, yet the major purpose of a high-level language is supposed to be to shield the programmer from all machine details. The solution to this problem is to design all debugging aids so that they communicate with the programmer solely in terms of the programming language and never in machine terms. The tools described in this section represent steps in this direction.

Interactive Tools

Most on-line debugging tools are the type that let the programmer interact with his program during execution. They provide the functions of allowing the programmer to interrupt the program, establish *break-points* in the program (preplanned points at which execution is to be interrupted), display and alter variables in *symbolic* terms (i.e., by name rather than machine address), step the program through its execution statement-by-statement, and obtain symbolic dumps of the program's storage.

One such symbolic debugging tool is IBM's PL/I Checkout Compiler [7]. The programmer communicates with the tool only in terms of the *source* language. He can set breakpoints at particular PL/I statements, alter the value of variable A by typing "$A = 2;$", and obtain a statement-by-statement execution trace of the program. The programmer can obtain selective descriptive dumps about such conditions as all activated procedures, all files, all pointer variables, and the status of all tasks and on-conditions. The Honeywell Multics PL/I compiler provides a similar set of symbolic debugging functions [8]. IBM provides similar tools for such languages as FORTRAN and COBOL [9]. Because of its generality and uniformity, the APL language provides an ideal debugging environment by making the programming language and the debugging language equivalent.

Debugging tools such as these are useful when the program is being examined in a test environment, but because they require special compilation options they are usually not applicable to debugging a system that is running in production mode. In developing a large complex software system it is worthwhile to consider incorporation of debugging aids directly into the system. For instance, IBM's OS/VS1 and OS/VS2 operating systems contain a debugging aid called DSS (Dynamic Support System [10]. DSS allows service personnel to interact with the system while it is in production mode. Breakpoints can be set at particular instructions and the system can be requested to stop when a particular register or storage location is modified.

The EXDAMS System

One interactive tool that deserves particular mention is EXDAMS (Extendable Debugging and Monitoring System) [11]. EXDAMS is unique in terms of the functions it provides and the way these functions are implemented.

EXDAMS is an interactive tool using CRT terminals. Although the terminal user may see himself as interacting with his program while it is executing, he is actually interacting with a *history tape* of the program. EXDAMS first stores the program's source code and symbol table on a file. It then executes the user's program, building a history tape containing a trace of execution flow and the results of all assignment statements. When the user is ready to debug his program, his program is "executed" through a "playback" of the history tape. A sample of the many available debugging functions are listed below:

1. The user might say, "Show me the statement that set variable A to 33.3." EXDAMS displays a segment of the source code on the screen and intensifies the appropriate statement.
2. The user can specify a list of variables whose values he wishes to examine. These variables become column headings on the CRT screen and EXDAMS "plays back" the program, showing how these variables change over time.
3. The user can watch his program execute. As each statement executes, it is brightened on the screen and, if it is an assignment statement, its value is also displayed. In doing this the user can run his program in either a forward or reverse direction.

Language Features

In addition to the debugging tools mentioned above, programming languages often contain debugging aids as extensions to the language. PL/I contains the powerful CHECK condition, which causes an interrupt to be generated or a message to be written whenever a specified variable is modified or a statement with a specific label is executed. For instance, the statement

(CHECK(TRAN,TABLE,I)): DIST: PROC;

causes a message to be issued whenever the DIST procedure alters the values of variables TRAN, TABLE, or I.

A language with additional features is PL/C [12], a compatible subset of PL/I. In addition to having the CHECK condition, PL/C also checks each variable to ensure that it is set before being referenced and checks all subscripts for out-of-range conditions. PL/C also allows the programmer to place permanent debugging statements in his program; these are treated as comments or executable statements depending on a compilation option. For instance, the statement

/*4 PUT SKIP(3) LIST('HIT POINT 32',ICOUNT);*/

is interpreted as a comment unless COMMENTS=(4) is placed on a control card, which turns this statement into an actual PUT statement. This method could be improved further by allowing the programmer to activate the statement at execution time instead of at compilation time.

PL/C also provides a useful storage dump when an error is encountered. The dump contains a list of all variables and their current values, a list of variables that were never referenced, execution frequency counts of all labeled statements and entry points, and a list of the last 18 transfers of control.

Dumps

As mentioned earlier, the simple hexadecimal or octal dump is a poor excuse for a debugging aid. These primitive dumps contain an enormous amount of irrelevant data and usually display the data in the wrong numerical form, forcing many organizations to establish classes solely in the art of dump reading. Symbolic dumps such as that provided by PL/C are desirable but they require a close association between the dump program and the compiler.

A dump program developed at Ohio State University has shown that useful nonsymbolic dumps are feasible [13]. This dump is produced by the operating system when a program interruption occurs in an application program. The intent of the dump is to print only those data that are relevant to the problem, to convert the data to their proper numerical form, and to assist the programmer by predicting the probable cause of the interruption. The dump prints all floating-point registers in base 10 scientific notation instead of the machine's hexadecimal "excess 64" form. The failing instruction is "disassembled" (printed in assembly language form instead of machine language form) and a description of the program interrupt is printed.

The significant feature in this dump program is its attempt to predict the actual error that led to the program interruption. This was done by analyzing a large number of previous errors to determine what types of programming errors commonly cause what types of interruptions. The dump program analyzes the type of interruption, the instruction that caused the interruption, and the location of the instruction and uses this information to suggest a probable error. For instance, if the interruption code is OC4 (an attempt to address protected storage) and general register 15 contains the hexadecimal value 02005000, the dump program deduces that the application program was attempting to read from an unopened file and it prints a message to this effect along with control block information about the file.

Intelligent dump programs like this one could be extended to recognize common faults in the use of particular languages. For instance, if a FORTRAN subroutine is passed an array as an argument but the array is not declared as such in a DIMENSION statement in the subroutine, most compilers assume that subscripted references to the array are function calls and the system ends up attempting to execute the array. An intelligent dump program could easily recognize this situation and predict the error.

Information Tools

Often during the debugging of a large system a programmer needs answers to question such as, "What other modules reference this field in this record?" or "What modules call this module?" A number of information gathering and retrieval tools have been developed to answer these and other questions.

The ASES tool discussed in Chapter 11 provides part of this capability by storing information about the program in a data base and providing answers to questions such as, "What statements use and/or modify this particular variable?" The Cross-Program Analyzer option of Applied Data Research's AUTOFLOW II program produces reports or answers queries on such situations as finding all statements that reference a specific variable, finding violations of installation-defined programming standards, finding all statements that reference a particular file, or finding all modules that call a given module.

Audits and Traces

The last set of debugging aids consists of functions within the software system that supply information to the programmer in the event of an error. The active and passive fault-detection functions described in Chapter 7 detect and record information about errors and hence fall into this category. Data base and teleprocessing systems often maintain audit trails or journals containing a copy of each data base and terminal transaction for purposes of recovering from hardware or line failures and tracking attempts to violate security rules. These audit trails are also invaluable to the debugger.

Large-scale real-time systems should contain functions to record the system's internal data flow. This can be implemented at various levels, for example by recording all calls between subsystems, levels of abstraction, or even individual modules. A record is constructed for every call containing the names of the calling and called modules and the input and output data transferred. The records can be saved on a trace tape or stored in a cyclic buffer so that only the last N (e.g., 100) records are maintained.

MONITORING THE DEBUGGING PROCESS

One of the best ways to improve software reliability in current or future projects is the obvious but often overlooked process of learning from previous mistakes. Each error should be carefully studied to determine why it occurred and what should have been done to prevent it from occurring or to detect it earlier. It is rare to see an organization or a programmer perform this valuable analysis, and when it is done it is usually only a cursory analysis such as placing errors in such categories as design errors, logic errors, interface errors, or other meaningless groups.

Time must be devoted to studying the nature of *every* detected error. I must emphasize that error analyses should be largely *qualitative* rather than simple "bean-counting" exercises. The following questions should be answered to understand the underlying causes of errors and to improve the design and testing processes:

1. Why did the error occur? The answer must pinpoint the original source of the error as well as the final source of the error. For instance, the error might have been made during the coding of a particular module but the underlying cause might have been an ambiguous point in a specification or a correction to a prior error.
2. How and when was the error found? Since we have just made a significant accomplishment, why not profit from the experience?
3. Why was the error not detected in one of the design or code reviews or in an earlier testing phase?
4. What should have been done in the design and testing processes to prevent this error from occurring or to detect it sooner?

In addition to collecting this information to learn from mistakes, a formal procedure for reporting and fixing errors is necessary to ensure that detected errors in production systems or systems under test are not overlooked and that corrections are made in a controlled manner. Almost every organization has such a procedure, so it is not necessary to outline one. A desirable aid to these procedures is a program that controls and monitors error corrections. For example, IBM uses a program called SMP (System Modification Program) [14], which assists in inserting modifications and removing incorrect modifications, records the status of each module, and maintains an audit trail of all modifications.

Another way to learn from software errors is from the mistakes of other organizations, for instance by examining software error studies in the computing literature. Unfortunately, this is not a viable alternative; such error studies are scarce for several reasons. Most companies view programming error data as confidential information. Most of the studies that do get published are simple "bean-counts" (e.g., "32% of our errors were logic errors"), rendering them almost useless. Finally, different studies count errors differently (e.g., it is often not clear whether compilation, walk-through, unit test, and user-detected errors are included), making comparisons among projects almost impossible. There are, however, some exceptions. Endres [15] gives an interesting study of errors found during the testing of a release of IBM's DOS/VS operating system. Shooman and Bolsky [16] analyze the resources expended during the testing and debugging of a small program, and Craig [17] analyzes errors from three large software systems.

REFERENCES

1. A. R. Brown and W. A. Sampson, *Program Debugging.* London: Macdonald, 1973.

2. R. F. Mathis, "Teaching Debugging," *SIGSCE Bulletin,* **6** (1), 59–63 (1974).

3. G. Polya, *How To Solve It.* Princeton, N.J.: Princeton University Press, 1971.

4. G. M. Weinberg, *The Psychology of Computer Programming.* New York: Van Nostrand Reinhold, 1971.

5. H. Sackman, *Man-Computer Problem Solving: Experimental Evaluation of Time-Sharing and Batch Processing.* New York: Auerbach, 1970.

6. J. D. Gould and P. Drongowski, "A Controlled Psychological Study of Computer Program Debugging," RC 4083, IBM Research Div., Yorktown Heights, N.Y., 1972.

7. *OS PL/I Checkout Compiler: Programmer's Guide,* SC33-0007, IBM Corp., White Plains, N.Y., 1971.

8. B. L. Wolman, "Debugging PL/I Programs in the Multics Environment," *Proceedings of the 1972 Fall Joint Computer Conference.* Montvale, N.J.: AFIPS Press, 1972, pp. 507–514.

9. *IBM OS COBOL Interactive Debug and (TSO) COBOL Prompter: General Information,* GC28-6454, IBM Corp., White Plains, N.Y., 1974.

10. *OS/VS Dynamic Support System,* GC28-0640, IBM Corp., White Plains, N.Y., 1973.

11. R. M. Balzer, "EXDAMS—Extendable Debugging and Monitoring System," *Proceedings of the 1969 Spring Joint Computer Conference.* Montvale, N.J.: AFIPS Press, 1969, pp. 567–580.

12. H. L. Morgan and R. A. Wagner, "PL/C: The Design of a High-Performance Compiler for PL/I," *Proceedings of the 1971 Spring Joint Computer Conference.* Montvale, N.J.: AFIPS Press, 1971, pp. 503–510.

13. B. M. Kirsch, "An Improved Error Diagnostics System for IBM System/360–370

Assembler Program Dumps," OSU-CISRC-TR-74-3, Ohio State University, Columbus, Ohio, 1974.

14.   *OS/VS System Modification Program (SMP)*, GC28-0673, IBM Corp., White Plains, N.Y., 1974.

15.   A. B. Endres, "An Analysis of Errors and Their Causes in System Programs," *IEEE Transactions on Software Engineering*, **SE-1** (2), 140–149 (1975).

16.   M. L. Shooman and M. I. Bolsky, "Types, Distribution, and Test and Correction Times for Programming Errors," *Proceedings of the 1975 International Conference on Reliable Software*. New York: IEEE, 1975, pp. 347–357.

17.   G. R. Craig et al., "Software Reliability Study," RADC-TR-74-250, TRW Corp., Redondo Beach, Ca., 1974.

Additional Topics in Software Reliability

CHAPTER 14

Management
Techniques
for Reliability

If you are a project manager and have turned to this chapter expecting to find a compact discussion of management techniques that can influence software reliability, you are making a mistake. It is impossible to separate issues into "purely managerial" and "purely technical" categories, and for this reason almost every chapter in the book discusses ideas that should be of concern to the project manager. The purpose of this chapter is to discuss a few management ideas that did not naturally fit into the other chapters.

A question that the nonmanagerial reader may have at this point is: why even discuss the subject of management in a book on software reliability? How can anything that my manager does or does not do influence the number of errors in my program? The reason is simple: software reliability requires a management commitment as well as a technical commitment. Studies of software projects have shown that management expertise (or the lack of it) is often the primary factor in the success of the project. A recent informal survey in a major computer company indicated that programmers feel that more serious software errors are caused by administrative problems than by weaknesses in the design, implementation, or testing processes. (Realize, or course, that this response is at least slightly biased.) The three major administrative problems listed were (1) pressure to begin coding before the design is complete because of tight schedules, (2) insufficient emphasis on programmer education (particularly in the use of the programming language), and (3) poor matching of programmers' abilities with job assignments.

ORGANIZATION AND STAFFING

Of all the variables connected with project organization and staffing, the most important consideration is minimizing the number of people involved. Although many managers realize that many of the most successful projects contained a surprisingly small number of people and that the "Mongolian horde" approach [1] (tackling problems by adding waves of people) rarely works, it is rare to see a manager who is actually committed to these ideas. When a project appears to be in trouble, the usual "solution" is to add additional people rather than the more sensible solution of reducing the number of people involved. In addition to positive effects on cost and schedule (e.g., see Brooks [2]), minimizing the number of people has a positive effect on reliability by reducing the number of communication paths and hence the number of translation errors.

Most projects require the headcount to reach a peak during the module design and coding phase. Staffing to this peak too early in the project should be avoided. One problem that may be encountered by staffing too early is that the system design will be compromised; the system will subconsciously be structured to reflect the organizational structure of the project.

Another problem that often occurs with early staffing of a large project is that the programming manager may say to the design manager, "Put my 50 programmers to work on your external specification so that we can shave a few weeks from the schedule." Such a suggestion is unwise for several reasons: the external design must be done with a minimum of people (a maximum of two was suggested in Chapter 4), and external design requires a completely different set of talents. If for some reason the programming organization is staffed at an early point in time, there are valuable activities for this organization to perform without becoming a Mongolian horde in the external design and architecture processes. These activities include education, experimenting with alternative designs of the program logic (it *is* possible to do this before the external design is complete), development of special programming tools, project sizings, and development of algorithms.

Lest the reader receive the impression that staffing is a simple matter, consider a question with a contradictory answer: should the same group of people perform all of the design steps? Based on the preceding discussion, the answer might be yes, for this would tend to minimize the project headcount and reduce the number of communication problems. However, there are several overriding reasons why one group of people should not have the responsibility of all design phases. Giving separate people the responsibility for two successive design stages usually results in better documentation and double-checking of the design (a group receiving the output of a prior design stage is highly motivated to find errors). Probably the most important reason is a point made in Chapter 4: each design stage requires specialized training and experience. The requirements, objectives, and external design stages require a thorough understanding of the user environment and skills in systems analysis, operations research, man–machine psychology, and so on. The system architecture and program structure design steps require knowledge in such areas as file design, levels of abstraction, general systems theory, and composite design. The steps of module external and internal design and coding require expertise in the programming language, algorithms, structured programming, and so forth. It is unlikely that any one person possesses all of these talents.

Whenever different people are involved in each design stage, an important consideration is continuity between stages. A common mistake is to assume, for instance, that the external designers or analysts can be transferred to another project as soon as the external specification is "done." A specification is rarely "done" before the end of the project because of errors and design changes. The key designers must remain with the project to the very end. Specification errors and inevitable design changes that occur toward the end of the project are the most risky changes and require the attention of the original designers. Also, as mentioned in Chapter 12, the external designers make ideal members of the system test organization.

Before leaving the subject of design, another consideration that must be discussed is a formal design change process. The purpose of a formal design change process is to ensure that decisions are made by the appropriate people and that all ramifications of a proposed change are understood. Assume that we made some design decision X early in the project and that subsequent to this, ten decisions were made based on the outcome of decision X. If someone proposes a change to decision X, it is important to have a project-wide review of the proposed change so that the ten other decisions are also identified and examined.

One danger in using a design change procedure in a large project is going overboard by trying to control the design at too low a level. In a large project only the objectives, external design, system architecture, and data base design should be controlled with a formal change process.

The testing processes are the part of the project that requires the most management planning and attention. One key organizational consideration is to form separate testing organizations. As mentioned in Chapter 10, the development organization must not have the responsibility of testing its product. The development organization is normally too close to the product, too bound by schedules and budgets, not likely to be highly skeptical of its work, and not highly motivated to find errors. In addition, testing requires a set of skills that are much different from programming skills. Testing also requires a different motivation and rewards system. Where programmers are usually rewarded based on the absence of errors in their product, test specialists must be rewarded for finding as many errors as possible, even to the extent of paying them on a commission basis (e.g., $100 for detecting an error of severity X).

In staffing a new project, managers often continue to promote a widespread "caste system" of programming jobs. High-level design jobs are viewed as jobs for only the elite, highly creative personnel, lower-level design and coding jobs are next on the scale, testing assignments are farther down the scale, and maintenance jobs are viewed as the lowest-class jobs, suitable for only the noncreative or inexperienced programmer. Not only is this attitude entirely wrong (it was said in previous chapters that system testing is the most creative software development task and debugging requires the best programmers), but it forces people with natural talents for testing and debugging into other jobs in order to advance their careers. An organization with such a caste system (and it may be there without one's knowing about it) should get an even balance of senior-level people and junior people in all jobs and make it apparent that equal professional advancement opportunities exist in each type of job.

One last staffing consideration is the distinguishing features of a good programmer. This consideration is obviously important in hiring programmers, establishing educational programs, and in matching the right skills to the right job. In surveying a group of managers about the attributes of a good programmer, one hears such answers as high analytic ability, pattern recognition abilities, algorithmic reasoning ability, mental concentration, and deductive reasoning. A survey of a group of more experienced managers might lead to additional perceptive answers such as professionalism, education in computer science fundamentals, ability to work under pressure, ability to work with other people, ability to adapt to change, neatness, perfection, and even a sense of humor. Each of these is, of course, part of the job of programming, but perhaps the most significant factor is *the ability to communicate*. Programmers spend about two-thirds of their time communicating (listening, reading, talking, and writing), and the microscopic translation model in Chapter 2 indicates that most software errors are due to man-to-man communication problems. This explains the interesting phenomenon that college graduates with English literature or music degrees (which are primarily communication skills) often turn into outstanding programmers. A major consideration in hiring and educating programmers must be communication abilities, both the ability for a programmer to express his own thoughts and ideas as well as the ability to understand the ideas of others.

PROGRAMMING LIBRARIANS

A fairly recent change in project organizations has been the concept of a *programming librarian*: a clerical or paraprofessional person who participates in the software project [3, 4]. The librarian becomes an interface between the programmer and the computer by performing much of the clerical work of the project (e.g., data entry and editing and executing test cases), maintaining a central library of program listings, source and object code, documentation, and test cases, and maintaining a chronological archive of all project activity and correspondence. The major advantage of the librarian concept in terms of software reliability is the central control of the current versions of the project's code and documentation, eliminating the common problem of massive stacks of listings in the programmers' offices where no one is sure of the current "official" version or status of the program. If a program library system is used, the librarian is usually the sole user of this system, thus reducing the number of programming tools that must be understood by each programmer. The librarian also often serves as a secretary and draftsman, typing and filing correspondence and producing graphical documentation such as decision tables, program structure diagrams, and HIPO charts from rough sketches.

In spite of its advantages, the librarian concept also has a few disadvantages:

1. A valid criticism of programmers is that they have insufficient experience in the end-use of their products. For instance, it is important that every programmer constructing a new operating system have some experience using existing operating systems, both as a system operator and a terminal user, for this gives him or her a better understanding of how his decisions affect the users of his product. If the librarian concept is taken to the extreme, programmers will have no direct contact with computers, which is certainly an undesirable situation.

2. On some projects librarians have the responsibilities of performing complex editing functions (e.g., "change every occurrence of variable XVELOCITY to YVELOCITY in my program") and even correcting syntax errors. The former is dangerous because it often requires professional expertise; the latter is undesirable because it contradicts the attitude of precision programming (professional programmers should not make syntax errors).

3. It is not clear that all the time spent by programmers on clerical tasks is unproductive time. Because programming is primarily an intellectual task, programmers seem to need frequent diversions to change their perspectives and to allow their subconsciouses to work on problems. The programmer you see walking over to the computing center to pick up a listing may not be wasting his time; he may be solving a problem during his walk.

4. It is difficult to keep the librarian's workload constant. During some stages he or she may be completely overwhelmed with work and become a bottleneck in the project; during other stages he may have insufficient work to do.

Fortunately, none of these problems is insurmountable, and with proper management foresight the programming librarian can be a valuable addition to project organizations.

Arguments about the worth of the librarian concept often resurrect the old argument about whether batch or terminal-oriented systems are more "productive" for programmers. If productivity means "the speed with which a programmer writes his program," then there is evidence that interactive systems are advantageous. If productivity represents the total cost of the product (and hence, as discussed in Chapter 1, becomes closely related to reliability), then interactive programming systems are likely to be undesirable (this feeling is shared by others, e.g., [5]). Programmers who use batch systems are forced to plan their activities carefully in advance, but this careful planning is often neglected in an interactive environment, leading to tendencies to "experiment" at the terminal. Interactive systems tend to force the programmer to think too quickly and carelessly and seem to encourage an environment of sloppy programming.

Of course, much of this question disappears if a programming librarian is used, because the librarian becomes an interface between the programmer and the computer. A librarian does not need an interactive system because he is rarely capable of "interacting." A librarian who uses an interactive system usually uses it as a batch remote-job-entry system; he may enter updates to a source module and initiate a test run, but he does not interact with the system (i.e., if something goes wrong he reports back to the programmer). It may be argued that this is not the case for interactive debugging tools, for in this situation the programmer and not the librarian must interact with the system. However, Chapter 13 mentioned some evidence implying that the best way to debug a program might be without the use of a computer.

PROGRAMMING TEAMS

Another recent change in project organizations is the idea that programmers should work in formal teams, putting an end to the traditional view of programming as being a highly individualistic activity. Programming teams have proved to have many significant benefits: communications among programmers are improved, teams develop group standards for quality and self-control, team members learn a great deal from one another, egoless programming is encouraged because programmers view their product as a team, rather than an individual, accomplishment, and continuity is more easily maintained when an individual unexpectedly leaves the project. Three common variations of the programming team concept are discussed here: the chief programmer team, the specialist team, and the democratic team.

The *chief programmer team* concept was originated by H. Mills of IBM [3]. The team is headed by a chief programmer: a senior-level programmer who is highly skilled and experienced. The chief programmer performs all of the design tasks, writes the code for all critical modules, and performs the integration and testing of the team's code. He is also the primary interface to outside organizations such as other teams and the user organization, thus reducing the number of lines of communication among project members. The chief programmer is assisted by a *back-up programmer*: a programmer with similar skills who performs such activities as researching design alternatives, planning, and participating in the design, coding, and testing activities. The other permanent member of the team is a programming librarian. The remainder of the team is transient and depends on the particular stage of the project. For instance, a systems analyst might be added to the team during the external design stage and two to five programmers might be added for the coding stage.

A major advantage of the chief programmer team is getting senior-level people back into the main stream of the software business. In many programming organizations the highly experienced personnel are totally disassociated from the development projects. People often view advancement in the software field as escaping from "coding jobs" as soon as possible. This attitude has forced many highly technically qualified people into management positions or into staff jobs that are detached as much as possible from the software development tasks. The chief programmer concept attempts to correct this situation by establishing valuable and respected professional positions in software projects.

The chief programmer team can also have several disadvantages. Skeptics often say that chief programmer teams are fine for chief programmers but uninspiring for everyone else because programmers are often shuffled around from team to team, eliminating their sense of responsibility and accomplishment. This attitude is reflected in a number of discussions of the subject: "Other programmers are added to the team only to code specific well defined functions . . ." [6] and "programmers may easily move from one project to another and yet get immediately down to details . . ." [7].

For the concept to work, the chief programmer must be a highly respected senior-level programmer. Forming a team of programmers with relatively equal experience and appointing one of them as the chief often leads to failure because of the jealousies created. Even when the chief programmer is highly respected, there is often a significant amount of jealousy within the team because of the feeling that the chief is privy to special information. Because of the nature of the position, proponents feel that the chief programmer needs management training and in fact must be a manager [6]. This is certainly a controversial idea because it could easily inhibit information flow and rapport within the team.

A second variation, the *specialist team,* has been proposed by Brooks [2]. The major difference between this team and the chief programmer team is that the team members remain with the team for the entire project and each member of the team has a special assignment that takes advantage of his particular talents. This team is led by a chief programmer, but this chief programmer writes *all* of the code and documentation for the team's product. The team also has a back-up programmer who researches alternatives, serves as a devil's advocate for the chief programmer, and interfaces with other programming teams on the project. Brooks also suggests that the team have an administrator: a person who is solely concerned with budgets, physical space, machine time, and personnel problems. A fourth member of the team is a documentation editor. Although the chief programmer produces all of the documentation, the editor has the responsibilities of editing and clarifying the documentation and supervising its production.

The specialist team also contains a programming librarian as in the chief programmer team. An additional member of the team is a toolsmith: a person responsible for designing and developing (or acquiring) any programming or testing tools needed. The team also contains a test specialist who is responsible for writing all of the necessary test cases and developing any simulation or scaffolding code. The final member of the team is a language expert: a person who researches various programming techniques and algorithms.

A third type of programming team is the *democratic team* [8]. This team is different in that it has no formally appointed leader or initial individual assignments. Particular team members tend to rise to the occasion (become an informal leader) when the team enters a stage for which that team member is most qualified. The team makes its own work assignments based on the talents of the members. Hence this team tends to concentrate on the strengths of its individual members. One big difference between this team and the chief programmer team is that the democratic team stays together from project to project. When a project is completed the team is not broken up; it is assigned as a whole to a new project. This means that the rapport, working relationships, and group standards within the team are maintained from project to project.

The programming team is a valuable concept because it recognizes that programming is largely a social activity rather than an individual activity. However, as is the case for almost everything, programming teams do have a few disadvantages. The work of each individual programmer is less visible to the project manager, making performance evaluations more difficult. In the teams with a formal leader, the leader can become an interface between the manager and the other team members, leading to significant morale problems. (Of course, neither of these disadvantages is present if the chief programmer is also the manager.) Physical facilities may also have to be altered to encourage the team environment. Rather than using the traditional physical facilities where one or two programmers are in an office or where every programmer in the organization sits in one huge partitioned room, one might consider altering the office arrangements so that each programming team is placed in a single room of sufficient size.

There is no single "right" team organization for all environments, and in fact many companies use variations of these three basic organizations. If a chief programmer who has the respect of the team cannot be located, the democratic team is probably the best alternative. On the other hand, there may be a group of programmers who have difficulty working in a "leaderless" democratic environment, implying a need for a chief programmer team.

THE ELEMENTS OF A GOOD MANAGER

Of all the aspects of project management, probably the most important one in terms of software reliability is *management commitment*. Many programmers feel that managers pay only lip service to reliable software and that the only things managers are really committed to are meeting a schedule and a budget. Unfortunately, this feeling is often accurate. The typical project manager is primarily measured on meeting his schedule and budget and rarely measured on the number of software errors in the end-product. If this is the case, then the manager cannot help but reflect these priorities to his employees. One way to correct this situation is to evaluate managers, as well as programmers, on the reliability of the product.

An ongoing argument in programming project management is the question of how technically capable a manager should be. At one extreme, people believe that the manager should be an administrator and a personnel manager and have little if any technical knowledge about software development. At the other extreme, people believe that the manager should be the technical leader of his organization, possibly even a chief programmer. One clue to the answer to this argument comes from a study of Department of Defense software projects, which showed that the factor that correlated most closely with the success of the projects was the technical know-how of the project managers [9]. A manager must be knowledgeable about the technical aspects of software development to set objectives, make tradeoffs, evaluate the use of new tools and techniques, and accurately evaluate his programming staff. Of course, this technical capability should not be carried to the extreme where the manager is telling the programmer how to do his job. One definite requirement for a project manager is the ability and the commitment to read and evaluate the products of the people working for him or her, including their code, specifications, test cases, and so on. Requiring the project manager to read each programmer's code gives the manager a better understanding of the programmer's work and also in turn leads to more readable code.

Chapter 3 emphasized the importance of *project objectives,* that is, directions for the programming organization in making tradeoffs between such factors as efficiency, adaptability, schedule, reliability, code readability, and so forth. Not only does the good manager explicitly identify these objectives, but he lets his programming organization establish them, for experience has shown that people are more highly motivated to achieve their own objectives than they are to achieve the objectives of others.

In most management schools or courses, a considerable amount of time is spent emphasizing the fact that a manager must be prepared to say *no* to his or her manager. What many managers fail to recognize is that programmers in turn have a right to say no, particularly when they are placed in a position of compromising their own ethics, such as asking them to deliver a software system when they are fairly certain that it still contains critical errors, or asking them to meet an unreasonable schedule that compromises the quality of their work. One should also realize that programmers may belong to professional organizations such as the ACM, IEEE, or ACPA that have codes of ethics for their members, and that occasionally these codes of ethics conflict with organizational objectives. If you are a manager do you understand the codes of ethnics of these professional organizations?

As a final note, remember that programmers must be treated as professional human beings. Essential reading for every manager at every level in the software business is Weinberg's *The Psychology of Computer Programming* [8].

REFERENCES

1. J. L. Ogdin, "The Mongolian Hordes versus Superprogrammer," *INFOSYSTEMS,* **19** (12), 20–23 (1972).
2. F. P. Brooks, *The Mythical Man-Month: Essays on Software Engineering.* Reading, Mass.: Addison-Wesley, 1975.
3. F. T. Baker, "Chief Programmer Team Management of Production Programming," *IBM Systems Journal,* **11** (1), 56–73 (1972).

4. E. Yourdon and R. Abbott, "Programmers are Paid to Program: Enter Program Librarian," *INFOSYSTEMS*, **21** (12), 28–32 (1974).

5. J. Martin, *Design of Man-Computer Dialogues.* Englewood Cliffs, N.J.: Prentice-Hall, 1973.

6. F. T. Baker, "Organizing for Structured Programming," in C. E. Hackl, Ed., *Programming Methodology.* Berlin: Springer-Verlag, 1975, pp. 38–86.

7. C. L. McGowan and J. R. Kelly, *Top-Down Structured Programming Techniques.* New York: Petrocelli/Charter, 1975.

8. G. M. Weinberg, *The Psychology of Computer Programming.* New York: Van Nostrand Reinhold, 1971.

9. B. W. Boehm, "Keynote Address—The High Cost of Software," *Proceedings of a Symposium on the High Cost of Software.* Menlo Park, Cal.: Stanford Research Institute, 1973, pp. 27–40.

CHAPTER 15

Programming
Languages
and Reliability

The final representation of a software system is thousands or even millions of programming language statements. In some respects, the design of the language itself is not of vital importance because the majority of the significant software errors are created before the program is coded in some programming language. However, even the most trivial errors in using a language can sometimes lead to disastrous results. In a FORTRAN program controlling the United States' first mission to Venus, a programmer coded a DO statement in a form similar to the following:

$$DO\ 3\ I\ =\ 1.3$$

The mistake he made was coding a period instead of a comma. However, the compiler treated this as an acceptable assignment statement because FORTRAN has no reserved keywords, blanks are ignored, and variables do not have to be explicitly declared. Although the statement is obviously an invalid DO statement, the compiler interpreted it as setting a new variable DO3I equal to 1.3. This "trivial" error resulted in the failure of the mission. Of course, part of the responsibility for this billion-dollar error falls on the programmer and the test personnel, but is not the design of the FORTRAN language also partially to blame?

The main reason that programming language design has an effect on software reliability is that professional programmers spend more time examining existing programs than they spend writing new programs. (The word "professional" here denotes any person whose primary job is producing programs for use by other people.) The activities of debugging, maintaining, and extending programs are largely dependent on reading and understanding a program as it is represented in a programming language. Hence the design of programming languages does have a significant bearing on software errors.

The intent of this chapter is to point out flaws in existing languages and suggest solutions for future languages. Although the PL/I language is used to illustrate most of the flaws, this does not imply that PL/I is a poor language. The design of PL/I began in 1963, before the "programming revolution" began, and many of PL/I's flaws are also present in other languages. PL/I is discussed because it (or a dialect of it) is taught in many computer science curriculums (so readers might be more familiar with it than with other languages such as COBOL or RPG), PL/I was designed more recently than most of the other widely used languages, and it was designed for use on a wide variety of applications.

One conclusion that is becoming apparent is that a general-purpose programming language is infeasible. "General-purpose" does not necessarily mean applicability to a wide range of applications: it is taken here to mean applicability for use by a wide variety of people such as professional programmers, analysts, amateur or occasional programmers (e.g., a chemical engineer who occasionally writes a small program to solve some problem), and students being introduced to the concepts of programming. A language that is designed for such a wide audience must have conflicting objectives such as ease of learning, ease of use, ease of extending the language, ease of extending programs written in the language, resistance to programming errors, machine independence, efficient object code, and efficient compilation. If a language attempts to satisfy all of these goals, it will undoubtedly be less than ideal for each particular type of audience. The most successful programming languages are ones whose design was oriented to specific audiences (e.g., the BASIC language was designed for teaching university students and RPG was designed for commercial programmers having little or no formal data processing education).

In this chapter we consider issues in languages designed for use by professional programmers on projects where reliability is of primary importance. In such languages goals such as ease of learning, ease of use, speed of coding the program, and compiler efficiency are of little concern. The primary goals in this case are the readability of programs written in the language, the lack of error proneness in the language, and the ability to represent clearly and simply the program's function and logic. Some language efforts have started with similar goals. For instance, the system language for Project SUE (a language designed for implementing operating systems) was based on the following two design principles [1]:

1. The main function of a language is communication between people and it is essential that this communication be clear, convenient, and unambiguous. As systems grow larger, this communication becomes more crucial.

2. The importance of high-level languages in the construction of systems comes at least as much from the errors and "clevernesses" that they prevent as from the powerful operations that they make convenient.

As is the case with almost every area of software development, the following suggestions on language design are based on intuition and experience rather than on empirical evidence. Language design is one of the few areas in which controlled experiments are feasible but surprisingly few experiments have been performed. Two notable exceptions are the Rubey experiment for the U.S. Air Force [2] and the Gannon experiment at the University of Toronto [3]. The purpose of the Rubey experiment was to compare PL/I to three other languages. Seven different applications were selected and two programs were coded for each, one in PL/I and the other in JOVIAL, FORTRAN, or COBOL depending on which one seemed best suited to each application. The general conclusion was that PL/I is superior or equal in all application areas, but the value of the experiment is the wealth of quantitative and qualitative data produced about the programming errors that occurred.

The Gannon study was a statistical experiment using 51 programmers (university students but with reasonable experience) and two languages. The first language was TOPPS, an expression-oriented language designed to encourage and teach the use of asynchronous processes. The second language, TOPPSII, was specifically designed for the experiment. Numerous constructs in TOPPS were hypothesized as being error-prone and were redesigned in TOPPSII to statistically test the differences. In this study, 1248 errors were analyzed according to the cause of the error and the persistence of the error (the time until the error was detected). Both of these studies confirm many of the suggestions in this chapter.

For many years the subject of language design was considered to be the design of the language's grammar or syntax. For instance, the specifications of the many forms of ALGOL are primarily concerned with syntax and, to a lesser extent, semantics, and some of the semantics are explicitly left as "implementation defined." However, it is important to realize that in the complete design of a language (called a "language system" by Nicholls [4]) the grammar is only one of many considerations. Other factors such as semantics, compiler listings, diagnostic messages, run-time error detection, testing and debugging features, documentation, compile-time facilities, and intermodule symbol resolution (e.g., linkage editing) must receive equal consideration in the language design.

UNIFORMITY

One of the most important principles in language syntax and semantics is uniformity. A language construct that appears in several contexts should have the same syntax and semantics (e.g., if I/O statements and assignment statements can contain subscript expressions, the rules should be identical in both cases). A single language construct should not have multiple meanings [e.g., in many languages the statement $I = A(B)$ can mean "set I equal to the B-th element of array A" or "pass B to function A and set I equal to the returned value of A"]. The syntax of different language constructs should be as similar as possible (all PL/I statements begin with a keyword *except* the assignment statement).

Languages should also obey the informal law of least astonishment, which implies that the language must not "trick" the programmer. One of the most perplexing violations of this is the default rules in PL/I. To maintain some compatibility with FORTRAN (in itself a questionable objective), many PL/I compilers will default variables beginning with the letters I through N to binary integer variables as shown by the first two lines in the example below. However, notice what happens when the programmer explicitly states part of the defaulted attributes. The default rules suddenly change so that in one case he gets a decimal number with five decimal digits of precision and in another he gets a floating-point number with 21 binary digits of precision.

Coded DECLARE
Statement for I   Attributes Assigned

none	AUTOMATIC FIXED BINARY(15,0) REAL
DECLARE I;	AUTOMATIC FIXED BINARY(15,0) REAL
DECLARE I FIXED;	AUTOMATIC FIXED DECIMAL(5,0) REAL
DECLARE I BINARY;	AUTOMATIC FLOAT BINARY(21) REAL
DECLARE I STATIC;	STATIC FIXED BINARY(15,0) REAL

Most languages have striking examples of nonuniformity. In FORTRAN the slash ($/$) character is used as a separator in the DATA and blank COMMON statements, yet parentheses are used as separators in the EQUIVALENCE statement. In most specification types in the FORMAT statement the field length follows the type character (e.g., F8.0, A6, and I5) but for two types the type character follows the field length (e.g., 4X). In IBM's implementations of PL/I, variable names can be up to 31 characters long, but procedure names and names of global variables can only be up to seven characters long (and to make matters worse, if the names are longer than seven characters they are truncated by taking the first four characters and the last three characters). Programmers are often taught to use extra parentheses to clarify expressions because extra parentheses are overlooked by the compiler. In PL/I this rule is generally true but there are unfortunate exceptions. The following two CALL statements are semantically different; the first specifies a call-by-reference and the second specifies a call-by-value.

CALL AMOD(X);
CALL AMOD((X));

Languages can also be complicated by assigning multiple meanings to a single operator, such as PL/I's use of the equal character for assignment and comparison. The statement "$A = B = C;$" means "set A to one if B equals C or to zero if not." Also, notice how this expression is interpreted differently in two different contexts:

A = B = C;   is the same as A = (B = C);
IF A = B = C   is the same as IF (A = B) = C

The IF statement does not mean what it appears to mean. The IF expression is true if A is equal to B and C has the bit value one, or if A is not equal to B and C has the bit value zero.

In a form of the DO loop, PL/I allows a list of expressions to be specified so that the loop is executed once for each expression, and the iteration variable takes on the value of the ith expression for the ith iteration. Hence one might expect the loop

```
DO I=0,I=1;
    PUT DATA(I);
END;
```

to be executed twice and the values 0 and 1 to be printed. That expectation is half right; the loop executes twice but the value 0 is printed both times. I leave the reader with the exercise of explaining why (it is related to the nonuniform meaning of the equal sign).

Some languages give the programmer the alternative of terse abbreviations. This practice should be eliminated because it reduces the readability of the program, introduces multiple constructs with identical meanings, and occasionally the abbreviations themselves are not uniform. For instance, the PL/I keywords PROCEDURE, VARYING, and REDUCIBLE have the abbreviations PROC, VAR, and RED, but the keywords SEQUENTIAL, FIXEDOVERFLOW, and CONTROLLED have the abbreviations SEQL, FOFL, and CTL.

One last area of nonuniformity is not one of syntax or semantics but of the object code environment. Suppose we are developing a new PL/I program (or in any other language for that matter) and we discover that we already have some FORTRAN and COBOL subroutines that could be incorporated. Could we call them from the PL/I program? The answer is usually no, not without a great deal of difficulty. The execution-time environments of different languages are highly incompatible, even when the compilers are written for the same computing system by the same software company.

One solution to many of these problems is to apply the idea of conceptual integrity discussed in Chapter 4 to language design. Conceptual integrity implies that the language should have a single set of coherent harmonious functions and constructs. Any "feature" that appears to be inconsistent in syntax, semantics, or in any other way must be excluded from the language. It was also mentioned in Chapter 4 that achieving conceptual integrity requires an extremely small design team (a maximum of two decision makers was suggested). As evidence of this, three highly uniform languages, APL, PASCAL, and the system language for Project SUE, were designed by one or two people.

SIMPLICITY

For precision programming the programmer must have complete mastery of his programming language. The language must be small enough to allow the programmer to have a complete understanding, yet it must encourage the clearest possible statement of the programmer's thoughts. The language must not encourage obscurity nor increase the programmer's opportunities to make mistakes. Alternatives must be minimized so that the programmer is not given many ways of doing the same thing.

One proposed way [4] of achieving simplicity is incorporating the "magical number seven" (proven to have a significant bearing on a human's discrimination and short-term memory capabilities) in language design. At each point the programmer should be faced with seven or less decisions in coding a language statement. That is, there should be a maximum of seven statement types, seven optional keywords within each statement, seven data types, seven operators, and so forth. This is achieved by eliminating alternatives or by introducing additional levels of hierarchy into the language structure.

PL/I is the best example of a programming language that violates most of the goals mentioned above (and COBOL is a close second). It is unlikely that any PL/I programmer could claim mastery of the language. PL/I contains over 30 basic data types, and some of these appear to do more harm than good. One of these data types is the LABEL variable, which allows the program to dynamically alter its structure, resulting in an obscure program. For instance, the following program shows how a "dynamic GO TO" can be constructed.

DECLARE XLAB LABEL;

.
.

XLAB=ALAB;

.

XLAB=BLAB;

.
.

GO TO XLAB;

This GO TO is much worse than the normal GO TO because the reader has no idea of what statements it may branch to without tracing the execution flow of the program.

PL/I contains many desirable features, but it suffers by having too many features. It seems that the PL/I language could have been an exceptionally good language if only three changes were made: about 80% of the language features were eliminated, the automatic data conversions (discussed in a later section) were completely eliminated, and the documentation was better written and better organized.

Language simplicity does not imply infinite generality; it implies clarity and integrity of language concepts. A reasonable measure of simplicity is the size of the language reference manual. A simple language is not necessarily one that is not powerful; APL is probably the best example. The system language for Project SUE has powerful constructs such as a block structure, a variety of data types including arrays and structures, compile-time macro facilities, IFTHENELSE, DO, CASE, and ASSERT statements, and explicit storage allocation, yet a formal description of its syntax takes only three pages [5].

DATA DECLARATION

An important consideration in language design is the method in which a programmer declares or defines the data in his program. Identifying the attributes (e.g., size and type) of each variable is important because it allows the compiler to detect certain errors (e.g., attempting to add a character string to a decimal number) and it serves as an important form of documentation about the program (understanding the data is the first step in understanding a program).

The first rule for data declarations is to require the explicit declaration of all variables. APL is weak in this area since it does not permit any form of data declaration. In FORTRAN (and in many other languages) any variables that are not explicitly declared receive default declarations. For instance, the typographical error in the statement

INDEX = INDEZ + 1

to increment INDEX will not be detected by most compilers. The compilers will assume that INDEZ is another variable and it will probably have an unpredictable value, leading to an error that may be difficult to locate. If one FORTRAN subroutine passes an array as an argument to another subroutine and the corresponding parameter in the called subroutine is not explicitly declared, the compiler assumes that every subscripted reference to the array is a call to a function subprogram, leading to an attempt to execute the array!

An interesting extension of this explicit declaration rule was made in the system language for Project SUE [1]. In this language the use of any constants with values greater than two is prohibited. Any constant greater than two must be explicitly declared and assigned a name. This minimizes the use of "mystery values" in programs and is an example of the enforcement of good programming style through language design.

A second recommendation for data declarations is that default rules be eliminated (so that the programmer must explicitly state all attributes of a variable) or, alternatively, the default rules should be extremely simple. I have already given an example of the complex default rules in PL/I. A common source of errors in the Rubey experiment [2] was the surprising default rules in PL/I. PL/I compounds this weakness in additional ways. There is a DEFAULT statement that allows the programmer to alter the default rules. Certain PL/I compilers even go to the extent of giving the programmer the option of not receiving the compilers' listings describing how it applied the defaults! To be fair to PL/I, the default rules were originated to make life easier for the amateur or occasional programmer, but this is another example of why a good general-purpose language is probably impossible.

A related problem in language design is described as *duplicity* [4]: situations where the program does not do what it appears to do. The most common occurrence is when references to a particular variable actually cause other variables to be referenced. For instance, there is no guarantee that the FORTRAN statement

$$A(J) = 1.0$$

alters an element in array A. This statement could even alter an element in another array if the value of J is beyond the extent of array A. The on-conditions in PL/I are a second example of duplicity because a condition could arise in the execution of a particular statement that causes an on-unit to receive control and alter some additional variables. A third example of duplicity is the use of a single storage area for multiple variables by using such constructs as the EQUIVALENCE statement in FORTRAN, the REDEFINES clause in COBOL, or the DEFINED attribute in PL/I. Whenever a statement alters one of these variables, the others automatically change. Needless to say, constructs that lead to duplicity also lead to obscure programs and should be avoided in languages.

The issue of uniformity also applies to the area of data declarations.

PL/I has a desirable property of allowing operations to be applied to entire arrays and structures as well as single variables. For instance, the following assignment statement sets all ten elements of A to zero.

```
DECLARE A(10) FIXED DECIMAL(5,0);
A = 0;
```

Variables can also be initialized in the DECLARE statement, so one might expect that the following statement has the same effect:

```
DECLARE A(10) FIXED DECIMAL(5,0) INITIAL(0);
```

Unfortunately, it does not; it only initializes the first element to zero. The attribute INITIAL ((10)0) is needed to initialize all elements. Notice that this requires us to state "10" twice, which is bound to lead to an occasional error when we are altering the size of the array.

DATA TYPES AND CONVERSION

There seems to be a trend in languages to give the programmer a broad selection of data representations. For instance, PL/I has over 30 data types and, if one considers that many of these types can have a large number of precisions (number of bits or digits in the data item), the programmer is faced with selecting among several thousand alternative forms. This trend must be reversed because it leads to unnecessary complexity, lack of machine independence, arbitrary decisions by the programmer, and pathological data conversion rules.

In real arithmetic (not complex numbers) PL/I offers decimal fixed-point with 240 different precisions, binary fixed-point with 992 different precisions, decimal floating-point with 33 different precisions, and binary floating-point with 109 precisions. Almost all of these possibilities could be eliminated without any loss of function. For instance, binary floating-point numbers (which have the form 11010.11011E2B) could be eliminated as well as binary fixed-point numbers.

There is no need to give the programmer so much control over the selection of the internal data representation (binary versus decimal) and the precision of the number, nor is there even a need to state whether the number has a fixed-position or floating decimal point. The APL language is proof of this; where PL/I has thousands of numerical forms, APL has just one. APL stores this single arithmetic data type in one of three internal forms (bit, binary, or floating point), depending on its use in the program. If a variable takes on only values of zero and one, it is stored as a bit. If a variable has only integer values, it is represented as a binary integer. If a variable has fractional values, it is stored as a floating-point number. Furthermore, APL changes this internal form dynamically based on how the variable is being used in the program.

A major reason for the simplicity of APL is its limited data types. There are only two data types (numbers and characters) and two ways of organizing data (scalars and arrays). However, APL has probably carried this simplicity too far. The useful concept of a *structure,* an organization concept in PL/I and COBOL that can be used to represent a file record with heterogeneous fields, is missing from APL. In perhaps an example of overgeneralization, APL represents entities such as statement labels as scalar variables, meaning that a programmer can perform such tricks as using a statement label as a variable in an assignment statement.

An important part of a high-level language is the elimination of the concept of a linear sequential storage and the introduction of the concept of disjoint variables. One data type that contradicts this is the *pointer variable,* a variable whose value is the address of another variable. The pointer concept as implemented in PL/I is an error-prone construct because it gives the programmer direct access to machine storage. If a pointer variable points to a data area in storage and the data area is freed, the pointer is not "dereferenced"; it continues to point to that machine location. This has led to subtle programming errors and has encouraged tricky programming. Hoare [6] considers the introduction of the pointer variable as "a step backward from which we may never recover."

If a language has a pointer construct, it should be constrained in at least two ways: when a data area is freed, any pointers to it should be "dereferenced" (given null values) and pointers should be declared as pointing to a specific data type or variable name to allow the compiler to detect certain assignment errors. ALGOL 68 and the system language for Project SUE have implemented the latter constraint.

A better solution is to eliminate the concept of a pointer. Pointer variables are generally used to implement linear lists (tables, stacks, and queues), multilinked lists, and trees. Rather than giving the programmer the dangerous flexibility of pointers, these data structures could be directly supported by the language. For instance, the system language for Project SUE contains the valuable data structure called a *set* and associated operators such as union, intersection, difference, containment, and equality [7].

One advantage of having different data types is that the compiler can detect such errors as adding a number and a character string. PL/I is weak in this area in three respects: not only does it have thousands of data types, but it does no checking for inconsistent data types and its conversion rules are unbelievably complex. In PL/I it is possible to mix real numbers, complex numbers, bit strings, and character strings in one assignment statement, although the result is often hard to predict.

PL/I automatic data conversion occurs in any expression involving variables of different types or precisions. The conversion rules occupy many pages in the language manual [8] and are so complicated that even experienced PL/I programmers will probably not guess the answers to the examples presented here. The PL/I expression $25 + 1/3$ yields the value $5.333\ldots$ but the expression $25 + 01/3$ yields the correct answer $25.333\ldots$, showing that the belief that leading zeros are meaningless is not always correct. In the following program,

```
DECLARE (I,J) FIXED BINARY (31,5);
I = 1;
J = 1;
I = I + .1;
J = J + .1000;
```

the final value of I is 1.0625 and the final value of J is 1.09375, showing that *trailing* zeros are also meaningful.

In the following program, to where is execution transferred?

```
DECLARE B BIT(1);
B = 1;
IF B = 1 THEN GO TO Y;
         ELSE GO TO X;
```

By now the reader may have decided to bet against his intuition, and if so is correct; execution transfers to label X. The reason is the conversion of the fixed-decimal constant 1 of precision (1,0) to a bit data type in the assignment statement and to a fixed binary data type in the comparison. It is not my intention to explain the conversion rules here but merely to illustrate their effects. As one more example, try guessing the final value of B in the program below.

```
DECLARE B BIT (5);
B = 1;
```

B has the bit string value '00010'B.

PL/I data conversions in procedure-calls can be extremely error prone. Suppose procedure A calls procedure B passing it an argument X. The normal parameter mechanism is call-by-reference (the address of X is passed to B). However, if the type or precision of the argument differs from that of the corresponding parameter in B, an automatic conversion of X is done, the converted value is placed in a temporary location, and the address of this temporary location is passed to B. If procedure B is supposed to alter the value of X, X will never change; only the value in the temporary location will change. All of this happens without any warning from the compiler and it leads to extremely subtle errors.

These examples lead to the conclusion that no automatic data conversions should exist in a language. Any attempt to mix data types in an expression should be flagged by the compiler. Of course, it is occasionally necessary to convert a variable to another type, but explicit functions should exist in the language to do so. ALGOL does not fully adhere to this recommendation, but it does present a reasonable compromise. In ALGOL only "widening" is permitted [9]. An integer can be automatically converted to a real (floating-point) or a complex number, or a real number can be converted to a complex number, but implicit conversions in the opposite direction are prohibited.

PROCEDURES AND DATA SCOPING

Another important aspect of programming languages is the degree to which the language supports desirable properties of system and program structure as discussed in Chapters 5 and 6. Concepts such as levels of abstraction, high module strength, and loose module coupling cannot be fully realized without proper language support.

One basic construct that must exist in the language is the module or external procedure. A module is a closed subroutine that can be separately compiled and has the potential to be called from anywhere within the program. Most languages provide this concept; one notable exception is ALGOL.

An important concept that must be supported by languages is the informational-strength module, as discussed in Chapter 6. This module has multiple entry points where each entry represents a closed subroutine. The entries must be independent from one another (e.g., variable and parameter names must be local to the code for the entry point) except for the data structure that the module is hiding, which must be known to all entries. PL/I does the best job of supporting this concept, but by examining Figures 8.2 and 8.7 several weaknesses can be noted. One entry point must arbitrarily be designated as the "main" entry point (the PROCEDURE name), thus distorting the concept that all entry points are peers. The only way to isolate the code for each entry point is by enclosing them in BEGIN blocks, which introduces some execution inefficiency. Also, the language does not permit the ENTRY statement to be enclosed in the BEGIN block, meaning that the parameter names are not local to the entries.

A data type that is associated with the use of the informational-strength module and should be present in languages is the concept of a *name*. Notice in the design of the loader in Chapter 6 that the name ESTAB is passed among many modules but only one module knows anything about the structure of ESTAB. The only way of implementing this in PL/I is to declare ESTAB as a pointer variable, but this may lead to problems because of the generality of the pointer concept. To properly support composite design, languages should introduce the *name* data type: a method of passing a variable or data structure among modules without knowing anything about its attributes or format. A module that declares a variable as a *name* should not be permitted to alter the variable or use it as anything but an argument or parameter.

The CALL statement in languages can be improved in a significant way. Part of the task of designing module interfaces is the specification of which arguments are inputs and/or outputs, but this distinction is not reflected in most languages. An improvement can be made if the CALL statement is changed to a form such as

CALL FINDTOK IN(XSTRING) OUT(SIZE,TOKEN)

Not only does this improve the readability of the program, but it also allows certain errors to be detected. For instance, all arguments that are specified as inputs but not outputs could be protected against alteration in the called module.

One dangerous practice in using CALL statements should be prohibited by the language. The following two statements are another example of duplicity because M and N in the called module have been assigned the same storage area by the CALL statement.

CALL X (I,I);

.

.

X: PROCEDURE (M,N);

The compiler should flag any multiple uses of the same argument name in a CALL statement.

The last area of interest in the relationships between language and system structure is *data scoping*: the methods in which data can be shared among modules or procedures when the data is not transferred as arguments. Chapters 5 and 6 explain that use of global data in a program is undesirable, but this does not necessarily imply that languages should eliminate the concept. The use of global data or data scoping is occasionally warranted, but it must be done under carefully controlled conditions.

One basic rule is that a variable must be local to a single module or procedure unless the programmer explicitly says otherwise. APL is weak in this area because it adopts the opposite principle; unless the programmer explicitly says that a variable is local to a given module (APL function), the variable becomes a global variable. This is a common cause of insidious bugs where a programmer consistently uses a variable name such as I as a loop control in many APL functions but in one or more of the functions he neglects to state that I is local.

In most other languages all variables default to local, but in languages where the concept of *internal procedures* (closed subroutines within modules) is provided (e.g., PL/I, COBOL, and ALGOL) the rule is usually violated. If a variable is used in an internal procedure but not explicitly declared, the variable is shared with the enclosing procedure. Wulf and Shaw [10] have built a strong case against this scoping practice. Of course, if the suggestion is adopted that all variables must be explicitly declared, this problem disappears.

Several principles should be adopted to control data scoping and global data. All data should be local to the procedure in which they are declared unless the programmer explicitly says otherwise. No variable should be globally known to two procedures unless both procedures designate it as such. Every global variable should be "owned" by a single module that can state which other modules can access the variable and what type of access each module can have (e.g., read-only access).

CONTROL STRUCTURES

Since the advent of structured programming, most language research has been focused on program control flow, primarily on the elimination of the GO TO statement. The interest has gone to the extent of prompting a satirical proposal for a COME FROM statement [11]. Although the GO TO statement is often the cause of overly complicated program logic, all uses of the GO TO are not harmful and in fact the GO TO is occasionally desirable [12].

Knuth [12] gives a good perspective on the concern over the GO TO statement: "But there has been far too much emphasis on *go to* elimination instead of on the really important issues." The Rubey experiment [2] seems to confirm this. Disregarding punctuation errors, there were 266 errors encountered and the most common cause (119 errors) was errors in data, file, and format descriptions. It is not clear how many of the remaining 147 errors would have been prevented by the absence of the GO TO statement; for instance, only 32 errors were due to sequence control and decision mistakes.

One popular extension to the traditional control structures is the CASE statement. The CASE statement is essentially a multiway IF statement, allowing one of n groups of statements to be executed based on the value of an index variable. For instance, ALGOL-W has a CASE statement where one of n blocks is selected based on the value of the index variable. However, the language definition states that the value of the index variable must be less than or equal to n. Of course, there is no guarantee that this will be true, and the program's behavior in this event is undefined. A CASE statement should always contain an ELSE condition that specifies a block to be executed when no other block is selected.

Although the CASE statement is a popular language issue, it does not seem to offer much of an advantage over a sequence of IFTHEN statements. Also, the use of a numerical index from 1 to n will not be useful in most real situations (e.g., one may want to take four actions depending on whether TRANCODE has the character value ADD, UPD, DEL, or DIS).

Problems in control structure may occur in subtle and simple ways. PL/I contains an END statement that is used to denote the ends of statement groups such as DO loops, DO groups, and BEGIN blocks. The helpful feature of such a statement is that the compiler can detect missing ENDs by comparing the number of DOs and BEGINs to the number of ENDs. However, PL/I defeats this checking by the "feature" of *multiple-closure ENDs*. If an END is followed by a label (e.g., the procedure name), then all missing ENDs are generated by the compiler at the point of this END (hence the term multiple-closure END). The consequences of this are often disastrous and, in particular, this was a common source of errors in the Rubey experiment. The multiple-closure END has no place in a programming language; its only use is to encourage sloppy programming. To generalize from this example, compilers must avoid making guesses or assumptions about the programmers' intentions.

Languages should prohibit the program from modifying itself, but most languages allow this to be done in one form or another (e.g., as previously mentioned, the label variable in PL/I is a way of modifying a GO TO statement). COBOL contains a nasty violation of this: the ALTER statement. The COBOL statement

ALTER ROUTINE-1 TO PROCEED TO END-ROUTINE

says that the GO TO statement in paragraph ROUTINE-1 is to be modified to say GO TO END-ROUTINE.

Needless to say, a language must provide the constructs needed for structured programming (e.g., DOWHILE and IFTHENELSE) and these control constructs must be designed in a clear and uniform way. The APL language is weak in this respect; not only does it lack these basic constructs, but the control constructs that it does provide tend to be obscure. For instance, in the following two APL statements, the first statement says, "if X is equal to Y go to statement 6" and the second statement says," if X is equal to Y then go to statement 6, else return."

$$\rightarrow 6 \times \iota \ (X=Y)$$
$$\rightarrow 6 \times \ (X=Y)$$

An experimental attempt has been made to correct these deficiencies by adding the conventional structured programming control constructs to APL [13].

DATA OPERATIONS

Of course, the ultimate purpose of a programming language is to perform operations on some set of data. The power of a language's data operations has a positive effect on software reliability by reducing the amount of code that has to be written by the programmer. PL/I allows operations to be performed on entire arrays or structures or on cross sections of arrays (e.g., a particular row or column), thus allowing the programmer to do in one statement what might have taken him an entire DO loop in FORTRAN. The power of APL largely stems from the uniform way its operators apply to vectors and arrays as well as scalars.

One common source of errors is the use of logical operators such as *and* and *or*. For instance, if one wants to determine if the value of I is one or two, there is a strong tendency to code

$$\text{IF } I = (1 \text{ OR } 2)$$

which often has an effect exactly opposite to what was intended. The expression above might cause the constants 1 and 2 to be converted to bit strings, the bit strings to be *or-ed* together (yielding a bit string of value three), this bit string to be converted to the data type of *I*, and the comparison to be made. The test could result in a *true* condition if *I* was three and a *false* condition if *I* was one! A reasonable suggestion [3] is to eliminate the *and* and *or* operators and replace them with the built-in functions ALL and ANY. The test for *I* would then be written

$$\text{IF } I = \text{ANY } (1,2)$$

Before the APL language there was general agreement that expressions should be evaluated from left to right. In APL the evaluation proceeds from right to left, so that the expression $3 - 1 + 2$ has the value 0 instead of 4. APL fans will argue that this right-to-left convention is more natural, but one of the reasons for this convention is to allow APL assignment statements to be nested within assignment statements, in itself a questionable practice. Because many other areas (e.g., writing, mathematics, circuit diagrams) use the left-to-right convention, the left-to-right convention seems less error prone and there is some experimental evidence confirming this [3].

COMPILE-TIME ERROR DETECTION

In Chapter 8 it was stated that the professional programmer must write his program so that he expects it to compile successfully on its first compilation. One reason for this was that few if any compilers are capable of detecting every syntax error. Any undetected syntax errors become logic errors. Language designers and compiler writers have seemed to adopt the attitude that programmers are perfect. Whenever a language specification uses the phrase "must be," the specification must contain a description of the action to be taken by the compilers when the "must be" is not true. This description is rarely present. Compilers writers are often guilty of believing the "must be" phrases in the specification, leading to a compiler that takes some undefined and unpredictable action whenever the program being compiled violates a "must be."

As an example, the FORTRAN language states that the initial value in a DO loop must be greater than zero. This means that the following program should be invalid:

```
L = 10
DO 20 I = 0,L

20 CONTINUE
```

The IBM FORTRAN H compiler does not detect the error and the code it generates causes the loop body to execute only once. On the other hand, the WATFOR compiler flags this as an error [14].

The best thing that a compiler can do for software reliability is to detect all syntax errors. Compiler projects would benefit by adopting the following objective of the Ditran compiler [15]: "Any condition prohibited by the specifications of the language or any condition prohibited by the machine implementation must be detected and not allowed to produce some undefined result." A full 56% of the run-time errors in the Rubey experiment could have been detected by the compilers if the compilers strictly enforced the language definitions and if the languages had less error-prone syntax and required full and explicit declaration and initialization of all variables [16].

To give the compiler an adequate opportunity to detect syntax errors, the language should be designed so that common syntax errors lead to syntactically invalid programs. Frequently made syntax errors should not result in the program statement being recognized as syntactically valid but with a different meaning than that intended by the programmer (e.g., typing a period instead of a comma in the DO statement at the beginning of the chapter transformed it into a valid assignment statement).

Compilers for professional programmers (contrasted with amateur programmers) should never attempt to automatically correct syntax errors or simply overlook the statement in error in order to produce an object program that the programmer may execute if he wishes. Such correction steps are often incorrect and they encourage sloppy programming. Many of the options in current compilers should also be eliminated. For instance, a programmer should not have the options of suppressing parts of the compiler listing or suppressing error messages.

Optimizing compilers are fine except when they introduce new errors into the program being compiled. For instance, IBM's

FORTRAN H compiler optimizes the following program by moving the SQRT function call to before the IF statement.

```
DO 11 I = 1,5
DO 12 J = 1,5
IF (B(I).LT.0) GO TO 11
12 C(J) = SQRT(B(I))
11 CONTINUE
```

Also, many potential situations for optimization are situations where the programmer actually made a mistake. For instance, an optimizing compiler might examine IF statements to see if the THEN clause and the ELSE clause are the same, meaning that the IF and one of the clauses can be deleted as in the following situation:

```
IF  A = B  THEN  A = A/2;
        ELSE  A = A/2;
```

This situation is more likely a programming error than a candidate for optimization. A good optimizing compiler might consider occasionally writing the message, "I am optimizing this piece of code but it looks suspicious to me. Please examine it to ensure that it is what you intended."

A good compiler can also analyze the source program in other ways for potential errors. For instance, it is possible for a compiler to detect situations where a variable is being used before it is ever initialized. The compiler can detect situations where a variable is being set and then set again without being referenced (although this is just a potential error). For instance, the sequence of statements starting with an assignment to X, one or more statements that do not reference X and do not branch or receive a branch, and then another assignment to X probably represents an error.

Compilers can detect additional errors if data declaration statements are extended to specify admissible values for variables. For instance, the system language for Project SUE allows the following data declarations:

```
TYPE angle = (0 TO 359);
TYPE direction = (north,east,south,west);
DECLARE angle a;
DECLARE angle b;
DECLARE direction movement;
```

This allows the compiler to detect invalid assignments to the variables *a*, *b*, and *movement*. Of course, the compiler cannot detect all of the invalid assignments (e.g., those involving parameters, input/output data, or complex computations), so this checking could be extended to the execution environment.

One disadvantage of separately compiled modules is that the compiler cannot detect inconsistent interfaces. However, most computing systems contain a function (often called a linkage editor) that builds a program from its object modules. The linkage editor should check for intermodule errors such as instances where the number of arguments is unequal to the number of corresponding parameters or where an argument and its corresponding parameter are different data types.

EXECUTION-TIME ERROR DETECTION

The "must be" argument presented earlier also applies during the execution of a program. If a language specification says "must be" about some semantic condition, one might expect that any violations will be detected during execution, but this is rarely the case. Most languages state that a subscripted reference to an array element cannot exceed the bounds of the array, but if an array bound is exceeded it is rarely detected and yields unpredictable results. The FORTRAN language states that the value of an index variable for a computed GO TO cannot exceed the number of statement numbers in the GO TO. However, five FORTRAN compilers from different computer manufacturers generate five different actions for the following program:

```
I = 5
GO TO (11,12,13,14),I
```

One compiler generates a wild branch, another generates a branch to statement 14, another skips to the statement following the GO TO, the fourth goes to statement 11, and the fifth detects the error and terminates the program.

Some compilers generate extra tests to detect error conditions when the program is compiled for "debugging mode" but remove the tests when the program is compiled for "production mode" (for reasons of "efficiency"). As Knuth and Hoare put it, this is like a sailor who wears his life jacket while training on land but then leaves it behind when he goes to sea [12].

One useful language statement for execution-time error detection is the *assertion statement,* which might take a form such as

ASSERT (0<INDEX<100,ORDER<ONHAND+INTRANS)

The assertion statement can be used to cause the compiler to generate defensive code at the beginning of each module or at other critical areas in the program. A standard error action could be defined for instances when the assertion is not true. The assertion is also useful as documentation when modifying or debugging the program.

REFERENCES

1. B. L. Clark and J. J. Horning, "Reflections on a Language Designed to Write an Operating System," *SIGPLAN Notices,* **8** (9), 52–56 (1973).

2. R. J. Rubey et. al., "Comparative Evaluation of PL/I," ESD-TR-68-150, U.S. Air Force, Bedford, Mass., 1968.

3. J. D. Gannon and J. J. Horning, "Language Design for Programming Reliability," *IEEE Transactions on Software Engineering,* **SE-1** (2), 179–191 (1975).

4. J. E. Nicholls, "Complexity and Duplicity in Programming Languages," TR-12.101, IBM United Kingdom Laboratories, Hursley, England, 1972.

5. B. L. Clark and J. J. Horning, "The System Language for Project SUE," *SIGPLAN Notices,* 6 (9), 79–88 (1971).

6. C. A. R. Hoare, "Hints on Programming Language Design," STAN-CS-73-403, Stanford University, 1973.

7. B. L. Clark and F. J. B. Ham, "The Project SUE System Language Reference Manual," CSRG-42, Computer Systems Research Group, University of Toronto, 1974.

8. *OS PL/I Checkout and Optimizing Compilers: Language Reference Manual,* SC33-0009, IBM Corp., White Plains, N. Y., 1972.

9. S. H. Valentine, "Comparative Notes on ALGOL 68 and PL/I," *The Computer Journal,* **17** (4), 325–331 (1974).

10. W. Wulf and M. Shaw, "Global Variable Considered Harmful," *SIGPLAN Notices,* **8** (2), 28–34 (1973).

11. R. L. Clark, "A Linguistic Contribution to GOTO-less Programming," *DATAMATION,* **19** (12), 62–63 (1973).

12. D. E. Knuth, "Structured Programming with go to Statements," *Computing Surveys,* **6** (4), 261–301 (1974).

13. R. A. Kelley, "APLGOL, an Experimental Structured Programming Language," *IBM Journal of Research and Development,* **17** (1), 69–73 (1973).

14. S. Siegel, "WATFOR . . . Speedy Fortran Debugger," *DATAMATION,* **17** (22), 22–26 (1971).

15. P. G. Moulton and M. E. Muller, "DITRAN—A Compiler Emphasizing Diagnostics," *Communications of the ACM,* **10** (1), 45–52 (1967).

16. D. K. Kosy, "Approaches to Improved Program Validation Through Programming Language Design," in W. C. Hetzel, Ed., *Program Test Methods.* Englewood Cliffs, N.J.: Prentice-Hall, 1973, pp. 75–92.

CHAPTER 16

Computer Architecture and Reliability

Computer architecture (the machine instruction level of a computer) has an indirect yet important effect on software reliability. Throughout the book the reader has seen many situations where reliability and efficiency clash with one another. By properly designing the computer itself, one can minimize this clash; programming languages and software systems can be designed with reliability as the primary goal, and the underlying computer can then be designed to execute this software in an optimal manner.

Before continuing with this idea, there is one relationship between computer hardware and software reliability that is so simple and obvious that it is often overlooked:

The biggest contribution that computer hardware can make to software reliability is continuing the trend of getting faster and cheaper.

Because of the clash between efficiency and reliability, reliability measures are often discarded for the sake of efficiency, for example omitting defensive code because it makes the program slower, avoiding high modularity because of the overhead of CALL statements, avoiding run-time checks by compilers because of their overhead, and using obscure programming tricks to squeeze a millisecond or two from the program. However, if the hardware processor were infinitely fast and had a price of only a few dollars, the clash would disappear because most efficiency concerns would have no justification.

Technological forecasting is always a risky matter, but forecasts that have been made paint an encouraging picture of the future [1]. It seems perfectly plausible to say that in 15 years from now the cost/performance ratio of processors will decrease by 100 times. As an indication of this, 1975 was the year of the arrival of central processing units with a production cost of under 100 dollars. Processors should be so inexpensive in the near future that the concept of multiprogramming (interleaving the execution of several programs on one processor) will probably disappear; instead, each executing program will be assigned one or more dedicated processing units. This cost/performance trend will benefit software reliability by making program efficiency a minor issue.

In the past, computer architects designed processors with little or no apparent knowledge of what programs are, what languages will be used, or how the compilers will be constructed. Studies have shown that many compilers use only a small subset of the instructions in the machines' instruction sets. In short, most computing systems have been designed in a bottom-up fashion. This has led to what Gagliardi calls the *semantic gap* [2]; the data and operations supported by the machine are rarely closely related to the data and operations in the programming languages. Computer architects are now beginning to realize that the gap between high-level languages and the machine instruction set must be closed; computer architectures must be oriented toward the programming languages. Not only does this have a positive effect on efficiency, but it has a positive effect on software reliability as will be illustrated later. This leads to two basic principles for computer architecture:

1. Computer architecture is not a separable art. The first step in designing a computer system is choosing or designing the programming languages to fit the end-use applications. The second step is designing the machine architecture and compilers and interpreters together, making the proper hardware–software tradeoffs among them. In doing this the real issue is not the number of instructions in the instruction set or the speed of any particular instruction, but the relationship of the machine architecture to the languages and compilers.

2. Machine or assembly language programming must be prohibited. If it is prohibited, many of the current issues in computer architecture such as virtual machines and memory protection mechanisms are of little or no importance because most of the problems that they attempt to solve will never occur if all programs are written in high-level languages. If machine language programming is allowed, the hardware–software tradeoffs in the first principle are all for naught because the programmer can circumvent them. The reader may have the feeling that it is impossible to prohibit machine language programming; it is not if such programming is made very difficult and if the motivations for doing it are removed. Computer manufacturers can prevent machine language programming by treating it in the same way that many manufacturers treat microprogramming today: by providing no support, no assemblers, and making it an "at your own risk" situation.

Because of the first principle, nothing specific should really be said about computer architecture without first considering the overall system design, particularly the programming languages. However, one improvement in computer architecture is almost universally accepted: *the Von Neumann type of computer is no longer desirable.*

The Von Neumann computer model has two major characteristics: the memory is a single linear sequential storage device and the machine does not distinguish between program instructions and data. The latter characteristic implies that programs can modify themselves and that the interpretation of whether a memory word is a datum or an instruction lies solely within the program executing on the machine. The vast majority of computers today are based on the Von Neumann model.

The important point about the Von Neumann model is that most high-level languages have eliminated the need for it. The concept of discrete named variables has eliminated the need for sequential memory. High-level language programs are not supposed to be able to be self-modifying. There is a sharp distinction between the program's data (which cannot be executed) and the program's statements (which cannot be referred to as data). The semantic gap between instruction sets and programming languages is largely due to the Von Neumann orientation of machine architectures and the elimination of this concept in languages. The following sections discuss methods of closing this gap.

MEMORY STRUCTURE

In the Von Neumann machine there is no meaning explicitly attached to each word in memory; the meaning is implicitly attached by the program. If a program says, "branch to this location," the machine interprets the word at that location as an instruction. If the program says, "do a floating-point addition of these two words," the machine interprets those words as having the format of floating-point numbers and performs the operation. Note, however, that in many language systems the compiler must maintain explicit descriptions of the program's data to perform data conversions, run-time error checking, symbolic debugging, and symbolic dumps. It appears that a reasonable tradeoff is to design the machine to maintain these data descriptions, thus moving the memory structure of the machine closer to the programming language.

The first step in doing this is to make every word in memory self-describing [3], as shown in Figure 16.1. The term *word* is used to define the addressable unit of storage. As Figure 16.1 implies, a word should not have a fixed or uniform length.

A memory word has four basic components as shown in Figure 16.1. (Please note that this format is used to discuss basic principles; it does not represent a specific machine design.) The variable-length *data* component is the value of the word. When a program references a word in storage (e.g., for a computation or input/output), the program sees only the data component. The *type* component describes the interpretation (data type) of the data component. These data types would correspond to the data types in the programming languages; examples would be integer, floating-point, character string, pointer, instruction, and module. Feustel [4] suggests 32 possible data types.

The *descriptor* component describes the length of the data component and indicates whether the data component has a meaningful value (i.e., a null or non-null indicator). If the machine is to recognize more complicated data organizations such as arrays, structures, or lists, information about these arrangements of the data component would also be present.

The *trap* component introduces the concept of a *program-oriented* (rather than system-oriented) interrupt. The trap component could specify that a special routine should receive control from the machine if this word is fetched or altered by the program or if this word (an instruction) is executed. This component is used by debugging tools and for instruction tracing and mapping.

Figure 16.1   **Self-descriptive memory.**

A program that is executing manipulates only the data component of the words. Special machine instructions are provided to store or examine the other three components, but these instructions are only used by the compiler or loader, debugging tools, and dump programs. The capability to *nest* memory words is desirable to provide such structures as strings of instructions within a module word and heterogeneous arrays of data.

Before proceeding with this design, we consider a few of its advantages:

1. Everything in memory is self-identifying. Program bugs, such as an attempt to branch to an array or to store into an instruction, are caught by the machine. Attempts to perform an arithmetic operation on inconsistent data types, or inconsistencies between arguments and parameters, are detected by the machine.

2. Rather than having unique machine instructions for each data type (e.g., binary add, floating-point add, decimal add), the machine has *generic* instructions (e.g., only one add instruction). The type of computation performed depends on the type components of the operands. This simplifies the code-generation processes in the compilers and, with some innovative language design, might mean that a program's data representations can be changed without recompiling the program (analogous to the concept of *data independence* in data base management systems).

3. Meaningful memory dumps are possible because the dump program can represent the value of each word in its proper data type.

4. The trap concept allows many of the tools discussed in Part 3 (e.g., instruction execution mapping and breakpoints for debugging) to be efficiently implemented.

Although most existing computers adhere to the Von Neumann model, a few have incorporated self-describing data, although generally not to the extent described previously. For instance, the Burroughs B6500 word has a 48-bit data component and a 3-bit type component [5]. Each word in the Rice Research R-2 computer has 54 data bits, 4 type bits, and 2 software-defined trap bits [6]. Each word in the ISPL system has 3 type bits and a 1-bit trap [7].

The next vital part of a memory structure is a method of referring to each word. The term *pointer* is used here to describe the reference to a memory word, but the term pointer should not imply a sequential or linear relationship among memory words. The format of a pointer is shown in Figure 16.2.

Address	Auth.	Disp.

Figure 16.2   **Contents of a pointer.**

The *address* component of a pointer is some name or value that tells the machine which word is being referenced. The address could be a memory segment name or number or any other unique combination of bits for that matter. The bits in the address component have absolutely no meaning above the machine interface. Programs can neither create addresses nor alter them in any way. When the program requests the machine to allocate a word of memory, the machine returns a unique address to the program. This is the only way that an address is created.

The pointer also contains an *authority* component. Authorities would include read/write authority and read-only authority for the referenced word. The machine allows the program to make a copy of a pointer and optionally lower the authority setting in the copy.

The third part of a pointer is a *displacement* component. This is a method of pointing to a particular position within the data component of the referenced word such as a character within a character string or an element within an array.

A pointer can be stored in a memory word or a register; in this event it has a data type of pointer and would take the form of Figure 16.3.

The pointer is the only mechanism needed for memory protection. A program cannot reference a word unless it has a pointer to the word, and self-generation or manipulation of pointers is prohibited by the machine. This means that a program (or module) can only reference those words that it created or words for which it was passed pointers from other programs. Associating the authority with the pointer rather than with the data itself allows different authorities to be granted to different programs or modules. The improved CALL statement in Chapter 15 can easily be implemented with this mechanism. Arguments are passed to a module by passing a list of pointers. The authority is set to read-only in each pointer of an argument that is strictly an input to the called module.

Type	Desc.	Trap	Address	Auth.	Disp.

Figure 16.3   **Storing a pointer in memory.**

The pointer mechanism as discussed so far has one significant weakness. There is nothing to prevent a program from saving a pointer to a word that has been freed and then later intentionally or accidentally using this pointer to reference memory. This situation is both an error-detection weakness and a security flaw in the architecture. One solution to this problem is to design the machine so that every pointer assigned by the machine is unique. The machine (throughout its lifetime) will never reuse the same pointer value (of course, the machine will reuse the same physical space, but the machine must maintain a map between pointers and physical locations). Pointer uniqueness can be achieved by embedding some type of time stamp in the address field when the pointer is assigned. Pointer uniqueness solves the weakness mentioned above by allowing the machine to detect all uses of obsolete pointers.

The concept of associating addresses and authorities has been implemented in a few computer architectures. In the ISPL system each pointer contains a read/write capability [7]. Plessey's SYSTEM 250 contains a concept called a *capability* that gives a module a specified type of access to a specified storage range [8].

PROGRAM STRUCTURE

A second likely hardware–software tradeoff in closing the semantic gap between machines and languages is the recognition of programs by machines. Most current architectures contain no knowledge of programs; they are simply "instruction executers." For instance, the only aspect of IBM's S/370 architecture that has any relationship to the concept of a program is the primitive branch-and-link instruction used for subroutine linkages.

Because many current systems impose efficiency penalties on modularity, and because of the emphasis on modularity in earlier chapters, one possible improvement is to have the machine formally recognize the concept of a module and handle the complicated module linkage process. To do this, consider three new machine instructions: CALL, ACTIVATE, and RETURN. The CALL and RETURN instructions correspond to the CALL and RETURN/END statements in most programming languages. The ACTIVATE instruction corresponds to PROCEDURE, SUBROUTINE, or ENTRY statements; it is generated by the compiler at each entry point of every module and at the beginning of each block in block-structured languages. All state saving, argument transmission, and storage allocation will be handled by the machine instead of by compiler-generated linkages.

To illustrate the operation of this approach, assume that the machine maintains information about each activation of a module as shown in Figure 16.4. This information is called an *activation block*; it is similar to the software-maintained linkage in the MULTICS system called a *stack frame* [9], except that activation blocks are maintained within the machine and are never seen by the software. The activation block contains a fixed-size header and a variable-size body. The header contains a register save area, addresses of the previous and next activation blocks, and the address of the instruction to which a called module should return. The body contains all the storage needed for local variables and temporary storage in this module.

When a CALL instruction is executed, the machine saves the program registers and the return address (normally the address of the instruction following the CALL instruction) in this module's current activation block (a recursive module or a module that is being executed by more than one program could have multiple activation blocks). The machine then begins executing the module that was called. The first instruction in the called module should be an ACTIVATE instruction. This instruction allocates a new activation block of the proper size and links it to the previous one. When a RETURN instruction is issued, the registers are reloaded from the previous activation block, the current activation block is destroyed, and the machine resumes execution at the return address in the previous module.

Save area for program registers
Address of previous block in stack
Address of next block in stack
Return address in this module
Storage pool from which local variables and other temporary storage are allocated

Figure 16.4   **Activation block.**

This mechanism also applies nicely to the processing of machine interrupts. When an interrupt occurs the machine simulates a CALL instruction, thus saving the state of the interrupted program. To resume execution of the interrupted program, the operating system issues a RETURN instruction.

Critical on-line systems need the capability of having program maintenance performed without interrupting the system's operation. A method is needed to insert "repaired" modules into a program without having to reload or reinitialize the program. One necessity in achieving this requirement is eliminating the traditional "link-edit" process (the binding of modules before execution). Modules must be bound dynamically; the conversion of a module name to a pointer must be done when the CALL is executed. This dynamic binding could be performed by software (e.g., the LINK function in OS/360), but it seems likely that efficiency will dictate a hardware or micropro-grammed solution. To do this the CALL machine instruction might have two operands: the symbolic name of the module being called and a list of argument pointers. The machine maintains a correspondence between module names and addresses so that it can dynamically transform a name into an address.

This mechanism eliminates the need for a linkage editor, but it still does not completely solve the problem of on-line module replacement. For instance, it seems impossible to replace a module while the module is executing or while other modules are in the process of calling it. To replace a module the machine needs an instruction to "suspend" a module. When a module is suspended all calls to it are temporarily intercepted and any activations of the module are allowed to complete. When this is done the new version of the module is loaded into storage, the machine updates its name/address table, and the halted programs are allowed to resume. (Of course, there will be modules that are permanently active when the system or program is running; in these cases the only recourse seems to be to terminate the system).

DEBUGGING AIDS

The memory structure described previously provides an efficient mechanism for implementing most of the common debugging functions. A reference to a word whose read-trap indicator is on would cause the machine to invoke a predetermined software routine, passing it the data address, the name of the module and number (or displacement) of the instruction that made the reference, and a time stamp. A modification to a word whose write-trap indicator is on would generate the same action, and in addition the old and new values of the data component would be given to the software routine. If the execute-trap indicator is on in a machine instruction that is being executed, the software routine is passed the module name, the instruction number, and a time stamp. This simple mechanism provides the ability to set breakpoints on executions of particular instructions or references and alterations to particular memory words, to trace or map the execution flow of a program, and to record the data references of a program. In addition, the concept of self-defining data gives the machine the ability to detect uses of uninitialized variables, computations involving inconsistent data types, inconsistencies between the attributes of arguments and parameters, and references beyond the extents of arrays. The software system is also provided with the ability to produce meaningful storage dumps.

Another possible debugging aid by the machine is automatic range checking of variables. When a word is allocated the machine could be given lower and upper boundary values of that word, allowing the machine to detect any out-of-range values. However, since this would significantly increase the amount of storage needed (triple in the worst case) and impose a performance penalty on the machine (or the need for extra parallel hardware), this suggestion is somewhat questionable and requires further investigation.

HIGH-LEVEL LANGUAGE MACHINES

Perhaps the extreme step in computer architecture is completely closing the semantic gap by making the machine language a high-level programming language. Rather than having traditional machine instructions such as load, store, and add-register, the machine instructions might be PL/I DECLARE statements, assignment statements, DO statements, and so on.

There is nothing magical about this approach, and it has been implemented on a number of experimental machines. One must view the source program as being interpreted instead of compiled into primitive machine code, and then view the interpreter as being microprogrammed instead of being a software program. Actually, a high-level language machine would not execute a program in its "raw" source form; a machine is considered a high-level language machine if there is a one-to-one correspondence between machine instructions and statements in the high-level language (similar to viewing a conventional machine as an assembly language machine). A simple software translator or "assembler" is usually present to find syntactic errors, remove blanks, convert names to addresses, and rearrange statements into a more manageable form such as postfix notation.

The most widely known high-level language machine is probably the SYMBOL 2R computer [10, 11]. The SYMBOL machine was specifically designed to execute a special high-level language called SPL, a language that is a mixture of features from PL/I, ALGOL, and APL. The SYMBOL computer also has no operating system; all of the traditional operating system functions are performed by the machine (i.e., the operating system is a hardware logic network).

One could design a PL/I machine and this would be fine if the operating system were coded in PL/I and all of the applications were PL/I programs, but what would be done about executing COBOL or RPG programs on such a machine? This problem was solved in the innovative Burroughs B1700 computer [12]. The B1700 has no fixed machine language. When a COBOL program is dispatched by the operating system the machine transforms itself into a COBOL high-level language machine. When a FORTRAN program is dispatched the machine becomes a FORTRAN machine. When the operating system is executing the instruction set becomes the language in which the operating system is coded. These transformations of the instruction set are performed by switching among many different microprogrammed interpreters. Measurements on this system have shown that this form of program execution requires less memory space and is more efficient than the execution of compiled low-level machine language programs on comparable machines [13].

For the reader who is interested in studying this high-level language machine concept in more detail, Ref. 14 is a good starting point.

REFERENCES

1. R. Turn, *Computers in the 1980s.* New York: Columbia Univ. Press, 1974.
2. U. O. Gagliardi, "Software-Related Advances in Computer Hardware," *Proceedings of a Symposium on the High Cost of Software.* Menlo Park, Cal.: Stanford Research Institute, 1973, pp. 99–119.
3. J. K. Iliffe, *Basic Machine Principles.* New York: American Elsevier, 1968.
4. E. A. Feustel, "On the Advantages of Tagged Architecture," *IEEE Transactions on Computers,* **C-22** (7), 644–656 (1973).
5. *Burroughs B6500 Information Processing Systems Reference Manual.* Burroughs Corp., Detroit, Mich., 1969.

6. E. A. Feustel, "The Rice Research Computer—A Tagged Architecture," *Proceedings of the 1972 Spring Joint Computer Conference*. Montvale, N.J.: AFIPS Press, 1972, pp. 369–377.

7. R. M. Balzer, "An Overview of the ISPL Computer System Design," *Communications of the ACM*. **16** (2), 117–122 (1973).

8. K. J. Hamer-Hodges, "Fault Resistance and Recovery Within SYSTEM 250," *Proceedings of the First International Conference on Computer Communications*. New York: IEEE, 1972, pp. 290–296.

9. E. I. Organick, *The MULTICS System: An Examination of Its Structure*. Cambridge, Mass.: MIT Press, 1972.

10. H. Richards and C. Wright, "Introduction to the SYMBOL 2R Programming Language," *ACM-IEEE Symposium on High-Level-Language Computer Architecture*. New York: IEEE, 1973, pp. 27–33.

11. P. C. Hutchinson and K. Ethington, "Program Execution in the SYMBOL 2R Computer," *ACM-IEEE Symposium on High-Level-Language Computer Architecture*. New York: IEEE, 1973, pp. 20–25.

12. W. T. Wilner, "Design of the Burroughs B1700," *Proceedings of the 1972 Fall Joint Computer Conference*. Montvale, N.J.: AFIPS Press, 1972, pp. 489–497.

13. W. T. Wilner, "Burroughs B1700 Memory Utilization," *Proceedings of the 1972 Fall Joint Computer Conference*. Montvale, N.J.: AFIPS Press, 1972, pp. 579–586.

14. *ACM-IEEE Symposium on High-Level-Language Computer Architecture*. New York: IEEE, 1973.

CHAPTER 17

Proving Program Correctness

Probably the major weakness in all software testing methods is their inability to guarantee that a program has no errors. As discussed in Chapter 10, exhaustive testing of even the most trivial programs is an impossible task, and the best one can hope for in a realistic testing effort is to find a high percentage of the remaining errors. This might lead to the question of whether there is some method other than testing that can be used to guarantee that a program is error-free.

Based on our earlier definition of a software error, the answer is an emphatic *no,* and this answer is not likely to change in the future. However, there is a school of thought that says that programs can be proved "correct" by expressing the intent of the program in some formal logic system, using this expression and the source code of the program to establish mathematical theorems about the program, and then proving the theorems. Given that this is possible (which it is), then obviously the central consideration in this idea is establishing what the word "correct" means. If it means correct in relation to the users' needs, then such an approach would be invaluable. If it means correct in relation to the external specification, the approach would still be extremely valuable, but it would not guarantee the absence of all errors. If "correct" means correct in relation to a low-level specification such as a module external specification, the approach would still be worthwhile, but to a smaller degree.

The idea of mathematically proving program correctness is currently focused on proving that a subroutine is correct with respect to its interface specifications. By now the reader should realize that this does not guarantee the absence of all errors. Furthermore, as is shown in a later section, a subroutine could be proved correct with respect to this specification, yet it might not execute as described by the specification.

The question now concerns the value of such a proof if it is not really an alternative to testing. The answer is simple: an attempt to prove mathematically that a program is correct is a unique way of finding errors in the program, and any technique that can uncover errors must have some value. Furthermore, this concept is already having significant effects on many aspects of software development such as language design, design methodologies, and simply encouraging programmers to think in more formal and precise terms.

An interesting aspect of this field is that more literature exists in this area than in any other area of software reliability. This chapter represents only a partial survey of the field; for a more complete picture, see the references at the end of this chapter and the references in those books and articles. In these references there are a number of proofs of programs, including sorting and searching algorithms, elementary compilers, numerical analysis subroutines, kernels of operating systems, and editing routines.

THE METHOD OF INDUCTIVE ASSERTIONS

The most common method of proving programs is the informal method of inductive assertions, originated independently by Floyd [1] and Naur [2]. It involves generating a set of potential theorems (often called *verification conditions*), the proof of which ensures the correctness of the program.

The first step is writing *assertions* about the input conditions and output results of the program. These assertions are normally stated in some formal logic system; the one most widely used is the first-order predicate calculus. In the predicate calculus an assertion (or statement) is a logical variable or an expression that has the value true or false. A complete discussion of the predicate calculus is beyond the scope of this book, but the informal operations that are needed in this section are summarized in Figure 17.1. For the reader who wishes to pursue this subject in more depth, most texts on mathematical logic or artificial intelligence contain a complete and formal description of the first-order predicate calculus.

Before proceeding further an example is given to illustrate the proof process. Figure 17.2 is a subroutine that computes $Z = A^B$ where B is a non-negative integer (this example is from King [3]). Rather than simply multiplying A together B times, the routine performs the operation by generating successive squares of A and using the binary representation of B to select the appropriate powers. Each time through the loop a new power of A is computed (A, A^2, A^4, A^8, and so on) and, if the corresponding bit of B is a one, the power of A is selected for inclusion in the result. For instance, if B has the value 13 (binary value 1101), Z is computed as $A^8 \times A^4 \times A^1$. The routine does this with seven multiplications instead of 13 (there are other multiplications and divisions, but they are done by the value two, which usually compiles into a simple left or right shift instruction). The $Y = Y/2$ statement shifts the exponent to the right by one bit and the IF statement tests the rightmost bit for a one value. Since the algorithm is somewhat tricky (which

Connective	Example	Meaning
Disjunction	$p \wedge q$	p and q
Conjunction	$p \vee q$	p or q
Negation	$\neg p$	not p
Implication	$p \supset q$	p implies q Same as $(\neg p) \vee q$
Equivalence	$p \equiv q$	p is equivalent to q Same as $(p \supset q) \wedge (q \supset p)$
Universal quantifier	$\forall x\ (p(x))$	For all values of x p(x) is true
Existential quantifier	$\exists x\ (p(x))$	There exists some value of x such that p(x) is true

Figure 17.1   **Predicate calculus connectives.**

THE METHOD OF INDUCTIVE ASSERTIONS 313

```
POWER: PROCEDURE (A,B,Z)
  Z = 1
  X = A
  Y = B
  DO WHILE (Y≠0)
    IF (Y≠(2*(Y/2))) THEN Z = Z*X    IS Y AN ODD NUMBER?
    Y = Y/2
    X = X*X
  END
END
```

Figure 17.2   **Program to be proved.**

is why one wants to prove its correctness), the reader should walk a simple test case through it before reading on.

To better illustrate the execution paths in the program, it is translated into the flowchart in Figure 17.3. Points A1 and A2 represent the places where the input and output assertions are made. The input assertion represents all necessary input conditions to the program and the output assertion represents the desired result. They can be represented as the following statements:

A1: $(B \geq 0) \wedge (B$ is an integer$)$
A2: $(Z = A^B) \wedge (A,B$ are unaltered$)$

The second step in this proof method is generating the theorems or verification conditions to be proved. One way of doing this is to assume that A1 is true at point 1, look at the semantics of the program statement between points 1 and 2 and use these to transform A1 into an intermediate assertion at point 2, and continue this until an intermediate assertion (originally derived from A1) is developed at point 9. Now two assertions are available at point 9: the first one is the derived assertion (the input assertion as transformed by the program semantics) and the second one is A2, the output assertion. A theorem can now be written stating that the derived assertion at point 9 implies A2.

A second way of accomplishing this is to start with the output assertion and run it *backwards* through the program until it is transformed into a derived assertion at point 1. The theorem (verification condition) now becomes: A1 implies the derived assertion at point 1.

To generate the verification conditions one needs an axiomatic description of the programming language semantics. The hypothetical language in Figure 17.2 reduces to two types of statements (assignment and decision), so descriptions are needed of the way in which assertions should be altered when they are passed through the statements. The *backwards* method of generating verification conditions is preferable

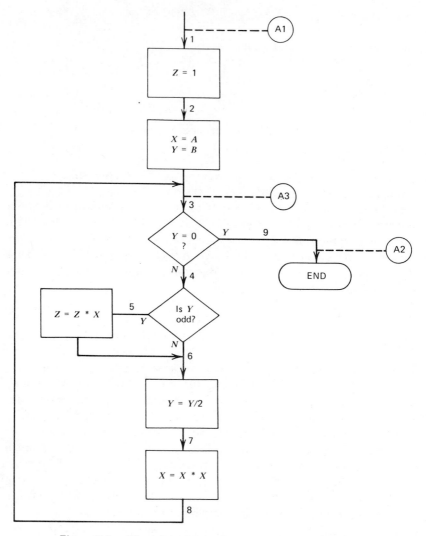

Figure 17.3   **Flowchart form of the program to be proved.**

because it gives a different perspective of the program flow (one can look at it as executing the program in reverse). Figure 17.4 illustrates the axioms for backwards transformations. The question that the axioms must answer is: If some assertion is true after the program statement, what assertion must have been true before the statement? If the assertion at point 2 in Figure 17.4 is $(S = X + 4) \wedge (X \geq 0)$ and the assignment statement is $X = X - 2$, then the derived assertion at point 1 is $(S = X + 2) \wedge (X \geq 2)$. In other words, you "undo" an assignment statement by taking the expression on the right side of the assignment statement and substituting it in the assertion for all occurrences of the variable on the left side of the assignment. To undo a decision statement the second axiom in Figure 17.4 is applied. If the assertion at point 5 is $X = 0.5MV^2$ and the decision g is $V > 1000$ then the assertion at point 3 is $(V > 1000) \supset (X = 0.5MV^2)$.

At this point it may seem that we have enough information to generate the verification condition, but one problem remains: determining how to handle the loop. The loop can iterate a variable number of times depending on the value of B. What we need is a third assertion (called an *inductive, loop,* or *invariant* assertion) within the loop so that we can use mathematical induction to prove the correctness of the loop. The inductive assertion should specify all of the properties of the program that are invariant at a selected point within the loop. By careful study of the program the reader should verify that the following assertion should be true at point 3 in Figure 17.3.

A3: $(Z*X^Y = A^B) \wedge (Y \geq 0) \wedge (Y$ is an integer$) \wedge (A,B$ are unaltered$)$

The trick in forming inductive assertions is specifying every meaningful invariant condition. Admittedly, this is the most difficult step in

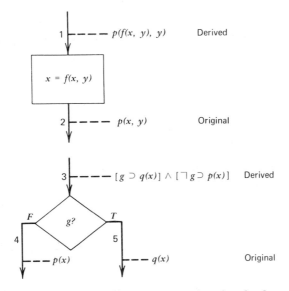

Figure 17.4   **Axioms for transforming assertions in a backward flow.**

the proof process. The usual tendency is to omit some invariant properties, but this is easily detected when the attempt is eventually made to prove the verification conditions. Defining the inductive assertions is always a valuable exercise even if you do not intend to prove the program's correctness, because it forces one to formalize his intuitive understanding of the logic of the loops.

At this point we have three assertions (or possibly more if the example had more than one loop). Rather than generating one verification condition to be proved, we generate a number of verification conditions in the following manner. Study the program flow and the assertions and identify all paths within the program that start with an assertion, end with an assertion, and have no assertions within the paths. These paths are called *tag paths* and Figure 17.3 has four:

1. From A1 to A3.
2. From A3 to A2.
3. From A3 to A3 for Y odd.
4. From A3 to A3 for Y even.

Verification conditions should be generated for each tag path; the proof of all of these verification conditions proves the correctness of the program. A verification condition is generated by taking the end assertion of a tag path and backing it all the way through the tag path. To examine one in detail let us find the verification condition for the third tag path. The assertion at point 8 is the same as the assertion at point 3 (which is A3) because there are no intervening program statements. At point 7 we get

$$(Z * X^{2Y} = A^B) \land (Y \geq 0) \land (Y \text{ is an integer}) \land (A,B \text{ are unaltered})$$

by substituting $X * X$ for X. At point 6 we get

$$(Z * X^{2(Y/2)} = A^B) \land (Y/2 \geq 0) \land (Y/2 \text{ is an integer}) \land$$
$$(A,B \text{ are unaltered})$$

by replacing Y with $Y/2$. The 2's in the exponent were not canceled because computer integer division is not the same as mathematical division [$2*(Y/2)$ is not always equal to Y]. At point 5 the derived assertion becomes

$$(Z*X^{1 + 2(Y/2)} = A^B) \wedge (Y/2 \geq 0) \wedge (Y/2 \text{ is an integer}) \wedge$$
$$(A,B \text{ are unaltered})$$

At point 4 we get

$$(Y \text{ is odd}) \supset [\text{previous assertion}]$$

and at point 3 we get

$$(Y \neq 0) \supset \{(Y \text{ is odd}) \supset [\text{previous assertion}]\}$$

We now have a verification condition stating that assertion A3 implies the assertion above. The three other verification conditions can be developed in a similar fashion; all four verification conditions are shown in Figure 17.5.

The next step is to prove the four verification conditions. To do this we should use the rules of inference from the predicate calculus, but informal arguments are usually sufficient. All of our theorems are of the form $p \supset q$ and the usual way of proving this is to show that q is true whenever p is true (the other ways are showing that q is always true or p is always false). The reader should have no trouble arguing the correctness of the first two verification conditions. The last two proofs are tricky so the proof of the third verification condition requires explanation. The $Y/2$, A, and B conditions should be apparent, so we are left with showing that $Z*X^Y = A^B$ implies $Z*X^{1 + 2(Y/2)} = A^B$ when Y is odd. Assume that the language (as is the case in most languages) rounds

1. $[(B \geq 0) \wedge (B \text{ is an integer})] \supset$
   $[(1*A^B = A^B) \wedge (B \geq 0) \wedge (B \text{ is an integer}) \wedge (A, B \text{ are unaltered})]$

2. $[(Z*X^Y = A^B) \wedge (Y \geq 0) \wedge (Y \text{ is an integer}) \wedge (A, B \text{ are unaltered})] \supset$
   $\{(Y = 0) \supset [(Z = A^B) \wedge (A, B \text{ are unaltered})]\}$

3. $[(Z*X^Y = A^B) \wedge (Y \geq 0) \wedge (Y \text{ is an integer}) \wedge (A, B \text{ are unaltered})] \supset$
   $\{(Y \neq 0) \supset \{(Y \text{ is odd}) \supset [(Z*X^{1+2 (Y/2)} = A^B) \wedge (Y/2 \geq 0) \wedge$
   $(Y/2 \text{ is an integer}) \wedge (A, B \text{ are unaltered})]\}\}$

4. $[(Z*X^Y = A^B) \wedge (Y \geq 0) \wedge (Y \text{ is an integer}) \wedge (A, B \text{ are unaltered})] \supset$
   $\{(Y \neq 0) \supset \{(Y \text{ is even}) \supset [(Z*X^{2(Y/2)} = A^B) \wedge (Y/2 \geq 0) \wedge$
   $(Y/2 \text{ is an integer}) \wedge (A, B \text{ are unaltered})]\}\}$

Figure 17.5   The four verification conditions to be proved.

down to the next integer when an integer division leaves a fractional part (e.g., $5/2$ is equal to 2). Hence $2(Y/2)$ is equal to $Y - 1$ because Y is odd and the proof is complete ($Y = 1 + Y - 1$). The fourth proof can be done in a similar way.

What we have shown is that the program is correct with respect to its input and output assertions, but only if the program terminates. We have not yet proved that the program will terminate (i.e., that it will not loop indefinitely). There is no general method of proving termination, but informal arguments are usually sufficient. In the example the program ends only when Y is zero. The input assertion states that Y is initially non-negative and Y is only altered in one place: in the loop where it is decremented by at least one during each iteration. This informally establishes that the program will terminate.

To summarize, the steps of an informal proof by inductive assertions are:

1. Translate the program into a flowchart (not absolutely necessary but it helps in identifying the paths).
2. Write the input and output assertions.
3. Locate each loop and specify an inductive assertion in each.
4. Identify the tag paths.
5. Generate the verification conditions using the semantics of the program statements.
6. Prove each verification condition. If you cannot, this means one of three things: either you were not creative enough, one of your assertions is incomplete, or you have detected a bug in that tag path.
7. Prove that the program will terminate.

This proof process is occasionally accused of being a fancy disguise for the common code reading or walk-through processes. To a large extent it is; the only difference is one of formality. The degree of formality is often a question of individual taste; for instance, London [4] proves five programs in a more informal and off-the-cuff manner than that described above.

It may also seem that this proof technique is oriented toward numerical programs. To some extent this is true, but with some ingenuity it can be applied to a large class of non-numerical programs. For instance, the output assertion of an algorithm to sort the elements of a vector M might state that, for all I, $M(I) \le M(I+1)$ and that the final M is a permutation of the original M. To prove an algorithm that searches a table T and returns the index I of an entry with the value X, the output assertion might be

$$[(X \in T) \supset X = T(I)] \wedge [(\neg(X \in T)) \supset I = 0] \wedge [T \text{ is unaltered}]$$

The reader probably realizes that a correctness proof is a lengthy process. The proof is always much longer than the program itself and the largest programs that have been tackled to date are only several hundred statements long. A later section discusses some methods of automating the proof steps to make the process less time-consuming.

The proof technique described in this section can be extended to an entire program by proving the program module by module. To do this the first step is specifying the input and output assertions for each module. When one is generating a verification condition within a module and encounters a CALL statement to another module, the assertions for the called module are used to define the semantics of the CALL statement.

WHAT CAN AND CANNOT BE PROVED BY PROOFS

As mentioned earlier, a correctness proof cannot guarantee the absence of software errors. Errors have been discovered in programs that were previously proved to be correct. However, this has not prevented researchers in the field from making such claims as, "it is an alternative to testing" and "it supplies conclusive proof that no bugs exist." To put this technique in perspective, the problems and weaknesses of mathematical proofs as well as their advantages are discussed. The weaknesses currently outnumber the advantages, but this does not imply that proof techniques are useless. Many (but not all) of the weaknesses will be solved by ongoing research efforts.

The primary weaknesses of proofs are that a proved program can still contain errors, proofs are difficult, tedious, and time consuming, and many of the constructs in the widely used programming languages are not amenable to proofs. The following list discusses these problems in more detail.

1. The program is proved only with respect to the input and output assertions. If the output assertion is wrong or incomplete, the program could be proved while errors remain undetected. Also errors created in the early design processes (objectives and external design) will not be detected by proofs.

2. The input assertion specifies the initial assumptions and environment of the program. There is no guarantee that these will hold when the program actually executes (e.g., the proof says nothing about the behavior of the program when the actual inputs do not meet the input assertion).

3. Incorrect interfaces (e.g., ordering the parameters and arguments in an inconsistent way or passing an argument in radians to a parameter in degrees) are usually not detected by proofs.

4. The proof itself could be wrong. A person proving a verification condition can easily make a mistake and show that the verification condition is true when it actually is not. In perhaps an extreme example, seven errors were later found in a 25-line program that had been proved and published in a professional journal [5]. All seven errors would have probably been found had the program been tested.

5. Perhaps the biggest weakness is the ease in which the language semantics can be misinterpreted. A particular statement in the program might not mean what one assumes it means. If one creates a bug by misinterpreting the meaning of a language construct while coding the program, the same mistake will likely be made while proving the program.

6. System and machine constraints such as round-off errors, overflow conditions, and other consequences of bounded computer arithmetic are usually omitted from proofs. There are ways of accounting for these constraints, but they tremendously complicate the proof.

7. Current proof techniques cannot adequately handle programs that perform input/output operations (e.g., a program that prints a report or updates a data base). As mentioned in Chapter 15, a large percentage of software errors (45% in the Rubey study) are related to input/output operations and data definitions.

8. Proofs of non-numerical programs are much more difficult than proofs of numerical programs. For instance, a proof of the small MATCHES subroutine in Chapter 8 would be extremely difficult.

9. Proofs will not detect unwanted side-effects or extraneous results. A "correct" program could still have an erroneous side-effect such as destroying a global data area.

10. Methods have yet to be devised to deal with such language constructs as parallelism, complex data structures, global variables, and scoping of variable names.

11. The difficulty of the proof is proportional to the richness and complexity of the programming language. A proof of a typical PL/I

program would be close to impossible because of PL/I's thousands of data types and the resulting subtle data conversions.

In spite of these problems, mathematical proofs have a number of significant advantages. Proofs can detect bugs, and these are bugs that might not have been detected by testing methods. Consider a program that compares three variables for equality by using the expression IF $(A = (A + B + C)/3)$. For certain values of B and C this expression does not produce the intended result. The bug would probably not be detected by conventional testing techniques, for it surfaces only for a small percentage of the possible values of the variables. Chances are also good that it would not be caught in an informal code reading or walk-through. However, it is very likely that an attempt to prove the correctness of the program would discover the bug.

Doing a proof forces the programmer to examine the program and specifications in great detail and to formalize his understanding of the program. The process of writing the input and output assertions (even if the programmer does not intend to prove them) is valuable as a formal method of expressing specifications and as a way of determining the defensive code needed in a module (i.e., code that checks the actual input conditions against the input assertion).

Program proofs also appear to have several indirect benefits. Because thorough specifications are a prerequisite, the programmer will be inclined to write his specifications more precisely if he later intends to prove the program. Because of the formalism involved, the programmer's overall attitude toward precision programming is often improved and the style and structure of his program are also favorably affected. Mathematical proofs are already influencing language designers by assisting in understanding language semantics and developing cleaner language constructs.

Because correctness proving is still in its infancy and because of the problems listed above, it cannot be recommended for use in most current projects. When it is used it can be a substitute for the code walk-through and unit test processes, but it cannot replace the remaining testing processes such as integration, function, system, and acceptance tests. However, proofs can be valuable today in certain critical situations where a project is willing to incur additional development costs for higher confidence in the product. If I were developing an operating system that contained a few modules that were absolutely vital to the system's operation, I would consider applying proofs to these modules in addition to the normal testing techniques. The same would apply to an application system such as an electrical utility system with a critical module that computes the billing rates or an algorithm that controls the transmission of power among companies.

For the reader who intends to apply the proof techniques, one of the testing axioms of Chapter 10 can be extended: you should not attempt to prove the program you wrote. This suggestion stems from the fifth problem discussed earlier; the programmer who made a mistake coding the program is likely to make the same mistake in the proof. Someone other than the programmer should specify the input and output assertions and generate and prove the verification conditions. However, because the inductive assertions require an in-depth understanding of the program's logic, it seems reasonable that the programmer should determine the inductive assertions and supply them to the person performing the proof.

FORMAL AND AUTOMATED PROOFS

Given the informal method of inductive assertions in the previous sections, the next logical step might be to formalize the method to the extent that it could be carried out by a program instead of by hand. In other words, can a program be written that accepts another program and its input and output assertions as input and provides the necessary proofs (or counter examples) as output? The answer is yes and no. Fruitful research has been performed along these lines, but the results are of no practical use today and will not likely be so in the near future.

Most approaches to this problem start by requiring the programmer to specify the input, output, and inductive assertions in the first-order predicate calculus (it may be possible to have the proof system generate the inductive assertions). The syntax and semantics of the programming language are stored in the system as axioms in the predicate calculus. The proof system identifies the tag paths in the program being proved and then uses the program logic, the assertions, and the axioms to generate the verification conditions. The proof system then uses the rules of inference of the predicate calculus combined with deductive and heuristic reasoning principles to attempt to prove each verification condition. Note that the existence of such a system would eliminate many of the problems discussed earlier such as human errors in interpreting language semantics and proving verification conditions.

The first component in a proof system is the verification condition generator. It must be capable of manipulating and simplifying logic predicates and interpreting the statements in the program, but the most difficult task is priming this system with the necessary axioms. Not only must every syntactic and semantic detail of the language be expressed as an axiom, but many commonplace principles such as addition and multiplication and the commutative and distributive laws of mathematics must also be written as axioms. A number of verification condition generators have been written for flowchart languages and subsets of APL, ALGOL, and FORTRAN. However, the process of reducing a complex language such as COBOL or PL/I to a set of axioms is an immense task and will probably not be done in this century.

The second part of a proof system is a mechanical theorem prover. Theorem provers fall in the realm of artificial intelligence because a human being uses a good deal of deductive, goal-setting, and reasoning maneuvers in proving a theorem. A proof system could prove a theorem by a trial-and-error method given an infinite amount of time and space, but of course this is impractical. Robinson's resolution principle [6] can theoretically improve the theorem-proving process significantly, but even this is too slow when the number of axioms is large (which would be the case for a practical programming language).

The classic effort in this area is King's program verifier [7], which appears to be the first implementation of a fully automated verification condition generator and prover. The system proves programs written in a very small subset of the ALGOL language and was used to prove the correctness of several small (less than 100 statement) programs. Although this was a milestone effort, it is a long way from being of any practical use.

Many research projects are underway with similar goals; one worth mentioning is the proof system by Good, London, and Bledsoe [8]. This system attempts to generate and prove verification conditions for programs written in the PASCAL language. The noteworthy feature of this system is that the human user can interact with the theorem prover. A time limit is set for the proof of each verification condition. If the system cannot complete the proof within this time it stops and asks the user for advice. The user can examine the incomplete proof and supply additional information or direct the system into a new line of reasoning.

This idea of interactive theorem proving seems necessary to make proof systems of some practical use within this century. Totally automated proofs of real programs coded in the widely used languages still remain an unreachable goal in the near future.

In the first section it was mentioned that specifying the inductive assertion within each loop is probably the most difficult chore in a correctness proof. Several research efforts have been directed toward this problem by attempting to automate the generation of inductive assertions. The VISTA system represents one of these efforts [9]. Given the source program (represented in a flowchart language) and the input and output assertions, VISTA generates some of the loop assertions or improves incomplete assertions. The system does this using a number of techniques. It examines the semantics of every loop to identify certain invariant conditions. It also propagates the other assertions to within the loop to add to the loop assertion. The final step is generating the verification conditions and attempting to prove them. If a proof fails, VISTA examines the reason for the failure, beefs up the appropriate loop assertion accordingly, and attempts the proof again. However, the major problem with this approach is that the program must be initially correct for this assertion generator to function correctly.

One automated tool that is both feasible and practical today is a *proof checker*. If a proof checker is given the steps in a human's proof as input, it can check the validity of each step against the known rules of inference. Hence a proof checker could examine a human proof for errors. But aside from the proof checker, automated proving systems are not likely to be feasible for practical programs for a long time.

ADDITIONAL APPLICATIONS OF PROOF TECHNIQUES

A large number of pioneering efforts have stemmed from the basic idea of mathematical correctness proofs. One of these is the idea of *symbolic execution* [10], a technique midway between traditional testing methods and correctness proofs. In symbolic execution the program is "executed" in some sense of the word, but it is executed interpretively with symbols as input values instead of real data. For instance, a symbolic execution of the program in Figure 17.6 would assign the algebraic expression $B + C*A$ to S after the execution of statement 1, T would have the value $C*A - B$ after statement 2, and when the procedure returns D is assigned the expression $2*B$. Hence the programmer now has a symbolic picture of the function of the subroutine.

One problem that immediately arises in symbolic execution is how

```
      CALL CALC(A,B,C,D);
        .
        .
        .
1     CALC: PROCEDURE(W,X,Y,Z);
2       S = X + Y*W;
3       T = S - 2*X;
4       Z = S - T;
5       END;
```

Figure 17.6 **Program for symbolic execution.**

to handle conditional statements such as IF statements that cause one of two paths to be taken based on the *specific value* of one or more variables. The solution is that the symbolic executer must take both paths. For instance, if the statement

```
IF P>N THEN DO...
        ELSE DO...
```

is encountered, execution must proceed down both paths because there is no way of knowing whether P > N is true or false. In proceeding into the THEN path the symbolic state of all variables is maintained and the condition P > N is added to the state of the program. In the ELSE path the current state of all variables is maintained and the condition ¬(P > N) is added to the program's state. This implies that the process of symbolic execution is almost identical to the process of generating verification conditions.

EFFIGY [11] is an interactive symbolic executer for programs written in a small subset of PL/I. When a conditional branch is encountered, EFFIGY saves the current state of the program and asks the user which path he wishes to explore. After a path has been executed the user can restore the state of the system to the beginning of the path and take the alternate direction. EFFIGY also provides a set of symbolic debugging features such as traces and breakpoints.

The advantage of symbolic execution is that a single execution of the program is equivalent to a large class of test runs with nonsymbolic data. Of course, symbolic execution is faced with the same problems that face verification condition generators, the primary one being the expression of the syntax and semantics of the programming language as a set of axioms.

A second application of proof techniques is the use of proofs *during* the design and coding stages rather than after. Dijkstra's original concept of structured programming embodied the ideas of structured code (top-down readability and the use of a limited number of control constructs), step-wise refinement (arriving at the final code through a number of small refinement steps), and informal arguments of the correctness of each refinement step [12, 13]. As the reader might have noticed, the last two aspects of structured programming have been largely overlooked in the past.

One approach to the use of proof techniques during the coding stage is first to write the assertions and then to fill in the code between the assertions. A methodology called *formal development* is being developed to do exactly this [14, 15]. A formal notation is provided so that the correctness of the logic can be established as it is written.

This idea of integrating the proof and coding processes is a worthwhile one because it encourages the programmer to formalize his ideas. Unfortunately, the techniques have not yet been generalized enough to make them easily applicable to the widely used programming languages. The reader who is interested in this concept is advised to review examples of the use of this approach (e.g., [16–18]).

Probably the ultimate goal of proof techniques is automatic program synthesis. If the programmer simply supplies the input and output assertions, it may be possible for a system to generate the code for the program and prove its correctness, thus eliminating the human coding stage. The motivation for such a system is the premise that it is easier for a programmer to describe *what* a program should do (its input and output assertions) than *how* the program should do it (its logic).

A program synthesizer is even farther off than an automated proof system because a synthesizer requires a large deal of artificial intelligence. Manna and Waldinger [19] discuss the knowledge and reasoning ability that must be present in a synthesizer. For instance, a synthesizer must decide on algorithms, generate loops and conditional tests, and debug the program that it is constructing. Rather than creating each new program from scratch, it should be able to draw on the results of previous syntheses. A number of primitive program synthesizers have already been developed. For instance, the PROW system can write LISP programs, given a predicate calculus specification as input [20].

Even if program synthesis proves feasible, it may not prove to be completely desirable because the valuable redundancy provided by after-the-fact proofs is eliminated. In a conventional proof the programmer writes the code from the specifications and someone else may write the assertions from the specifications and attempt the proof. If the verification conditions cannot be proved, a potential error has been uncovered (in the code or the proof). This redundancy (two translations of the specifications) is the primary value of proofs, but it is eliminated by automatic synthesis.

Except for the idea of informal manual proofs, the entire concept of proving program correctness is of no practical use today, but it is important to keep abreast of the field because it is bound to change the programming environment of the future. For a more complete survey and an extensive bibliography refer to Elspas [21].

REFERENCES

1. R. W. Floyd, "Assigning Meanings to Programs," in J. T. Schwartz, Ed., *Mathematical Aspects of Computer Science.* Providence, R.I.: American Mathematical Society, 1967, pp. 19-32.

2. P. Naur, "Proof of Algorithms by General Snapshots," *BIT,* **6** (4), 310-316 (1966).

3. J. C. King, "A Verifying Compiler," in R. Rustin, Ed., *Debugging Techniques in Large Systems.* Englewood Cliffs, N.J.: Prentice-Hall, 1971, pp. 17-40.

4. R. L. London, "Proving Programs Correct: Some Techniques and Examples," *BIT,* **10** (2), 168-182 (1970).

5. J. B. Goodenough and S. L. Gerhart, "Toward a Theory of Test Data Selection," *IEEE Transactions on Software Engineering,* **SE-1** (2), 156-178 (1975).

6. J. A. Robinson, "A Machine-Oriented Logic Based on the Resolution Principle," *Journal of the ACM,* **12** (1), 23-41 (1965).

7. J. C. King, "A Program Verifier," Ph.D. thesis, Carnegie-Mellon Univ., 1969.

8. D. I. Good, R. L. London, and W. W. Bledsoe, "An Interactive Program Verification System," *IEEE Transactions on Software Engineering,* **SE-1** (1), 59-67 (1975).

9. S. M. German and B. Wegbreit, "A Synthesizer of Inductive Assertions," *IEEE Transactions on Software Engineering,* **SE-1** (1), 68-75 (1975).

10. J. C. King, "A New Approach to Program Testing," in C. E. Hackl, Ed., *Programming Methodology.* Berlin: Springer-Verlag, 1975, pp. 278-290.

11. J. C. King, "Symbolic Execution and Program Testing," RC-5082, IBM Research Div., Yorktown Heights, N.Y., 1974.

12. O. J. Dahl, E. W. Dijkstra, and C. A. R. Hoare, *Structured Programming.* London: Academic Press, 1972.

13. E. W. Dijkstra, "A Constructive Approach to the Problem of Program Correctness," *BIT,* **8** (3), 174-186 (1968).

14. C. B. Jones, "Formal Definition in Program Development," in C. E. Hackl, Ed., *Programming Methodology.* Berlin: Springer-Verlag, 1975, pp. 387-443.

15. C. J. Date, M. A. McMorran, and G. C. H. Sharman, "Program Proving and Formal Development: A Tutorial Introduction," TR-12.127, IBM United Kingdom Laboratories, Hursley, England, 1974.

16. R. W. Floyd, "Toward Interactive Design of Correct Programs," *Proceedings of the 1971 IFIP Congress.* Amsterdam: North-Holland, 1971, pp. 1-4.

17. C. A. R. Hoare, "Proof of a Program: FIND," *Communications of the ACM,* **14** (1), 39-45 (1971).

18. C. B. Jones, "Formal Development of Correct Algorithms: An Example Based on Earley's Recogniser," *Proceedings of an ACM Conference on Proving Assertions About Programs, SIGPLAN Notices,* **7** (1), 150-169 (1972).

19. Z. Manna and R. J. Waldinger, "Knowledge and Reasoning in Program Synthesis," in C. E. Hackl, Ed., *Programming Methodology.* Berlin: Springer-Verlag, 1975, pp. 236-277.

20. R. J. Waldinger and R. C. T. Lee, "PROW: A Step Toward Automatic Program Writing," in D. E. Walker and L. M. Norton, Eds., *Proceedings of the International*

Joint Conference on Artificial Intelligence. Bedford, Mass.: Mitre Corp., 1969, pp. 241–252.

21. B. Elspas, K. N. Levitt, R. J. Waldinger, and A. Waksman, "An Assessment of Techniques for Proving Program Correctness," *Computing Surveys,* **4** (2), 97–147 (1972).

CHAPTER 18

Reliability Models

The field of hardware reliability has advanced to the point where a large set of mathematics has been developed to allow the engineer to predict the reliability of his product. These mathematics (primarily in the form of probabilistic models) are widely used in many areas of engineering for such diverse purposes as predicting the probability of success of space missions or the expected lifetime of a light bulb. Because of the relatively advanced state of hardware reliability, it is natural to try to apply this theory to software reliability.

Of all of the unknowns of software reliability, probably the most important one is the number of remaining errors in a program. If a reasonable estimate of this were available during the testing stages, it would help determine when to stop testing. If one knew the number of remaining errors in an installed program, he could estimate the cost of maintenance activities and establish a level of confidence in the program. Other related attributes for which estimates are desirable are the reliability of the program (the probability that the program will run for a given time before an error of a given severity occurs) and the mean-time-to-failure of the program. Measures of the program's complexity would also be useful to judge the quality of the design and to estimate the "ripple effect" (i.e., if a given module is changed, how this change ripples throughout other parts of the program).

A number of reliability models are discussed in this chapter. The first few are closely related to hardware reliability theory and contain significant assumptions about the underlying probability distribution of software failures. The next set of models produces similar results, but these models have no ties to hardware reliability theory. The last set of models is concerned with predicting the complexity of software systems. Because most of these models are probabilistic, the reader is expected to have a basic understanding of probability and statistics.

A RELIABILITY GROWTH MODEL

The most well-known reliability model is probably the one developed by Jelinski and Moranda [1] and Shooman [2]. Because it draws from hardware reliability theory, it is necessary to digress for a moment to introduce some reliability concepts.

Let $R(t)$ be the reliability function: the probability that no errors will occur from time 0 to time t. $F(t)$ is the failure function: the probability that an error will occur in the time interval 0 to t. Clearly, $F(t) = 1 - R(t)$. The probability density of $F(t)$ is $f(t)$ so that

$$f(t) = \frac{dF(t)}{dt} = \frac{-dR(t)}{dt}$$

A useful function to define is the *hazard function* $z(t)$: the conditional probability that an error occurs in the interval t to $t + \Delta t$, given that the error did not occur prior to time t. If T is the time that the error occurs then

$$z(t)\Delta t = P\{t < T < t + \Delta t \mid T > t\}$$

which from probability theory is equivalent to

$$z(t)\Delta t = \frac{P\{t < T < t + \Delta t\}}{P\{T > t\}} = \frac{F(t + \Delta t) - F(t)}{R(t)}.$$

By dividing both sides by Δt and taking the limit as Δt approaches zero we get $z(t) = f(t)/R(t)$ or $z(t) = [-dR(t)/dt]/R(t)$. This differential equation can now be solved for $R(t)$. By choosing the initial condition $R(0) = 1$ we get

$$R(t) = \exp\left(- \int_0^t z(x)\, dx\right)$$

and mean-time-to-failure (MTTF) is given by

$$\text{MTTF} = \int_0^\infty R(t)\, dt$$

One way of estimating MTTF is to observe the behavior of the program over a time period and plot the time between successive errors. Hopefully, one would discover a *reliability growth* phenomenon; as errors are detected and corrected the time between successive errors tends to become longer. By extrapolating this curve into the future one can then predict the MTTF at any point in time and predict the total number of errors (by estimating the number of errors that would occur before MTTF approaches infinity). However, such extrapolations involve a lot of guesswork and tend to be misleading. A better technique would involve having some knowledge of the underlying probability distribution of error occurrences, then using the measured error data to estimate the parameters of the probability distribution, and then using this model to predict future events.

Developing this model starts with identifying the behavior of the function $z(t)$. In most hardware models $z(t)$ starts by decreasing with time (the "burn-in" part of the system's life representing the detection and correction of design and manufacturing errors), then becomes constant over the majority of the system's lifetime (representing random failures), and then increases near the end of the system's useful lifetime (refer back to Figure 1.1). Hardware reliability theory is largely concerned with this middle period where the hazard rate is constant, leading to the familiar "memoryless" equation $R(t) = \exp(-ct)$ where c is some constant. The assumption of a constant hazard rate seems unrealistic for software because the hazard rate should decrease as errors are detected and corrected. Because of this, as shown in Figure 18.1, software has no single $R(t)$ curve; as errors are corrected the $R(t)$ function changes (and improves).

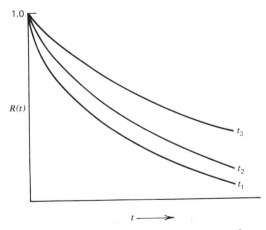

Figure 18.1   **Software reliability growth.**

This model starts with the assumption that $z(t)$ is constant (the time between failures is negative exponential) until an error is corrected, at which time $z(t)$ is again constant but with a reduced value. This implies that $z(t)$ is proportional to the number of remaining errors. A second assumption is that $z(t)$ is *directly* proportional to the number of remaining errors, that is, $z(t) = K(N - i)$ where N is the unknown number of initial errors, i is the number of errors already corrected, and K is some unknown constant. The behavior of $z(t)$ is shown in Figure 18.2. Every time an error is detected (the model assumes that no time elapses between the time an error is detected and the time that it is corrected), $z(t)$ is reduced by some amount K. The time axis t can represent calendar time or program operating time (or possibly be normalized by the usage of the program).

The parameters N and K can be estimated if some number of errors have already been detected (e.g., if one is part way through the testing phase). Assume that n errors have been detected and $x[1], x[2], \ldots, x[n]$ are the time intervals between these errors. Assuming that $z(t)$ is constant between errors, the density for $x[i]$ is

$$p(x[i]) = K(N - i) \exp(-K(N - i)x[i]).$$

By letting T be the summation of the x's and taking the maximum likelihood function of this equation, the following two equations are obtained:

$$\sum_{i=1}^{n} \frac{1}{(N - i)} = n/(N - (1/T) (\sum_{i=1}^{n} x[i]i)) = KT$$

Note that K and N in the above equations are estimators of the previous K and N.

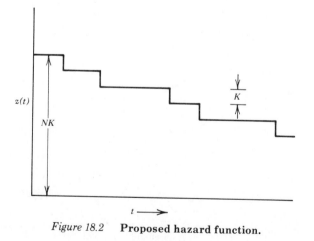

Figure 18.2   **Proposed hazard function.**

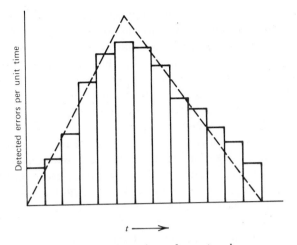

Figure 18.3 **The triangular extension.**

These two equations contain two unknowns, N and K. Given n detected errors with durations $x[i]$ between the errors, the equations can be solved for N and K by a simple numerical analysis program. N gives the primary result: an estimate of the total number of errors. Knowing parameter K allows the use of the equations to predict the times of occurrence of the $n + 1$ error, $n + 2$ error, and so on.

This basic model has been extended in various ways. For instance, the failure rate often increases over an initial period of time (as test cases are developed or as usage of the program increases) as shown in Figure 18.3 [3]. $z(t)$ then becomes

$$z(t) = K(N - \int_0^t p(x)\, dx)$$

where $p(x)$ is the error detection rate. A least-squares fitting technique can be used to approximate $p(x)$ by a triangle as shown in Figure 18.3. However, this extension to the model appears to have little predictive value because of the difficulty of postulating $p(x)$ before most of the errors have been detected.

Critique of the Model

Understanding and using this model first requires an understanding of its underlying assumptions. It makes many assumptions and all of them are questionable. Some, but not all, of the assumptions can be dealt with by extensions to the model.

One basic assumption made is that all errors have equal severity (e.g., that a system failure and a misspelled word in a message are equally significant). This assumption can be easily removed by categorizing the errors by severity and estimating a different N and K for each category. A second assumption is that all errors are corrected immediately (or that the program is not used until a detected error is corrected). The model also assumes that the program is not being altered (except for error corrections). A fourth assumption is that all corrections correct the detected error and do not introduce new errors. Miyamoto [4] has addressed this assumption by adding an error introduction factor. He also claims to have shown empirically that $z(t)$ is approximately proportional to the remaining errors, but he measures the remaining errors as the errors found by the end of the test period (making the unrealistic assumption that testing has uncovered all of the errors).

Of course, the major assumption is concluding that all programs have the $z(t)$ of Figure 18.2. This assumes that each error reduces $z(t)$ by a constant amount K, a phenomenon that is probably untrue but also probably a reasonable assumption to start with. The more interesting assumption is that $z(t)$ is constant between errors. Although it is reasonable to want to express software reliability in relation to time, one should recognize that it is not really a function of time. Software reliability is a function of the number of errors, the severities and locations of those errors, and the way in which the system is being used. Proponents of the constant $z(t)$ agree that the inputs to the system are not random and equiprobable, but they argue that the inputs appear to be random because the input domain is so large. However, others argue that $z(t)$ increases during the time between errors (Figure 18.4a), using the rationale that the program's inputs gradually close in on the remaining errors. There are others [5] who believe that $z(t)$ decreases with time (Figure 18.4b), arguing that the longer the program runs without encountering an error, the lower the probability of encountering one. Based on the earlier axiom that every time an error is encountered, the probability of encountering another one increases, one could postulate that $z(t)$ decreases between errors and it increases whenever an error is detected (Figure 18.4c).

All of the guesses of the behavior of $z(t)$ in Figures 18.2 and 18.4 show some reliability growth, but even this is not always the case in real programs, even in programs where corrections do not introduce more errors than they fix. The failure rate in a large system may tend to decrease when measured over several years, but large perturbations are bound to occur within this period. By analyzing the error detection rates from 14 different test phases in Craig [6], it was observed that the rates

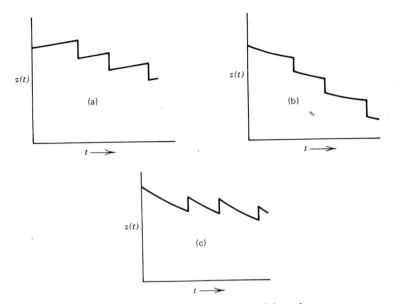

Figure 18.4   **Other proposed hazard functions.**

peaked at the beginning of five of the efforts, at the middle in five of the efforts, and at the end in four of the efforts.

To complicate matters further, one could argue that each program has its own unique distribution of $z(t)$ and even that each installation of each program has a unique $z(t)$. Richards [7] also points out that the $z(t)$ function for a single program could change with time or with the detection of each error.

As one last note (without trying to be overly negative, because research in this area is indeed worthwhile), the model described earlier seems to be overly optimistic. For instance, with $n = 10$ (10 detected errors) and times between those failures (in minutes) of

$$9 \quad 17 \quad 21 \quad 54 \quad 32 \quad 78 \quad 82 \quad 33 \quad 57 \quad 82$$

the model predicts 3.3 remaining errors ($N = 13.3$). Predictions for the time intervals between the 10th, 11th, 12th, and 13th errors are 135, 245, and 1265 minutes.

OTHER PROBABILISTIC MODELS

In addition to the basic model discussed in the preceding section, a number of other models have been devised. A Bayesian model has been proposed that accounts for the possibility that $z(t)$ may not decrease after every correction because of the possibility that corrections introduce new errors [5]. Schneidewind [8] removes the assumption that corrections are made immediately after error detections by proposing a model where the distribution of corrections is proportional to the distribution of error detections, but lagging behind it in time. A number of additional models have been proposed including a Markov model where the states in the Markov process change whenever an error is detected or corrected and the transition probabilities represent the error detection and correction rates [9].

A more general approach has been suggested by Schneidewind [10, 11]. He performed statistical tests on error data from 19 programs and found that these data fitted no single underlying probability distribution. An analysis of variance test on the MTTF of a single program in seven environments showed that the means were not the same, implying that the environment (i.e., the way the program is used) is a more significant factor than the number of remaining errors. These tests led to the conclusion that the reliability model must be tailored to each program in each particular environment. The first steps involve collecting some error data, guessing at the reliability function based on the shape of the frequency of the errors, estimating the parameters of the model, and performing goodness-of-fit tests on the model. Confidence limits are then determined for the parameters and the model, and the model is then used to predict $R(t)$ and its confidence limits. The last step is to compare the estimated $R(t)$ with the occurrences of new errors.

AN ERROR SEEDING MODEL

A completely different type of model that makes no assumptions about the behavior of the hazard rate $z(t)$ and is built on firm statistical ground is the error seeding model developed by Mills [12]. The model involves "seeding" the program with a number of known errors. These errors are randomly inserted within the program and an assumption is made that the indigenous (original) and seeded errors are equally likely to be detected in subsequent testing efforts. By testing the program for some amount of time and determining which detected errors are indigenous or seeded, it is possible to estimate N, the number of original indigenous errors.

Suppose that s seeded errors are inserted into the program and testing is allowed to proceed. Let $n + v$ be the number of errors detected by testing, where n is the number of detected indigenous errors and v is the number of detected seeded errors. Then the maximum likelihood estimate of N is

$$N = \frac{sn}{v}$$

For instance, if 20 errors are seeded in a program and, at a particular point in the test phase, 15 indigenous and 5 seeded errors have been found, the estimate of N is 60. Actually, N can be estimated after every error is found; Mills [12] suggests maintaining a graph throughout the test period of the number of indigenous errors found and the current estimate of N.

The second part of this model is concerned with stating and testing hypotheses about N. Let us assert that the program contains no more than k indigenous errors and then let us insert s seeded errors into the program. The program is now tested until all s seeded errors are found and at this time the number of detected indigenous errors is counted and represented as n. A confidence C is computed as

$$C = \begin{cases} 1 & \text{if } n > k \\ \dfrac{s}{s+k+1} & \text{if } n \leqq k \end{cases}$$

C is a measure of the confidence of the model; it is the probability that it will correctly reject a false assertion. For instance, if we assert that a program has no errors ($k = 0$) and we seed the program with four errors and detect these four errors without finding an indigenous error, C is 0.80. To achieve a confidence of 95% in this situation we would have to seed the program with 19 errors. If we assert that a program has three or less errors and we seed six errors and detect all six while finding three or less indigenous errors, the confidence is 60%. The formula for C has a firm statistical basis and is derived by Mills [12].

These two formulas for N and C form a useful error model; the first predicts the number of errors and the second can be used to establish a confidence in the prediction. However, one weakness is that C cannot be predicted until all of the seeded errors are detected (and of course this might not occur by the end of the testing phase). To overcome this, the formula for C can be modified so that C can be estimated after j of the seeded errors ($j \leqq s$) have been found [7]:

$$C = \begin{cases} 1 & \text{if } n > k \\ \dbinom{s}{j-1} \Big/ \dbinom{s+k+1}{k+j} & \text{if } n \leq k \end{cases}$$

In the previous example where $k = 3$ and $s = 6$, if we find 5 of the 6 seeded errors C drops to 33% instead of 60%. Another useful graph to plot during the testing process is the current asserted upper bound k for some fixed confidence such as 90%.

This error seeding model is both mathematically simple and intuitively appealing. It is easy to envision a program that performs the seeding by randomly selecting a module, inserting a logic error by changing or deleting statements, and then recompiling the module. The nature of the inserted errors must be kept secret, but the program must keep a log of its inserted errors so that we can later determine which errors are indigenous or seeded.

This seeding process is currently the weak point of this model because of the assumption that indigenous and seeded errors have the same (but unknown) probability of being detected. This implies that the seeded errors must be a reasonable sample of "typical" errors, but we do not yet understand programming well enough to know what these typical errors should be. However, in comparison to the problems surrounding the other reliability models, this problem seems relatively minor and solvable.

As one final note, error seeding has another useful benefit: it may have a positive psychological effect on testing efforts [13]. One reason that programmers have difficulty testing their own programs is that they tend to assume that each detected error is the last one. Error seeding may help to overcome this problem because the programmer now *knows* that his program contains yet-to-be-detected bugs.

SIMPLE INTUITIVE MODELS

In the quest for predictors of software reliability, there are a number of extremely simple models for predicting the number of software errors. Because of their simplicity they are often overlooked, yet they make fewer assumptions than the more sophisticated models and they are usable today.

One simple method involves starting a testing effort with two completely independent test groups using independent sets of test cases. These two groups (or people, depending on the size of the project) are allowed to test in parallel for some period of time and then their discovered errors are collected and analyzed. Let N_1 and N_2 represent the number of errors discovered by each group, and let N_{12} represent the number of errors that were detected twice (i.e., by both groups). This relationship is illustrated in Figure 18.5.

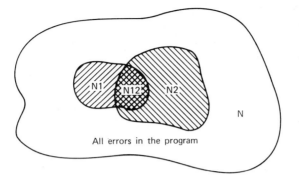

Figure 18.5   **Sets of errors found in independent tests.**

Let N represent the unknown total number of errors in the program. A testing effectiveness ratio can be stated for each group: $E_1 = N_1/N$ and $E_2 = N_2/N$. Assuming that all errors have the same chance of being detected (a big assumption but not entirely unreasonable), then we can look at any subset of the space N as approximating the total space. If group one found 10% of the total population of errors, they should have found approximately 10% of any randomly selected subset such as the subset N_2. In particular, we could say that $E_1 = (N_1/N) = (N_{12}/N_2)$. Substituting for N_2 we get $E_1 = N_{12}/(E_2 \times N)$ or

$$N = \frac{N_{12}}{E_1 \times E_2}$$

N_{12} is known and E_1 and E_2 can be estimated by N_{12}/N_2 and N_{12}/N_1. Hence we arrive at an approximation of N.

As an example, suppose that the two groups find 20 and 30 errors and by comparing these we notice that both groups found eight errors in common. E_1 is 0.27 and E_2 is 0.4, leading to an estimated N of 74 and an estimated 32 undetected errors ($74 - 20 - 30 + 8$).

Probably the simplest error estimation technique is to base the estimate on historical data, in particular the average number of errors per statement that programmers have made on previous projects. The literature on programming error rates is rather sparse, but based on the data that are available it appears that the industry average is about 10 remaining errors per 1000 program statements after the unit test phase has been completed. Hence, if there is no better information to use, one could estimate that a 32,000-statement program still contains 320 errors after the unit test phase.

This figure must be used with caution because it is only an average and it is based on data that were mostly gathered before the widespread use of newer programming technologies such as structured programming. Advocates of structured programming claim much lower rates, but because of the data processing community's well-known tendency to be optimistic, it seems safer to be pessimistic about error rates.

An interesting intuitive model has been developed within IBM to estimate errors in releases of OS/360 and its successors OS/VS1 and OS/VS2. A study of the error data for all components of OS/360 shows an extremely close fit to the equation

$$\text{CHANGES} = 23(\text{CPM}) + 2(\text{CM})$$

CHANGES is the total number of module changes because of errors. CPM (change-prone modules) is the number of modules that required 10 or more corrections. CM is the number of modules that required one or more corrections. This formula has proven to be a remarkably accurate predictor of errors providing that the parameters CPM and CM can be estimated. In using this on releases of OS/VS1, CM has been estimated as 90% of the number of new modules and 15% of the number of modified modules. CPM is often estimated as 15% of the new modules plus 6% of the modified modules. (All of these percentages are based on historical data.) Of course, there is no claim that this model is applicable to other programs or environments.

Because of the uncertainty in all of the models discussed so far, the only reasonable approach today is to use several of the models together and pool their answers. Data from previous projects can be used to estimate the number of errors in current projects. Two parallel test efforts can be established to use the earlier formula for N. Errors can be manually seeded into the program and the number of errors and a confidence can be estimated with Mills' model. The model developed by Jelinski, Moranda, and Shooman could also be used to produce a fourth prediction.

COMPLEXITY MODELS

Because of the close relationship between complexity and reliability, another set of models has indirectly addressed the question of reliability by focusing on the question of complexity. Rather than being based purely on statistics, the parameters of these models are selected attributes of the particular program being studied.

One model that estimates the complexity of a program is a model based on the measures of composite design in Chapter 6 [14]. To use this model one must first determine the strength of each module in the program and the coupling among every pair of modules. A table is provided that assigns each category of strength and coupling a quantitative value between zero and one (the high-strength and low-coupling categories have the values closest to zero). The model then assumes that the *first-order dependence* between every pair of modules is given by

$$D_{ij} = \begin{cases} 0.15(S_i + S_j) + 0.7\,(C_{ij}) & \text{if } C_{ij} \neq 0 \\ 0 & \text{if } C_{ij} = 0 \\ 1 & \text{if } i = j \end{cases}$$

D_{ij} represents the probability that module j will have to change when module i is changed if modules i and j are considered out of context from the remainder of the program (the relationship is assumed to be symmetric). S_i and S_j are the strengths of the two modules and C_{ij} is the coupling between them (D_{ij} is zero if there is no coupling).

The matrix D can be visualized as an undirected graph where the nodes are the modules and the edges represent the nonzero values of the first-order dependencies. This matrix does not represent a complete model of the program because of higher-order effects among modules (i.e., second-order, third-order, etc. dependencies). Given that a module A is changing, module B might require changing because of a change that ripples over any unique path in the graph from A to B or any combination of these paths. A second matrix, the *complete dependence matrix*, is computed to reflect the complete relationship between every pair of modules. This relationship is computed by the following steps:

1. Find every unique path in the graph (loops are excluded) between a pair of modules.
2. Compute the path probabilities (product of the edge probabilities).
3. Compute the relationship between the two modules using the path probabilities but treating them as non-mutually exclusive events. This relationship gives the probability of having to change one of the modules, given that the other must be changed (again the assumption is that the relationship is symmetric).

These computations are quite lengthy for even a small program, so programs have been written to perform these three steps.

An example of a complete dependence matrix is given in Figure 18.6. The elements are the intermodule relationships. For instance, if module A is changed, the probability of having to change module F is 0.11. By summing the elements in any row, one gets the expected

Modules

		A	B	C	D	E	F
M	A	1.00	0.21	0.32	0.30	0.04	0.11
o	B	0.21	1.00	0.11	0.08	0.20	0.21
d	C	0.32	0.11	1.00	0.53	0.02	0.24
u	D	0.30	0.08	0.53	1.00	0.02	0.13
l	E	0.04	0.20	0.02	0.02	1.00	0.04
e	F	0.11	0.21	0.24	0.13	0.04	1.00
s							

Figure 18.6   **A complete dependence matrix.**

number of modules that must be changed given that a particular module is changed. For instance, if module C is changed, the expected number of other changes is 1.22. By excluding the diagonal, subtracting each element in a row from 1.0, and taking their product, one gets the probability that a module can be changed without having to change any other modules. For instance, if module A changes there is a 0.32 probability that no other modules need to be changed. A rough measure of the program's complexity can be obtained by summing all of the elements in the matrix and dividing by the number of modules.

The answers from the model and the fact that it is based on key structural attributes of the program are appealing, but the model is based on many unsubstantiated assumptions. The model has not been validated because it has not been possible to devise a reasonable method to do so (validating this model to empirical data is much harder than it first appears to be). A related model based on a linear algebra solution was proposed by Haney [15], but this model leaves the determination of intermodule relationships up to the ingenuity of the user.

A number of research efforts are underway to model the complexity of a program based on properties of the code. Sullivan [16] proposes several models with the premise that the difficulty of understanding a program at any particular point within its logic is proportional to the number of concepts that are active within the program at that point. A number of measures are proposed based on directed graph representations of the program's control flow and data structure.

REFERENCES

1. Z. Jelinski and P. B. Moranda, "Software Reliability Research," in W. Freiberger, Ed., *Statistical Computer Performance Evaluation.* New York: Academic Press, 1972, pp. 465–484.

2. M. L. Shooman, "Operational Testing and Software Reliability Estimation during Program Development," *Record of the 1973 IEEE Symposium on Computer Software Reliability.* New York: IEEE, 1973, pp. 51–57.

3. M. L. Shooman, "Probabilistic Models for Software Reliability Prediction," in W. Freiberger, Ed., *Statistical Computer Performance Evaluation.* New York: Academic Press, 1972, pp. 485–502.

4. I. Miyamoto, "Software Reliability in Online Real Time Environment," *Proceedings of the 1975 International Conference on Reliable Software.* New York: IEEE, 1975, pp. 194–203.

5. B. Littlewood and J. L. Verrall, "A Bayesian Reliability Growth Model for Computer Software," *Record of the 1973 IEEE Symposium on Computer Software Reliability.* New York: IEEE, 1973, pp. 70–77.

6. G. R. Craig et al., "Software Reliability Study," RADC-TR-74-250, TRW Corp., Redondo Beach, Ca., 1974.

7. F. R. Richards, "Computer Software: Testing, Reliability Models, and Quality Assurance," NPS-55RH74071A, Naval Postgraduate School, Monterey, Ca., 1974.

8. N. F. Schneidewind, "Analysis of Error Processes in Computer Software," *Proceedings of the 1975 International Conference on Reliable Software.* New York: IEEE, 1975, pp. 337–346.

9. A. K. Trivedi and M. L. Shooman, "A Many-State Markov Model for the Estimation and Prediction of Computer Software Performance Parameters," *Proceedings of the 1975 International Conference on Reliable Software,* New York: IEEE, 1975, pp. 208–215.

10. N. F. Schneidewind, "A Methodology for Software Reliability Prediction and Quality Control," NPS-55SS72111A, Naval Postgraduate School, Monterey, Ca., 1972.

11. N. F. Schneidewind, "An Approach to Software Reliability Prediction and Quality Control," *Proceedings of the 1972 Fall Joint Computer Conference.* Montvale, N.J.: AFIPS Press, 1972, pp. 837–847.

12. H. D. Mills, "On the Statistical Validation of Computer Programs," FSC-72-6015, IBM Federal Systems Div., Gaithersburg, Md., 1972.

13. G. M. Weinberg, *The Psychology of Computer Programming.* New York: Van Nostrand Reinhold, 1971.

14. G. J. Myers, *Reliable Software Through Composite Design.* New York: Petrocelli/Charter, 1975.

15. F. M. Haney, "Module Connection Analysis—A Tool for Scheduling Software Debugging Activities," *Proceedings of the 1972 Fall Joint Computer Conference.* Montvale, N.J.: AFIPS Press, 1972, pp. 173–179.

16. J. E. Sullivan, "Measuring the Complexity of Computer Software," MTR-2648-V, Mitre Corp., Bedford, Mass., 1973.

CHAPTER **19**

Software Support
Systems

In prior chapters a number of tools have been
mentioned that were developed to assist the
programmer with various aspects of his or her
job. These tools ranged from commercially
available products to private tools developed by
individual organizations to research efforts, and
included test tools (e.g., static code analysis,
code coverage monitors, terminal simulators),
debugging tools, and correctness-proof tools.
This potpourri of tools brings two questions to
mind: are there not other aspects of the
software development process that need
automation, and is there not some method of
unifying these tools into a single programming
support system?

PROGRAM LIBRARY SYSTEMS

The view many of us have when we are
asked to picture a programmer's office is one of
disarray: cabinets reaching to the ceiling hold-
ing thousands of punched cards, stacks of specifications and listings filling the desk, and cof-
fee-stained boxes of punched cards, flowcharts,
and project workbooks piled on the floors. This
type of environment, although it is steadily
disappearing for several reasons (one of them

being the fire hazard), leads to an additional and unnecessary class of software errors. In such an environment no one is really sure of the latest version of the program. Managers have little indication of the status of the project. If a programmer becomes ill his piece of the project often disappears from sight. In addition, a large number of software errors are created because of simple clerical mistakes in handling the program. (I remember all too well testing a program the night before its demonstration, rushing to the printer and lifting its cover in my impatience to examine some test results, and watching with awe as the only card deck of the 3000-statement FORTRAN program splattered across the computing center because I had placed the card tray on the printer!).

The programming librarian concept is a step toward solving these problems. However, the simple addition of a librarian to perform the clerical tasks is not a complete solution. The opportunities still remain to lose or mishandle card decks, misplace listings, and be exposed to risks such as fires or a sudden disappearance of the librarian. One solution to these problems is an automated program library or support system. By storing all of the project's work products (e.g., source code, object code, test cases, documentation) in a data base, the opportunities for clerical and logistical errors are reduced. Project visibility and auditing can be enhanced by report generators that analyze data within this data base. If all of the organization's programming tools can be incorporated into this single system, the project gains the advantages of a single integrated data base and standardization of the programming environment.

This section surveys a number of program library systems. In no way does it represent a complete survey; the intent is to illustrate the advantages of such tools and to examine some unique solutions to sources of software errors.

The PANVALET System

The PANVALET system produced by Pansophic Systems is a widely used library system. It operates in interactive or batch mode on any of the IBM operating systems on the S/360 and S/370 computers.

The PANVALET data base contains files to hold source code, object code, JCL (job control language), and program data. A variety of editing commands are provided to manipulate these files, for instance adding, deleting, or changing records, copying one file to another, and printing a file. A global scan/replace function can be used to search for and/or alter a character string in one file, all files of a given type (e.g., all COBOL source files), or the entire library.

A particularly useful feature in PANVALET is the concept of *file versions*. Any file (e.g., the source code for PL/I procedure CALCXYZ) can have multiple versions. Hence one version can represent the current production copy of the module and a second version could be used by a programmer testing a modification to the module. One version of every file in the library can be tagged as the *production* version. There is absolutely no way to alter the production version of a file. The only way to make a change is to create a new version and copy the production version into it. This facility is useful in controlling program modifications.

The files can be hierarchically structured with an *include* facility. That is, file *A* could contain indications that it includes the contents of files *B*, *C*, and *D*. Whenever file *A* is used (e.g., compiled), it is expanded by logically copying files *B*, *C*, and *D* into it.

Another valuable part of the data base is a directory of information about each version of each file. Each directory entry contains the status of the version (e.g., production status), the dates of the last access and last update to the version, the number of statements, and the type of the last action taken against the version. A number of reports are provided such as a listing of the directory and a cross-reference listing showing which files include other files and which files are included in other files.

A frequent problem in program maintenance is examining a program's object code in a dump or examining a program's compilation listing and not being able to relate this to the corresponding source code version of the program. PANVALET solves this problem by inserting the version number and date of last change into the compiler's listings and into the object modules.

PANVALET also contains a number of library maintenance reports and functions. Backup copies of the library can be made periodically for protection against disasters. Deleted files are automatically copied to a backup tape before the space is deleted to allow recovery from accidental or premature deletions. Infrequently used files are spooled to an archive tape and retrieved when needed. Three levels of security access can be given to any file to protect it from unauthorized use.

The System Building System

SBS is a program library system developed for use within IBM [1]. Its file types include source code, object code, link-edit information, data, documents, and entities called *groups*.

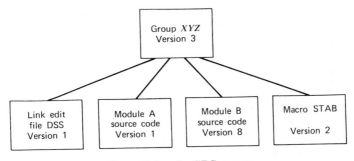

Figure 19.1   **An SBS group.**

Like PANVALET, SBS provides the concept of multiple versions of the files, but it solves the problem of maintaining synchronization between the object and source code in a different manner. To understand how this is done, we must first discuss the *group* type of file. The group file is essentially a bill-of-material specification for a program. As shown in Figure 19.1 it simply names the materials for the program (in this case two modules, one macro that is needed for the compilation of one or more of these modules, and the link-edit directions). When a user directs SBS to build version 3 of program XYZ, SBS automatically compiles the necessary module versions (if their object code files are empty) and performs the link-edit process. Synchronization of source and object code is done in the following manner: whenever a source code file is updated, SBS automatically deletes the object code file for the file version and deletes the object code for any group of which this file version is a part. This ensures that the object code for any version of a module or group (program) will always correspond to the current copy of the source code.

The Software Factory

The previous two systems provide a number of convenient functions for storing, updating, and compiling programs, but they are mainly oriented toward the coding and maintenance stages of a programming project. In particular, they do not explicitly support other phases such as requirements definition, design, and testing. The Software Factory, probably the most ambitious support system yet developed, attempts to integrate tools for the entire development process into a single system.

The Software Factory was developed for use within the System Development Corporation [2]. The best place to start describing the system is at its data base as shown in the center of Figure 19.2. The

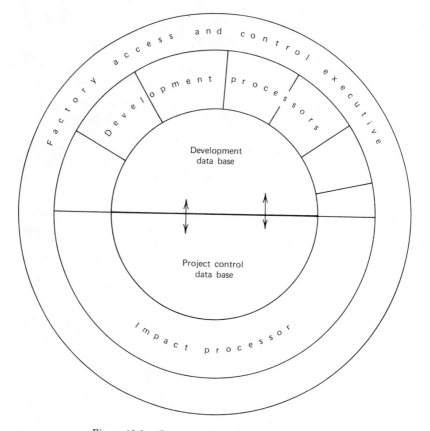

Figure 19.2   **Layers of the Software Factory.**

system has two data bases: the bulk (development) library and the relational (project control) data base. The development library consists of files containing source code, object code, load modules, link-edit control statements, and test cases, and these files may have multiple versions. The project control data base contains information pertinent to the management of the project and the overall structure of the program being produced. This data base records the schedules and resource estimates of each activity within the project, descriptions of the user requirements and the hierarchical structure of the program being produced, design change and error correction activity, dependencies on other projects, and so on. Most importantly, relationships among all of these items are maintained, allowing queries to be made concerning the relationships. A project manager could determine what user requirements are related to a particular program module, what design changes affect a particular module, what program modules are being developed by a particular project activity, the number of errors made by a particular programmer, and so forth.

Surrounding the data bases is a set of development tools. These include compilers, linkage editors, utility programs, documentation tools, test tools, and a special processor called IMPACT. Surrounding these processors is the FACE component. FACE is the command language interface between the users and the processors. It also gathers control and status information from the processors and inserts it into the project control data base.

The function of the IMPACT (Integrated Management, Project Analysis, and Control Technique) processor is to assist the project manager in planning and monitoring production. Through the use of critical path methods it can be used to develop project schedules and study alternatives. As the project is underway, it tracks progress and resource expenditures, giving the manager greater visibility of the project's status. IMPACT is also used to query the project control data base in terms of the relationships described earlier, or to ask simpler questions such as the size of a module, the number of compilations that have been performed on a module, the number of reported errors against a module, or the test status of a module.

The Simon Monitor

Simon is a production tool developed by Mitre Corporation [3]. Unlike the other systems, Simon is not a library system; it is an *implementation monitor* with the purpose of collecting data about programming projects to gain insight into the programming process and study the effects of experiments.

Simon sits between the programmer and his tools (e.g., compilers, text editors, test tools). It analyzes every transaction and updates one of three files. The *entity file* contains information about the projects, programmers, program modules, documents, test cases, macros, and programming errors. The *relational file* maintains the relationships among the entities in the entity file, showing, for instance, what errors were found in what modules, what modules call what modules, and who coded what module. The *event file* records each event that occurs in the system (e.g., an update to a module, a compilation, a test run). The collection of all of this data contributes nothing to the reliability of the current project, but it is used to improve future projects by formulating and testing hypotheses about ways in which the programming process can be improved.

Other Desirable Features

The systems described above contain many valuable features but, as one might expect, they could contain even more. The following discussion describes a number of additional features that would be desirable additions to a program support system.

The key to any program support system is an integrated data base. Entities in the data base contain the source code, object code, macros, specifications, test cases, and programs (i.e., the *group* entity in SBS). Relationships must be maintained among the entities so that given one entity (e.g., a particular module), one can readily obtain the corresponding entities (e.g., its specifications and test cases). Data base relationships should also reflect the structure of the programs so that such queries as who calls module X, who does module X call, who uses macro Y, and what macros does module X use can be asked. Each version of a program that is constructed should have an associated parts list so that one could identify what versions of what modules and macros made up that version of the program. Program construction functions (e.g., a linkage editor) should ensure that the versions of all parts of the program are consistent. For instance, if a programmer is building a program in which two modules use the same macro, the system should check to see that these modules were compiled with the same version of the macro.

With this integrated data base, a number of useful tools come to mind. Source code could be scanned for violations of programming standards or use of error-prone language constructs. Programs could be written to draw the module call structure of any program or to trace and analyze the flow of data from module to module. (Such a program must allow for name changes in argument/parameter transmission and storage overlays. Allen [4] describes an experimental program that does this for PL/I programs.) A module interface checker can be provided to analyze the source code of calling and called modules to determine if the number and type of arguments match the number and type of parameters.

Provided that the system contains information about all projects and the people within those projects, the system could selectively disseminate information to project members that may be affected by a particular event. For instance, a programmer might be notified by the system when an error has been found in a module that adjoins (i.e., calls or is called by) one of his. A project manager could be notified when a scheduled activity is not completed on time. Alternatively, the system could be told to send notifications when particular activities are completed. For instance, programmer A could tell the system, "Let me know when programmer B finishes the unit test of module X."

An interesting concept that is related to these ideas is the concept of *promotion criteria*. At the beginning of the project the project manager might specify criteria to the system such as, "for a module to be promoted to a status of unit-tested, all of the unit test cases must execute correctly, 100% of the conditional branches must have been covered by testing, the standards-compliance and module interface check programs must have been run successfully, and the module must have been compiled with options A, B, and C." Once a module obtains this status, it is available for use in later processes such as function testing. Different levels of promotion could be devised for different entities such as modules and specifications (and a module might even be "demoted" whenever an error is found).

DESIGN AIDS

Noticeably missing from the previous section is any mention of tools to automate any of the software design processes. The reason for the lack of tools is quite simple: it is rather difficult to automate an operation that is not yet well understood by humans.

One small way to begin automating the design processes is to develop tools that check a completed design for inconsistencies and incompleteness. It is difficult to envision a tool that does this for the product's objectives or the external (user) specification, but it begins to sound feasible for the subsequent design processes such as the program structure design (Chapter 6) and the module external specification (Chapter 8).

One such tool is DACC (Design Assertion Consistency Checker), developed by TRW Corporation for the verification of module interface specifications [5]. For each interface DACC compares the arguments and parameters in terms of the number and order of the data items and their data types, format, units (e.g., pounds, meters per second, dollars), and valid ranges. DACC was used to check a design specification for a large-scale spacecraft system; it found seven definite errors (e.g., an argument was specified in degrees but the corresponding parameter was specified in radians) at a cost of $30 for computer time and several hundred dollars for entering the specification into a data base.

An experimental tool that verifies certain attributes of a program structure design has been developed at the IBM Systems Research Institute. The designer enters his design into the data base by describing each interface. An interface description names the calling and called modules and the input and output arguments. The arguments are described in abstract terms; for instance, the designer might state that the inputs for a particular interface are "the region code and a list of customer names." He also enters a description of the strength of each module and the coupling among the modules.

The program performs several types of verifications. It examines all interfaces entering each module to determine whether the numbers of input and output arguments for each interface are the same. It examines the program for inconsistent descriptions of module coupling. For instance, if modules A and B call module C, the tool would issue a warning message if A and C have one type of coupling and B and C have a different type of coupling.

The last type of verification attempts to locate incomplete interfaces. The tool examines each module and its surrounding interfaces. A list of the module's *total input space* is formed, which contains the input arguments from its callers plus the output arguments from all of the modules it calls. A list of the module's *total output space* is formed from the output arguments to all calling modules and the input arguments to all called modules. Each item in the output space is matched against the input space to determine if the output item is derivable from the input. A subsetting algorithm is used so that the tool would assume that output "customer name" is derivable from input "list of customer names."

Obviously, the report will contain many indications of potential problems that are not true problems. For instance, the program does not know the output "man number" is derivable from input "employee personnel record." However, the intent of the report is to give the designer a list of potential problems to check. If the designer desires to do so, he may prime the data base beforehand with established relations, such as the relation "man number can be drived from employee personnel record."

With this existing data base describing program structures, additional design tools can be devised. As an example, a query function has been added to allow the designer to ask such questions as, "What modules call module X" or "What is the interface to module Y?"

The design tools mentioned above focus on only a tiny portion of the overall design process, and one might envision tools that participate more directly in the design process. Cougar [6] and Teichroew [7] survey attempts to automate the requirements and systems analysis processes. The ultimate design tool might be one that, given a high-level functional specification, automatically produces the program's code and documentation. To most of us this sounds like a premise for a science-fiction novel, but Freeman [8] discusses the major obstacles and describes research efforts in this area. For the reader interested in pursuing this area, Winograd [9] provides additional ideas on what might be provided by future programming tools. For those readers involved in designing the user interfaces to programming tools, Overton [10] gives some useful human factors advice.

REFERENCES

1. S. P. DeJong, "The System Building System (SBS)," RC-4486, IBM Research Div., Yorktown Heights, N.Y., 1973.

2. H. Bratman, "The Software Factory," *Computer,* **8** (5), 28–37 (1975).

3. J. A. Clapp and J. E. Sullivan, "Automated Monitoring of Software Quality," *Proceedings of the 1974 National Computer Conference.* Montvale, N.J.: AFIPS Press, 1974, pp. 337–341.

4. F. E. Allen, "Interprocedural Analysis and the Information Derived by It," in C. E. Hackl, Ed., *Programming Methodology.* Berlin: Springer-Verlag, 1975, pp. 291–321.

5. B. W. Boehm, R. K. McClean, and D. B. Urfrig, "Some Experience with Automated Aids to the Design of Large-Scale Reliable Software," *IEEE Transactions on Software Engineering,* **SE-1** (1), 125–133 (1975).

6. J. D. Cougar, "Evolution of Business System Analysis Techniques," *Computing Surveys,* **5** (3), 167–198 (1973).

7. D. Teichroew, "A Survey of Languages for Stating Requirements for Computer-Based Information Systems," *Proceedings of the 1972 Fall Joint Computer Conference.* Montvale, N.J.: AFIPS Press, 1972, pp. 1203–1224.

8. P. Freeman, "Automating Software Design," *Computer,* **7** (4), 33–38 (1974).

9. T. Winograd, "Breaking the Complexity Barrier Again," *SIGPLAN Notices,* **10** (1), 13–30 (1975).

10. R. K. Overton et al., "Developments in Computer-Aided Software Maintenance," ESD-TR-74-307, AMS Corp., Claremont, Ca., 1974.

Index